Acts of the international
symposium on rock art

Instituttet for
sammenlignende
kulturforskning

The Institute for
Comparative Research
in Human Culture,
Oslo

Serie A: Forelesninger

XXIX

Acts of the international
symposium on rock art

Korályu-Grotte, Kimberley-Division, Nordwest-Australien.
Wondjina-Köpfe; mehrfarbige Malerei. Kopie: Gerda Kleist, 1938/39.

Acts of the international symposium on rock art

Lectures at Hankø 6 - 12 August, 1972

Editor
Sverre Marstrander

Universitetsforlaget
Oslo - Bergen - Tromsø

© Instituttet for sammenlignende kulturforskning 1978
(The Institute for Comparative Research in Human Culture)
Oslo , Norway

ISBN 82-00-14194-2

UNIVERSITETSFORLAGET

Distribution offices:

NORWAY
Universitetsforlaget
Box 2977 Tøyen
Oslo 6

UNITED KINGDOM
Global Book Resources Ltd.
109 Great Russel Street
London WC 3ND

UNITED STATES and CANADA
Columbia University Press
136 South Broadway
Irvington-on-Hudson
NY 10533

Printed in Norway by
Harald Lyche & Co. A.s, Drammen

Contents

Introduction

On 6th March 1971, it was decided at a board meeting of The Institute for Comparative Cultural Research in Human Culture that the Institute should arrange a symposium on rock carving, to take place in the course of 1972. A committe responsible for further work on this matter was appointed on the same occasion. It consisted of the following:

Professor Dr. Sverre Marstrander, Oslo, chairman.
Professor Dr. Anders Hagen, Bergen
Statsstipendiat Dr. Erling Johansen, Fredrikstad
Professor Povl Simonsen, Tromsø

The board of the Institute emphasized the importance of including also non-Scandinavian scholars in the symposium. In November 1971, the chairman of the committee, Professor Sverre Marstrander, submitted the committee's plans for the symposium to the board of the Institute. It was decided that the symposium was to take place at Hankø near Fredrikstad, a well-known sea-side resort on the east coast of the Oslo Fjord, from 6th August until 12th August 1972.

Twenty-seven scholars from ten different countries attended the symposium. Six associated members also took part, so that thirty-four participated, including the secretary of the symposium.

List of members
(associated members marked with *)

Austria
Professor Hofrat Dr. Ernst Burgstaller, Institut für Landeskunde, Bahnhofstrasse 16, Linz a.d. Donau,
* Professor Dr. Josefa Burgstaller,
* Frau Helene v. Sick-Tenbruck,
* Frl. Maximiliane v. Sick-Tenbruck.
Bulgaria
Dr. Georgi I. Georgiev, Archaeologisches Institut der Bulgarischen Akademie der Wissenschaften, Sofia.

Denmark

Rigsantikvar Dr. P. V. Glob, Nationalmuseet, Copenhagen.

Museuminspektør Hans Langballe, Viborg Stiftsmuseum, 8800 Viborg.

Finland

Fil.lic. Pekka Sarvas, Arkeologiska Institutionen vid Helsingfors Universitet, Nationalmuseum, Helsingfors 10.

Germany

Dr. Gisela Asmus, Institut für Ur- und Frühgeschichte, Weyertal 125, 5 Køln.

Direktor Dr. Wolfgang Asmus, Niedersächsishes Landesmuseum, Am Marschpark 5, 3 Hannover.

* Frau Hannah Asmus

Professor Dr. Herbert Kühn, An der Goldgrube 35, Mainz.

* Frau Rita Kühn.

Dr. Agnes Susanne Schulz, Frobenius Institut, 6 Frankfurt a.M.

Italy

Professor Dr. Emmanuel Anati, Centro Camuno di Studi Prestorici, 25044 Capo di Ponte, Valcamonica.

* Signora Ariela Anati

Norway

Mag.art. Eva Fett, Historisk Museum, Universitetet i Bergen, Boks 25, 5014 Bergen Univ.

Førstekonservator Per Fett, Historisk Museum, Universitetet i Bergen, Boks 25, 5014 Bergen Univ.

Professor Dr. Gutorm Gjessing, Universitetets Etnografiske Museum, Frederiks gt. 2, Oslo 1.

Statsstipendiat Dr. Erling Johansen, Bauveien 1, Kråkerøy, 1600 Fredrikstad.

Stud.mag.art. Christian Keller, Kirkeveien 85, Oslo 3.

Universitetslektor Gro Mandt Larsen, Historisk Museum, Universitetet i Bergen, Boks 25, 5014 Bergen.

Professor Dr. Sverre Marstrander, Universitetets Oldsaksamling, Frederiks gt. 2, Oslo 1.

Professor Povl Simonsen, Arkeologisk avdeling, Tromsø Museum, 9000 Tromsø.

Museumsassistent Karl Vibe-Müller, Universitetets Oldsaksamling, Frederiks gt. 2, Oslo 1.

Spain

Professor Dr. L. Pericot-Garcia, Universidad de Barcelona, Barcelona.

Professor Antonio Beltran, Faculdad de Filosofia y Letras, Zaragoza.

Sweden

Professor Dr. Bertil Almgren, Institutionen för arkeologi, Uppsala Universitet, Gustavianum, 8–752 20 Uppsala.

Museichef Lili Kaelas, Arkeologiska Museet, Skärgårdsgatan 4, 414 58 Gøteborg.

Fil.kand. Jarl Nordbladh, Andra Långgatan 29, 413 03 Gøteborg.

Fil.kand. Jan Rosvall, Skjutbanegatan 37, 413 21 Gøteborg.

Intendent Dagmar Selling, Skepparegangen 22, 413 28 Gøteborg.

U.S.A.

Dr. Dale W. Ritter, 266 Cohasset Lane, Chico, California 92926.

Secretary of the symposium

Cand.philol. Bjørg Olsen, Universitetets Oldsaksamling, Frederiks gt. 2, Oslo 1.

THE DIARY OF THE SYMPOSIUM

Sunday 6th August: Arrival of the members.

Monday 7th August: The symposion was opened by the chairman of the Institute, professor Dr. Einar Molland:

In a short historical sketch Professor Molland stated that the founding of the Institute was due to the initiative of Professor Fredrik Stang, an outstanding lawyer. Stang's prime objective was that Denmark, Norway and Sweden, which had been neutral during the war, would have a step-up reestablishing international, scientific contact in the post-war period. As a medium through which his intentions could be realized, Professor Stang suggested founding institutes of pure research, which in turn would invite scholars from various countries to cooperate across national borders. These plans were realized only in Norway, where an institute along the lines of Professor Stang's model was founded in 1922.

During its more than 50 years of existence the Institute has issued more than 120 volumes in its three series of publications: lectures, monographs and reports. From the beginning, perhaps one of the most important activities of the Institute has been its publication, in series, of lectures given in Oslo under the auspices of the Institute by scholars of international repute. They cover such divergent fields as history of law, linguistics, history of arts, prehistoric archaeology, history of religions, folklore, among others.

Over the years the Institute organized a considerable number of lectures of this type, but for various reasons this tradition of lecture activity ceased in 1960. The Board of the Institute has now decided to try a new path by organizing symposia in which Norwegian scholars and prominent experts from abroad will participate together.

The Symposium on Rock Art at Hankø was the first of this kind the Institute has organized. Prehistoric rock art was chosen as the subject and this part of the country (county of Østfold) as a suitable meeting place, especially as a series of rock art specimina can be studied *in situ* in this area.

Professor Molland concluded by wishing members of the symposium pleasant talks, fruitful discussions and, not the least, good weather on the excursion days.

The first group of lectures dealt with problems of rock art in the North Eurasian area:

Herbert Kühn: Die Felsbilder Sibiriens.

Pekka Sarvas: Finnische Felsmalereien.

Wolfgang Asmus: Zur kulturellen Deutung der nordwestdeutschen Sonnensteine.

After luncheon the session continued with the following lectures:

Gutorm Gjessing: Rock art in Northern Fenno-Scandia and its Eastern Affinities.
Povl Simonsen: New Elements for Evaluating the Origin and End of North-Scandinavian Rock Art.
Sverre Marstrander: The Problem of European Impulses in the Nordic Area of Agrarian Rock Art.

Tuesday 8th August: Excursion by bus to localities of «hunters' carvings» in Oslo and Drammen. In Oslo the members visited the rock carving near the Maritime School at Ekeberg.

In the Viking Ship Museum at Bygdøy Professor Sverre Marstrander gave a short account of the Viking Ships and the Oseberg find.

In Drammen the rock carvings at Skogerveien were studied. Here the fine whale figure aroused especial interest.

The next point of the excursion, only some kilometers distant, was the carving at Åskollen, with its expressive big elk figure.

The trip continued along the west side of the Oslofjord, visiting the National Park at Borre near Horten, with its monumental grave mounds. It is generally believed that they are built over the forefathers of king Harald the Hairfair, the founder of the kingdom of Norway. Professor Sverre Marstrander told what we know about the grave field from literary sources and the rather scanty archaeological material.

Wednesday 9th August: The theme of the next group of lectures was: problems of rock art in Central Europe and the Mediterranean area.

Herbert Kühn: Die Stilbewegungen der Felsbildkunst in Europa.
Ernst Burgstaller: Österreichische Felsbilder.
Georgi I. Georgiev: Der Forschungsstand der alten Felsenkunst in Bulgarien.
Antonio Beltran: Les Rapports entre l'Art Rupestre Canarien et Atlantique à l'Age du Bronze.

The lectures after lunch also treated problems connected with other rock art areas.
L. Pericot-Garcia: An Element for the Chronology of West-European Rock Paintings.

Agnes Schulz: Rock Paintings in Northwest and North Australia.
Dale Ritter: Medicine Men and Spirit Animals in Rock Art of Western North America.
Herbert Kühn: Die Felsbilder vom westlichen Nord-Amerika.
Bertil Almgren: Changes in Bronze Age Religion in Sweden.

Thursday 10th August: Rock art excursion to localities in Borge and Skjeberg in Østfold. Statsstipendiat Erling Johansen and Professor Sverre Marstrander acted as guides during the visit to the classic carvings of Begby and Lille Borge in Borge parish, the recently found carving of Skjælin and the group of carvings on the estate of Hafslund in Skjeberg. At Lille Borge the members were busily occupied making experiments with mirrors reflecting the sunrays on to the figures in order to make them stand out more clearly on the surface of the rock.

The excursion continued to the carvings at Kalnes near Sarpsborg, discovered some years ago; further to the classic locality of Nedre Solberg in Skjeberg, with its famous symmetrical tree figure, already known in the last century, and finally to the carving of Post-Hornnes in Skjeberg with its magnificent fleet of shipsfigures.

Friday 11th August: Excursion to rock art localities in Northern Bohuslän. Professor Bertil Almgren acted as guide when visiting the carvings of Askeberget, Vitlycke, Lisleby, Bro utmark and Fossum, all of them localities well known from the classic corpus published by L. Baltzer.

During the excursion, Mrs. Hannah Asmus demonstrated a new method for making impressions of carved figures.

Saturday 12th August: The lectures of the last work session of the symposium treated general problems concerning recording, dating and interpretation of rock art:
Emmanuel Anati: Method of Recording and Analysing Rock Engravings.
Gro Mandt Larsen: Is the Location of Rock Pictures an Interpretive Element?
Jarl Nordbladh: Some Problems Concerning the Relation between Rock Art, Religion and Society.
Jan Roswall: An Attempt at a Framework for Visual Analysis of Rock Pictures.

Sunday 13th August: Departure.
According to the decision of the Board of the Institute, all lectures presenting new material have been included in the Acts of the sym-

posium, as far as the authors have handed in their manuscripts. In the cases where no manuscripts were to hand, the editor had to give the main points of the lectures as stated in the authors' own summaries. Some few lectures treating material already published in books or papers were rendered in the same way according to the financial frame set by the Institute.

It appeared rather difficult to get all manuscripts within reasonable time, but after many delays they could at last be handed over to the Institute in the autumn of 1975.

The calculation of the printing costs and linguistic control of all translated texts undertaken by the Institute have required extremely long time and the editor can only regret that the publishing of the acts of the symposium should be so delayed as in the present case.

Oslo in March, 1978.
Sverre Marstrander

Rock-pictures in northern Fenno-Scandia and their eastern affinities

BY GUTORM GJESSING

When, in the 1930's, Johs. Bøe, Eivind S. Engelstad and I published the entire Norwegian material of hunters' monumental art known until then,[1] and when, just before 1940, Gustav Hallström finally published his own investigations from 1907—1914 of the same material,[2] Norwegian archeologists apparently found that it was time to pause for a while and take a breath. Unfortunately Hallström found it necessary to publish this well-known material before publishing his Swedish material unknown to all of us. His second work on «Monumental art» covering the Swedish localities did not appear until 1960.[3] But be that as it may — now we must be grateful that this fascinating material has finally been published, too.

It seems as if our Norwegian colleagues have now recovered their breath, and once again the problems connected with this kind of art are being discussed.

Povl Simonsen has published a volume on the North-Norwegian petroglyphs and pictographs discovered after my own «Arktiske helleristninger i Nord-Norge» from 1932[4] and Anders Hagen has recently published the comprehensive and tremendously interesting West-Norwegian collection of panels at Ausevik, Sunnfjord, originally investigated by Johs. Bøe in 1935, and reinvestigated by Hagen in 1963—1966.[5] Simonsen and Hagen, moreover, have published some more popular writings on the subject. And in the younger generation the discussion seems to be lively and animated, although not yet expressed in print. Being, in fact, the only surviving member of the petroglyphic trio, or quartet if we include Hallström, from the 1930's, I would like to add my voice to the petroglyphic choir, conducted not least by a sound and fruitful desire for controlling, and perhaps especially revising hypotheses and views of the older generations.

My paper will be focussed on two questions, namely the chronology of the Nordland group of petroglyphs ground into the surface of the rock, which will be discussed more or less briefly, and mainly the question of eastern relationships of the monumental art in

North Fenno-Scandia. But this discussion depends to a large extent on some very general problems, which must be therefore outlined at the outset.

In art form and content are complementary. Consequently art forms cannot be profitably studied in isolation from their content, that is, in fact, from the whole eco-cultural situation. From this follows that motives in the rock-art from one eco-cultural sphere cannot be automatically compared to motives belonging to a different eco-cultural environment.

In the study of petroglyphs and pictographs we are, ideally, dealing with two entirely different ecological and socio-cultural spheres, different in terms of economy, sociopolitical organization, general culture, and certainly also of religious system, in short, two diametrically opposed world views. In South-Scandinavia: agriculture, a hierarchical socio-political organization and a form of religion closely interwoven with the whole socio-cultural weft. In North-Fenno-Scandia, on the other hand, we meet subarctic hunters and fishermen organized in small, more or less egalitarian local, social groups, probably with no political organization extending beyond the local groups. In some areas, particularly in Southern Norway, obviously also in southern Finland, the two cultures meet and intermingle, and consequently influence each other.

Nobody doubts that the petroglyphs of the agricultural south have a religious content, but where the northern art is concerned the interpretations have usually had a heavy list towards magic (hunting magic), — supposedly as a more «primitive» spiritual expression. This, of course, has not been, and cannot in any way be proved, and the more I have thought about rock-art, in relation to what we know of religious types from relatively comparable socio-cultural forms, the more convinced I have become that is it not a question of religion *versus* magic — the distinction between which is on the whole rather foggy — but of two entirely different forms of religions based on and themselves forming, in mutual interaction, very different world views.

With the domestication of certain animals «one of the most profound revolutions in man's relation to the world began ... the dethronement of the animal,» S. Giedeon says in his imaginative work, «The Beginnings of Art»[6], and he proceeds: «The animal was first regarded as a being higher than man himself, the sacred animal, the object of highest veneration. During the paleolithic era — which was above all, zoomorphic — the animal was the indisputabel idol». This is confirmed by several anthropological reports from hunters' and fishermen's socio-cultures. It is the original basis of totemism, and often animals are more than men because they can even transform themselves into men. Even as late as in the 18th century, missionaries complained of the Saames, who believed that the soul of animals was as sublime as the soul of man. In fact, the dethronement of the animal is an essential part of Gordon Childe's «food-producing revolution», the enormous consequence of which no archaeologist would deny.

In his important paper, «Acculturation»,[6b] Sol Tax's main postulate was that no acculturation has occurred among North-American Indians. «This leads me to what I think is the most important difference (between the Indians of North-America and of Meso-America) is that North American Indians are among the few people on earth who never became in any sense peasants.»

This explains the difference between the art of hunting socio-cultures of North Fenno-Scandia with the overwhelming majority of animal representations qualitatively far superior to the poor representations of man, and agricultural petroglyphs where man is the predominating motive together with domesticated animals, symbolic figures of various kinds, and, of course, ships. Moreover the

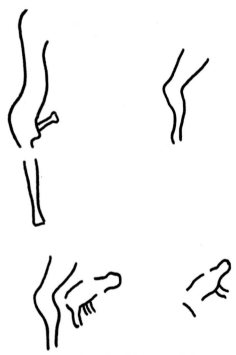

Fig. 1. Human representations. Bardal. Lower left: copulation scene.

copulation scenes at Bardal and in Karelia represent copulation *ex posteriori,* imitating animals (fig. 1). In one case the man apparently even has a horned animal's mask, showing the ritual meaning of the copulation.

Two of the Karelian examples are of particular interest because the copulation is synchronized with the delivery: the baby is newborn and still tied to its mother by the umbilical cord (fig.2)[7], showing the irrelevance to the artist of our dynamic and mechanical concept of time. Apparently this was the case with the macro-time concept

Fig. 2. Copulation and delivery. Karelia. (From Savvateev).

too. In contrast to the technologically more inventive agricultural societies, this irrelevance of a dynamic time concept was a general characteristic of hunters' socio-cultures which were what Marshall Sahlins called «the original affluent societies». That means societies in which people do not have more material needs than they are able to satisfy, and therefore do not have the same need for socio-cultural change as agricultural, and more especially industrial people have.[8] I may here add that one of the important results of the symposium, «Man the Hunter», held in Chicago 1966, was in Murdock's phrasing that «there is a surprisingly narrow range of variations in hunting and gathering culture with regard to social organisation»,[9] The Symposium covered all parts of the world, except Europe.

This means that the zoomorphic art of hunters is not tied to specific periods or areas, but in its inner meaning it is interwoven with world views of hunting people everywhere and at all periods where it is still a living world view. It was living in Eskimo art right up to the intrusion of European culturereligious concepts, in fact, right up till today. And the Saame (Lapp) Nils Jernsletten recently wrote: «Very many characteristics of the Saamish hunters' and fishers' culture are still living among reindeer-breeding Saames as well as the fisher- and small-farming Saames.»

Now to the chronology of the ground petroglyphs. On somewhat

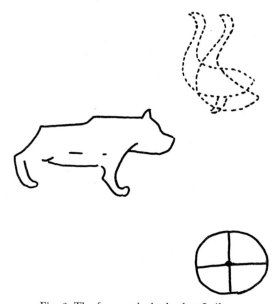

Fig. 3. The four-spoked wheel at Leiknes.

different premises both Hallström and I have dated the group to Mesolithic times, a dating which now seems to be seriously questioned. The doubts, to put it mildly, are based mainly on two points, namely my dating from 1932 of the petroglyphs at Sagelva, Hamarøy[10] and the occurrence of a big four-spoked wheel which I discovered in 1937 at the big panel at Leiknes, Tysfjord.[11] (fig. 3) Simonsen is in no doubt that this wheel was modelled upon the

18

Fig. 4. Illinois, USA. (Sketch from photograph).

Fig. 5. The Urals. (From Chernetzov).

wheels of carts, consequently it should not be older than the first use of carts with spoked wheels, that is, from the Bronze Age.[12] I have earlier discussed this argument in my unpublished opposition to Sverre Marstrander's doctorial disputation, and shall here restrict myself to a few points.

Spoked wheels, as well as circles of various types, such as plain, many-spoked, dotted, or concentric circles, often with rays suggesting them to be sun symbols, have an enormously wide-spread distribution in very divergent socio-cultural settings, upon which I shall not enter here. But it is important to note that four-spoked wheels occur in multitudes in petroglyphs from both American continents where the use of wheels was entirely unknown (Fig. 4) Four-spoked wheels as well as concentric circles were employed as decorative

19

elements in Siberian Neolithic and Bronze Age without carts and agriculture having belonged to the cultural inventory. The four-spoked wheel is, moreover, a known motive from petroglyphs and pictographs from the Urals[13] (fig. 5) and from the Angara region in eastern Siberia.[14]

I have, of course, no intention of transfering the philosophy of North American Indians to the four-spoked wheel at Leiknes, but both the number four and the circle had deeplying and important symbolic connotations among most, if not all, North American Indians. Four were the corners of the world and the four winds, and the circle was holy because it represented the boundary of the world from where the four winds came. In other words, here you have a concise and pregnant interpretation of the wheel. Obviously the four-spoked wheel at Leiknes may have had an entirely different symbolic meaning, or in fact, several different meanings; I merely mention this to suggest that we will be much freer in our interpretations if we throw out most of the archaelogists' South-Scandinavian myth, and instead concentrate on interpretations consonant with the eco-cultural setting into which this monumental art belongs. At any rate, the four-spoked wheel is completely valueless as a chronological means.

The hunters' monumental art almost certainly had some ritual connection with water, an almost universal symbol of fertility well known already in Magdalenien art. All Fenno-Scandian localities, except the two neighbouring ones at Flatruet and Grannberget in Härjedalen, are situated close to the sea, or to rivers or lakes. The same is the case with those by the White Sea, Lake Onega and the river Vyg, apparently also with all localities in the Urals and the Angara region, those recently discovered at the river Pegtymel, Chukot, N.E. Siberia and, more surprisingly, even those from Alaska and the Canadian west coast.

However, this does not permit us to use old shore-lines as a means of dating specific panels, although we have at least two panels, at Kirkely, Balsfjord, and Strand, Bjørnør, which can be demonstrated to have been tied directly to an old shoreline.[15] Therefore, I an perfectly willing now to admit that my former dating of the two reindeer at Sagelva is not tenable as isolated evidence. The carvings are situated in a way which to me at that time seemed inaccessible except from a boat. Hallström and others have suggested the possibility of the carvings having been made from the ice by means of a ladder which, in that case, must have been four and a half meters long. But the currents of the river are so strong that it never freezes. There is a rapid only 20 meters further upstream. (Gjessing: Arktiske helle-

20

ristninger etc. Pl.XXXVI, 2) Yet, when revisiting the locality in 1970 together with the participants of the Nordic Congress of Archaeologists, I saw my young colleagues managing to walk on the very steeply sloping rock, although I still doubt seriously that they would have been able to do the very tedious work of grinding the big animals into the hard gneiss, rich in quartz. But there is every reason to suppose that the Stone Age artists were considerably more experienced in moving around in difficult terrain, and also a good deal more trained in this kind of grinding than urbanized archaeologists of 1970 are.

Yet, there is one factor which has not been sufficiently appreciated by the doubting Thomases, but which to me seems rather important: Whereas all the hunters' pecked petroglyphs and the pictographs in the Trøndelag area and North-Norway are situated below the so called Tapes shoreline, all the ground ones have been found above this line, some of them at a considerably higher level. This remarkable general fact cannot be ignored. And as this is so, the stylistic peculiarities and the differences in dimensions of the representations must be considered, too. The specific stylistic character is nowhere as explicit as precisely at the Leiknes panel (Gjessing: Arktiske helleristninger etc. Pl.VIII) with a much more lively and also a more individualistic way of designing the animals, which can be seen, for instance, by the movements and the many and various ways of representing details such as antlers, hoofs etc. Moreover, the animals are generally decidedly larger than the pecked ones. Only the four biggest elks at Bardal are of relatively comparable style and size.[16] Without entering into the chronological questions in any detail, I am, therefore, still convinced that this group is older than any other known groups of petroglyphs in Fenno-Scandia.

Now over to my second, and main problem, namely the relationship to eastern types of rock-art, and here I must remind you of my introductory, general remarks, because it is to the east we must look for hunters' and fishermen's cultures.

I have already demonstrated the fallacy of comparing the four-spoked wheel to those from South-Scandinavian agricultural petroglyphs. There is, if possible, even less reason to suggest that representations of boats in a culture definitely depending on hunting and fishing are derived from boats and ships in an agricultural environment. Looking through Jurij Savvateev's recent, big monograph, «Zalavruga» is, in fact, a fantastic experience, not least because it shows how entirely integrated boats and bigger craft were in the hunter-fishermen's culture, with scores of dramatic scenes where one and the same whitefish *(beluga leucal)* is being harpooned from several boats. (fig. 6) There is no doubt since the harpoon-lines are seen running from the harpooneers into the animal.[17] The craft of the Karelian petroglyphs are of various dimensions, sometimes with only one hunter on board, but crews of one harpooner and twelve paddlers are not uncommon, and the crews are represented by short, vertical lines, exactly as in the Bronze Age ships from southern Scandinavia — and, in fact, it could scarcely have been done otherwise. The boats are of various types, most often filled in, but boats made in outline with vertical lines inside occur. Practically every one of the craft is equipped with an elk's head on the top of the prow.

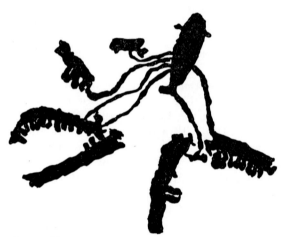

Fig. 6. Harpooning from six boats. (From Sabbateev).

Now, apart from the bear, the elk obviously had a very important religious significance in northern hunting sociocultures, since the *art mobilier* is entirely predominated by these two species, the bear particularly on ritual axes, the elk on knives of slate and many other objects, to a great extent including ritual axes, the remarkable ritual objects from burials at Olenij Ostrov, Lake Onega, published by N.N. Gurina, etc.[18] Over the whole world, craft have been conceived as living beings, very often with an eye or a head in the prow, and apparently related to specific significant religious concepts. I would remind the reader of the prows of many gigantic tankers today, which are still decorated with a figure head. Consequently there is no reason for associating these elks heads with the heads on ships from agricultural petroglyphs from South-Scandinavia. When these latter heads can be determined, they are always horses heads (Gjessing: Østfolds jordbruksristninger. Inst. f. Sml. Kulturforskning Serie B XXXVII, Oslo 1936 Pl.) connected with Indo-European fertility rites.[19]

Simonsen has compared two boats on a boulder from Gåshopen, Sørøy, Finnmark, to petroglyphs of craft from Båhuslen and Scania, primarily because of a short, oblique line running from the back of six members of the crew and reminding him of the swords of males from southern petroglyphs.[20] But as the shape of the boat cannot be used as evidence, since the same form occurs on petroglyphs as far east as in the Angara region, and even in Br. Columbia

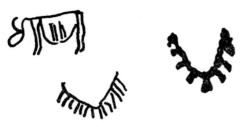

Fig. 7. Left: Lamtrøa, Nord-Trøndelag. Right: Lake Onega.

and Alaska, this short line can probably be interpreted in several other ways so much the more as bronze swords, of course, are most unlikely to have played any role in Finnmark at that time. The line might, for instance, represent something as prosaic as part of the costume.

Unfortunately comparisons with more eastern petroglyphs and pictographs have usually been confined to those from Lake Onega and the White Sea published by Raudonikas, in part also A. K. Linjevski's publication of other Karelian petroglyphs. By and large, however, these are so distinct from the Fenno-Scandian material, with a remarkable exception for the tremendously rich occurrences at Nämnforsen, Ångermanland, so admirably published by Hallström[21], that one suspects ethnic differences. But motives parallel to our own can be found even in these Northwest-Russian monuments, such as a curved line with fringes hanging down, which occurs twice at Lamtrøa, Bardal, and has a direct counterpart at Lake Onega.[22] (fig. 7)

The same motif, but turned upside down, occurs rather often in the rock-art from the Urals.[23] How important this turning upside down of the motif is, we do not know, but as our concept of time is

Fig. 8. Various motives from panels in the Urals. (From Chernetzov).

irrelevant to this monumental art, so is our concept of space, since we very often find animals etc. turned upside down or in any other direction. The wellknown novelist and dramatist Alexander Kielland, when visiting the panel at Bogge, Eirisfjord in 1903, wrote: «But what I admire most of all, is that this artist has hit upon the idea to throw one of the animals on its back, legs up. And I imagine a tremendous laughter through centuries has rolled over Eirisfjord by this fat animal lying on its back legs up, - a fancy of the artist which for that time equals the most supreme comic art which later became famous in art and literature».[24] (my translation).

The interesting fact of these Uralic figures is that in some cases they are placed directly above and apparently in direct connection with another figure. It may be an elk or a sun disk, or the two can be combined.[25] (fig. 8) Now, curiously enough the same figure is a well-known motif on pictographs from Salishan areas in Br. Columbia, but there it is, as a rule, placed above a human being. Even in the Uralic material, there is however, at least one instance where the figure beneath the curved line may possibly be a human being[26] (fig. 8) and, *vice versa*, there is in my Canadian material one example of a moose, the American elk, beneath the curved line. In the Urals there may be two or three parallel curved lines, in Br. Columbia there may be two.* This is so much the more remarkable as in the Uralic petroglyphs human masks also occur, very close to masks from Br. Columbia and Alaska.

Of course, I would not venture to suggerst a direct connection between areas so far apart from each other. My knowledge of Soviet literature is far too incidental for me to be able to tell in how much detail the distribution of petroglyphs and pictographs is known, because all of us who have worked in this line will know how accidentally this kind of art is usually discovered. Thus, during an archaeological expedition in 1967—68, eleven groups of extremely interesting petroglyphs were discovered almost as far east as the Chukchee Peninsula and close to the Arctic Ocean. They were published by N.N. Dikov only last autumn, and have been dated to the 1st millennium B.C. and onwards.[26b]

But the relationship between the Fenno-Scandian hunters' monumental art and that of the Urals is apparently much closer than to that of Northwest-Russia.[27] The style of the seminaturalistic Uralic quadrupeds (elks) is practically the same, the animals are made in outline and filled with vertical lines, sometimes only one in the

---

* The most probable interpretation of the Karelian and Norwegian examples would perhaps be that they were due to eastern influences, but that their symbolism was not properly understood by the carvers.

The Urals

Hinna

Nyelv

Fig. 9. Geometrical patterns.

middle of the trunk, as well-known in North-Scandinavia, too.[28] Elks with what I have called «the heart-and-life-line» also occur; the same, by the way, is the case with some animal representations filled with a geometrical pattern, in part meandering figures from the Angara region.[29] Moreover, there are geomatrical patterns related to those from Finland and Norway, in part rhomboid figures

Fig. 10. Confluence Tuba, Upper Jenissei, West-Siberia.

Fig. 11. Top: Verkhnaja Lena. Bottom: Angara.

of Andronovo-style, corresponding to the pictographs from Hinna and
Nyelv (fig. 9) There are also strongly schematized human beings, in
part horned, in part dancing rows as those from the Solsem cave
and from Valkeasaari, Finland.

My late friend Valerij Chernetzov, in his posthumous work on
the Uralic art, and also in a previous book,[30] was very much aware
of the relationship to Fenno-Scandian monuments, but he also points
to affinities with Siberia.

And, in fact, more or less the same semi-naturalistic style is well-
known also in pictographs and petroglyphs from Siberia, at least
from near the outlet of the tributary Tuba into the upper Jenissei,
north of Minussinsk,[31] (Fig. 10) from Verkhnaja Lena,[32] (fig. 11)
and from the Angara region. The rich material from the Angara region has been published in a big volume by Okladnikov.[35] Part
of this material is obviously late, with mounted horsemen etc.,
but the animals are comparable in style to Uralic and Fenno Scandia
petroglyphs and pictographs and are clearly Neolithic. These representations, painted in red or pecked — or both — are in part
made in outline, in part filled in, or the heads of the animals, mostly
elks, may be filled in while the rest of the animals is made in
outline, this is also a well-known trait in Scandinavian hunters'
monumental art. There seems to be no stylistic difference between
the petroglyphs and the pictographs, in some instances both techni-

27

ques, as mentioned, are applied to the same animal. In some cases of superimpositions the filled-in elks seems to have been made later than those made in outline, but these cases are too few to allow of a generalization. Sometimes, but rarely, the trunk of the animal is filled in with vertical lines or a geometrical pattern and with the «heart-and-life-line» motif (fig. 12). The vertical body lines are known also in animal representations from the Minussinsk-region.[34]

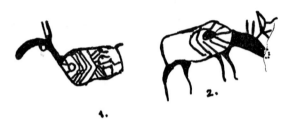

Fig. 12. 1. Balsfjord, Norway. 2. Angara.

Of course, there is very far from stylistic identity between the Angara art and the Uralic, let alone the Fenno-Scandian, since not only spatial but also ethnical factors have to be considered. Many of the Angara-elks are more naturalistic in postures, movements and in details; thus practically all of them have four legs and many have eyes and mouth, an even nostrils are represented. Beside elks, there are fishes and highly schematized human representations, some of them with horned masks, others dancing in a row in «Solsem style».[35] Boats also occur, with the hull formed as a horizontal line and with the crew represented by short, vertical lines, precisely as in South-Scandinavian petroglyphs. Ski-runners hunting elks are to be found, and also sun disks with rays. The latter seem, however, to belong to the younger, although not the youngest stratum.

It will almost certainly be objected that the exstremely long distances between these centres of monumental art preclude hypotheses on relationship, and such an objection is not easily met, to be sure. I am also well aware of the fact that my old idea of a circumpolar culture complex has been seriously questioned by both Scandinavian, Soviet and US-American scholars, precisely on these grounds.[36] But I wonder if this is not caused by these scholars having specialized in archaeology, and having judged the hypothesis from distributional studies of archaeological artifacts only. If they had supplemented their often intimate morphological knowledge of prehistoric artifacts with comparative ethnological and sociological knowledge, their questioning might possibly have faded away.

Generally I have a strong feeling that archaeologists are prone to overrate geographical distances as barriers to cultural influences, forgetting that concepts of time and space were entirely different from ours in these very sparsely inhabited regions. At all times people have travelled impressive distances. It is almost banal to remind you of Australians who would travel by foot some 300 miles to get a particular ochre necessary for proper ceremonial use, and Eskimos also have travelled several hundred miles, dog-sled by land or by sea in winter-time, umiak in the summer time. Everywhere in Arctic and Subarctic hunting socio-cultures, some idea could be found which could be fitted into their own cosmology, on the whole, their world view. As Fenno-Scandian *art mobilier* evidently belongs to the vast area of zoomorphic art, reaching way east to Mongolia and North-China the same may, of course, be the case with monumental art belonging to precisely the same spiritual sphere.

NOTES

1. *Johs. Bøe:* Felszeichnungen im westlichen Norwegen, Bergens Museums Skr. nr. 15, Bergen 1932; *Gutorm Gjessing:* Arktiske helleristninger i Nord-Norge, Inst. for Sml. Kulturforskn. Serie B-XXI, Oslo 1932, *Eivind S. Engelstad:* Østnorske ristninger og malinger av den arktiske gruppe, Ibid. Serie B-XXVI, Oslo 1934; *Gjessing:* Nordenfjelske ristninger og malinger av den arktiske gruppe, Ibid. Serie B-XXX, Oslo 1936.
2. *Gustaf Hallström:* Monumental art of Northern Europe from the Stone Age. I. The Norwegian localities, Stockh. 1938.
3. *Hallström:* Monumental Art of Northern Sweden from the Stone Age. II Nämnsforsen and other localities, Stockh. 1960.
4. *Povl Simonsen:* Arktiske helleristninger i Nord-Norge II, Inst. for Sml. Kulturforskn. Serie B-L-IX, Oslo, 1958.
5. *Anders Hagen:* Studier i vestnorsk bergkunst, Ausevik i Flora, Årbok fra Universitetet i Bergen. Humanist. Serie 1969 No. 3, Bergen 1969.
6. *S. Giedion:* The Beginnings of Art, Bolingen Series XXXV: 6 : 1, Washington D.C. 1962, p. 5.
6b. *Sol Tax:* Acculturation in *Anthony C. F. Wallace* (ed): Selected Papers of the Fifth International Congress of Anthropological and Ethnological Sciences 1956, Philadelphia 1960.
7. *Jurij Savvateev:* Zalavruga. Archeologischeskie pamjatkin nizovjaja reki Vjig, Leningrad 1970.
8. *Marshall Sahlins* in *Richard B. Lee & Irven DeVore* (eds): Man the Hunter, Chicago 1968, pp. 85 ff.
9. *George P. Murdock* in *Lee & DeVore:* Op. cit., p. 335.
10. *Gjessing:* Arktiske helleristninger, pp. 46 f.

11. *Gjessing:* Yngre Steinalder i Nord-Norge, Inst. for Sml. Kulturforskn. Serie B-XXXIX, Oslo 1942, p. 383, Fig. 206, *Simonsen:* Loc. cit. pp. 62 f.
12. *Simonsen:* Fortidsminner nord for Polarsirkelen, Tromsø — Oslo — Bergen 1970, pp. 64 f.
13. *U. Chernetzov:* Naskalnie Izobrazenia Urala, Archeologia SSR Svod. Archeologicheskih istochnikov B. 4812, Moskva 1971, fig. 53.
14. *A.P. Okladnikov:* Petroglifii Angarii, Moskva - Leningrad 1966.
15. *Gjessing:* Nyoppdagete veideristninger i Nord-Norge, Viking 1938, p. 139. *Gjessing:* Nordenfjelske ristninger etc., pp. 16 ff.
16. *Gjessing:* Op. cit. Pls. LVIII-LXI.
17. *Savvateev:* Zalavruga, Figs. 48, 64, 92.
18. *Hallström:* Monumental Art II, Figs. on p. 315.
19. *Gjessing:* Hesten i forhistorisk kunst og kultur, Viking 1943, p. 11.
20. *Simonsen:* Arktiske helleristninger II, p. 52.
21. *Hallström:* Monumental Art II, pp. 128 ff.
22. *Gjessing:* Nordenfjeldske ristninger, p. 1. LXVIII, *Hallstrøm:* Monumental Art II, Fig. on p. 348.
23. *Chernetzov:* Op. cit., Figs. 30, 42, 51.
24. As quoted by *Gjessing:* Arktiske helleristninger, p. 7.
25. *Chernetzov:* Op. cit., Fig. 42.
26. *Chernetzov:* Op cit., Fig. 49 : 3b.
26b. *N.N. Dikov:* Naskaljnie Zagadki drevnev Chukotki, Moskva 1971.
27. *Chernetzov:* Op. cit. Figs. 40, 110, 133, 136.
28. *Chernetzov:* Op. cit. Fig. 43 : 2.
29. *Okladnikov:* Op. cit., Pl. 55 : 4.
30. *Chernetzov:* Op. cit., Fig. 44 : 1, 46 : 9, 50 : L, 51, 50 : 19.
31. *H.G. Bandi & Johs. Maringer:* Kunst der Eiszeit. Levante Kunst. Arktische Kunst, Basel 1952, fig. 92.
32. *Okladnikov:* Neolit i bronzovjij vek Pribalkalia, Moskva - Leningrad 1950, fig. 92.
33. *Okladnikov:* Petroglifii Angarii.
34. *Bandi & Maringer:* Op. cit., Fig. 191.
35. *Okladnikov:* Petroglifii Angarii., Pls. 94, 85, 88, 90, 108 : 2, 109 : 5.
36. *Kr. Møllenhus:* Steinalderen i Søndre Helgeland, Det Kgl. Norske Videnskapers Selsk. Skrifter 1958 nr. 1, Trondheim 1958, *A.J. Brjusov:* Eines der Merkmale des gemeinsamen Ursprungs der vorgeschichtligen Stämme im europäischen und westsibirischen Teil der Sovjetunion, Finskt Musum 1955, Helsingfors 1955, *Chester Chard,* oral information.

New elements for evaluating the origin and end of northern Scandinavian rock art

BY POVL SIMONSEN

The traditional chronology for the development of the socalled Arctic Monumental Art of Northern Scandinavia is as follows:

First a *phase I* with naturalistic animal-figures full scale, produced in grinding technique.

In *phase II* the figures are more stylized, on a somewhat smaller scale, with more variation in the motives, where we now meet human beings, boats, geometric signs etc., and the technique is one of hewing the lines.

The *phase III* ought to be figures on a still smaller scale, still more stylized, so that a zoological name for the animals now is impossible. We see a division of the art into more parallel styles, some of them geographically limited, others coexisting in the same area. The smallest and most stylized animal figures, for instance, have been called the *Trøndelagen-style*, whereas figures with a geometric filling-out of the body have been named the *East-Norwegian style*.

In *Western Norway* we see quite a different style on the sites of Vingen and Ausevik, and in North-Norway all the different styles coexist. In this pase III, apart from the narrow, hewn lines, we meet the wide, battered lines, and the oldest rock-paintings also occur now.

Finally in *phase IV*, we have figures where the whole of the interior of the figures is hewn out, creating a basrelief, others where the whole of the body is only one single line, and animals without legs or in other ways zoologically defective have obviously in spite of this been looked on as finished works of art. No direct continuity from the latest rock-carvings and rock-paintings of the North-Scandinavian type to still later art has ever been found.

The dating has always been random. Gjessing believed in a very early start, 5000—6000 B.C., so that one could suggest a connection to the Kleinkunst of the Maglemose-peoples. And a tradition going back to Late Paleolithic art was not impossible. While the South-Scandinavian farmer's art, according to Glob, must be presumed to have a southern origin in the Early Bronze Ages, the North-Scandinavian hunter's art has a different and far older origin. It has developed independently in Northern Scandinavia. Chronologically its later phases run parallel with the farmer's art, both of them being extinct round 400—200 B.C.

It is not my intention here to break down this construction. In its main features, I think it will remain for still some decades. But in recent years some material has been published which lays some of the details open to debate. This new material throws light especially on the questions:

1. When did the Arctic rock-carvings begin?
2. What was the relation between the two art-traditions in Scandinavia in their last phase?
3. The possibility of some continuity over to certain later types of art?

Some of this material has been debated at the Nordic Prehistoric congress at Tromsø 1970, later published by Anders Hagen in his book on the Ausevik-sites, and by me in my paper in the Festskrift to P.V. Glob. Other material is up to now unpublished, and still other problems and solutions have appeared orally at the congress mentioned and on its excursions to the sites in question. In this lecture I shall try to derive some main lines from all this.

1. The beginning of North-Scandinavian rock-art

That the beginning of the North-Scandinavian hunter's art should be placed as far back as in the middle of the Mesolithic is a theory which requires proof. Over the whole of this early distribution area the beginning of the Neolithic — or better: the Subneolithic — means a radical change in many respects, in trade- and influence-routes, in culture, in food-gathering and social structure. Is it really possible that this could happen without the least disturbance to the quiet continuity of the development of art? I do not think so. And before this change the area was divided into two rather different cultural provinces, Komsa to the north, Fosna to the south. Is it really possible that an artstyle can have its first outspring on both sides of a cultural borderline? I do not think so. In fact, the theory of the early beginning is indeed very weakly founded. Its most prominent argument is the locality of *Sagelv* in Hamarøy, where the figures are found on a steep rock-face over a waterfall. Gjessing argued that in practic it had only been possible to hew at this place at times when the sea still had a level higher than the top of the waterfall, 48 m over modern sea-level, so that men could work either from a boat or from the winter-ice. In 1970 a prominent group of archaeologists, among them also Gjessing himself, visited the place. After a discussion all of them agreed that the argument could not be kept up. The surface of the rock is not steeper than that is should be possible to walk on it bare-footed with caution, if necessary anchored from the top with a rope. Two students demonstrated the possibility. Thus this argument no longer holds good.

In 1971 Tromsø Museum held, near Narvik, a course in the handling of rock-carvings. As a demonstration-site we used the locality *Forselv* in Skjomen. The last day we dug out a larger area of the

rock in the hope of finding more figures. We succeeded, and some
of the new-found animal figures were placed so low that their lower
parts were hidden under a natural layer of marine sand. Its surface
is 31 m above the sea, which ought to prove a date around 2000 B.C.
The figures are not of the oldest style, but of my phase II. Parallel
observations could be made when I worked at the *Kirkely*-locality
near Tromsø in 1960. Already before the last war Gjessing had here
demonstrated that the lower part of the lower figures had been worn
by water after being hewn. Now it turned out that these figures had
been covered by a natural layer of marine gravel. The surface of
this layer is 19 m over the sea, which at this place means a date around
1000 B.C. Presumably this is a deposit from the subatlantic trangres-
sion, a slight rise of the sea-level in the North of Norway in the
last millennium B.C. The figures in the lower row are late, of the
so-called East-Norwegian style of my phase III. This fits in very
well. But if it is so that we can prove that these figures were hewn
right down to their contemporary coast-line, the figures of the upper
row cannot be very much older, because of the rising of the land,
which was fast just then. This upper row is stylistically earlier, from
my phase II, and so it can hardly be older than from around 2000
B.C. Together these two geological observations ought to give a hint
to the effect that phase III is not older than 1000 B.C., phase II
not older than 2000 B.C. For phase I we have no proofs, but to measure it a span of perhaps 3000—4000 years would be out of proportion with the length of the later phases. So, a beginning of this art
around 3000 B.C. is a most likely hypothesis, in the Early Neolithic
of South-Scandinavian chronology. The whole of the history of this
art then ought to take place within a much shorter span of years
than stipulated by the traditional chronology. And then it probably falls totally inside the Subneolithic period of the North-Scandinavian Stone Age, i.e. within a relatively uniform culture province
with a relatively quiet development. In this I do no include the
South-Scandinavian localities of the hunter's art, because it is obvious
that they belong to its later phases. This «short chronology» is a
working hypothesis, wich in my opinion is much more credible
than the «long chronology».

2. *The relation between the two rock-carving styles*
As mentioned above I take it granted that the two Scandinavian
types of rock-art had separate origins, and for a long time showed
parallel and separate development. But in recent years, some signs
have appeared in favour of the theory that they finally more or
less flowed together and mixed. This can have different results:

1. On the west coast of Norway, it obviously resulted in a mixing of the styles, so that at last it is quite impossible to tell to which type every single figure belongs. The site of *Ausevik* is typical in this respect, but other examples are also known. In North-Norway a figure in «Ausevik-Style» is found on the *Forselv*-locality near Narvik, hewn later than the other figures on the same rock-face.

2. Another form of mixing is when both of the styles, the hunter's art and the farmer's art, are to be found at the same locality, and there must be contemporaneous.

   For instance, we have cup-marks and a snake-figure at *Kirkely* near Tromsø, wheel-crosses at *Leiknes* near Narvik, *Gråbergan* near Tromsø, and *Gåshopen* on Sørøy, possible foot-prints at *Slettjord* near Narvik, all of them elements from the farmer's art intruding into the hunter's art. The opposite may also very well have happened, as when representations of fishing implements and wild animals or boats of Arctic types appear on South-Scandinavian localities, for instance in Västmanland on the northern side of lake Mälaren, or round Norrköping in Östergötland.

3. A third way of mixing is seen in the expansion of the farmer's art northwards right up to the North Cape, which is much further north than the northern limit of farming and of bronze-culture. Here I mention two large blocks with cup-marks, one in *Steigen,* south of Narvik, the other on *Sørøy* near Hammerfest. Then on *Isnesstoften* in the Altafjord we have a stone with a femal figure, and on *Gåshopen* on Sørøy another with two boats with many men onboard, boats of shapes otherwise quite unknown in North Norway. Nor must we omit the rock-paintings in *Transferdalen* near Alta, on *Kjeøy* outside Harstad, and in the *Solsem*-cave near Namsos which contain elements which I relate to southern influences, namely human figures.

All these foreign traits must have come from the South, cup-marks, wheel-crosses, ships with men, snake-figures are all typical South-Scandinavian elements. And that they are late in the North can partly be proved: The stones at *Gåshopen* are found only 3 m over sea-level, and must be from the centuries around zero, the *Solsem*-cave can by finds in the cave-floor be dated to the Late Bronze Age; the cup-marks and the snake at *Kirkely* are assosiated with figures from my phase III; and so on. Can we give any natural explanation of what happened? I think so.

It is a common theory that agriculture in Norway in Early and Middle Neolithic may have been introduced by one or more immigrations; so for a while there was an ethnic difference between farmers and hunters. But in the Late Neolithic and the Bronze Age agriculture expanded to many areas, where we must think of an aboriginal hunter-population changing their way of life to that of farmers. In due time the ethnic as well as the cultural dualism disappeared, and large groups of people lived in an agriculture on a huntsman-substrate. Should not such a development naturally result in a state where also these groups had a mixed religion and, in consequence, also a mixed art? And could not that open up the vast region of hunting and fishing North-Scandinavia to influence from foreign religion and art on a completely new scale?

3. The continuity from rock-carvings to later art
Finally some words about the very end of the rock-carvings or — better — of the problem: Did this art end at all or did it transform itself to new shapes? It is well known that cup-marks have been shaped and used for sacrifices in South Norway right up to only 200-300 years ago. Also that the *Kårstad*-carving — now in the garden of Bergen Museum — has a combination of a ship in true rock-carving style and an inscription in the old futhark, which means the Migration Period. In Östergötland there exist more combinations of rock-carvings and runic inscriptions. But otherwise there is obviously no continuity from the rock-carvings to either the Gotlandic pictoral stones, nor to the runic-figured stones on the Swedish continent. What about the North-Scandinavian hunter's art? Here is has often been stressed that there are strong resemblances between the latest carvings in the Trøndelagen-style and the painted figures on the Lappish magic drums from the 16th and 17th centuries. But a connection has been denied because of the long chronological lacune. This lacune perhaps will be filled in the future.

On the mountain *Aldon* on the north side of the Varangerfjord — «Aldon» is Lappish for: «Sacrificial place for sacrificing femal reindeer» — there was a holy stone, to which the Lapps have sacrificed at any rate since the 16th century, presumably much earlier. Now it has been removed, but we know its original place. Only about 20 m from there, a rock-carving of two reindeer was found a few years ago, its style undoubtly being late rock-carving style, but nearer to the drum-paintings than any other known rock-carving. A little to the west, at *Gullholmen* in the mouth of the Tana river, many figures have been found in 1973, so low that they must be later than around A.D. 1400. A couple of reindeer and two seals are recognizable, but most of the figures are obscure. The hewing technique is battering as on the late rock-carvings, but lack of patination certifies that the site is not very old. Here we also have a written source, telling us that we are on a holy place from the pre-Christian era of Lappish culture. But does any knowledge about Lappish practice of hewing or engraving pictures in the rocks really exist? Not a written or oral tradition, but perhaps a concrete. The publications of Gjessing and Hallström often mention «false rock-carvings», which are said to be «modern or near-modern», and are not described more closely. No one has ever taken up a study of them and tried to find out if they are really falsifications or if they are works of art which is genuine, although not rock-carvings in our sense of the word. In 1971 from *Glomfjord* south of Bodø an area with a lot of figures of Lapps was reported. In 1973, on the *Aldon*-mountain, about 150 m from the rock-carving and the sacrifical place, a representation has been found, showing a Lapp girl in an old-fashioned national costume, killing a wolf with a spear. Beside this is a figure of a ship with two masts, but the hull itself of a traditional, North-Norwegian type extinct at least a century ago. In 1971 I visited yet one more locality, in *Mathisdalen* in Alta, and this was of exactly the same type.

If these really are only falsifications, how could their style be exactly the same from one end of North-Norway to the other? But how else to explain the phenomenon? Does it merely mean that the Lapps throughout the Middle Ages and later centuries on some occations made pictures, which by pure chance are like rock-carvings either in motive or in technique? Or is there really a continuity from the most recent known rock-carvings in North-Norway, presumably from around the year O, and through more than a millennium up to the oldest known Lappish art? We do not know yet. But I think it necessary to submit the problem, else we shall never arrive at a solution.

REFERENCES

G. *Gjessing:* Arktiske helleristninger i Nord-Norge; Institutt for sammenlignende Kulturforskning, serie B, vol. XII, Oslo 1932.

G. *Gjessing:* Nyoppdagete veideristninger i Nord-Norge; Viking, vol. II, Oslo 1938.

P.U. *Glob:* Helleristninger i Danmark; Kbhn. 1969.

A. *Hagen:* Studier i vestnorsk bergkunst; Årbok for Universitetet i Bergen, Hum. serie 1969, no. 3, Oslo.

G. *Hallström:* Monumental Art of Northern Europe from the Stone Age; Sthm. 1938.

P. *Simonsen:* Arktiske helleristninger i Nord-Norge II; Inst. f. sam.lign. Kulturforsk., serie B, vol. XLIX, Oslo 1958.

P. *Simonsen:* Sydskandinavisk i Nordskandinavien; Kuml 1970, Kbhn.

Bonde-Veidemann: Bofast — Ikke Bofast; Tromsø Museums Skrifter XIV, Tromsø 1973.

Gibt es bei den Felsbildern von Fossum/Bohuslän Anzeichen für die Annahme von Wettermagie?

VON GISELA ASMUS

Die Langlebigkeit alter Bräuche überrascht in der Volkskunde immer wieder. Sehr häufig handelt es sich dabei um abgesunkene religiöse Vorstellungen aus vorchristlicher Zeit. Speziell in Fastnachts-Bräuchen und im Karneval — worauf bereits O. Almgren (1934) für die Bedeutung von Schiffen verwiesen hat — ist solch altes Kulturgut erhalten geblieben. Auch in Kinderspielen finden sich noch häufig Reminiscenzen alten Brauchtums, oft allerdings nur noch in der äusseren Form, während der eigentliche Sinngehalt verlorenging.

Ein Beispiel für die Zählebigkeit solch überkommener Bräuche könnte man in einem Zeremoniell des rheinischen Karnevals, dem «Stippeföttche», erblicken. Es handelt sich dabei um eine Zeremonie der Karnevalsgarden in der Uniform der alten Kölner Statsoldaten. Dem Aufzug voraus reitet ein «Offizier», hinter ihm auf dem gleichen Pferd, aber Rücken an Rücken — sodass der eine nach vorn, der andere nach hinten blickt, sein Adjutant. Auf Kommando stellen sich die «Funken», wie die Soldaten genannt werden, reihenweise so auf, dass jeweils 2 im Wechsel dos à dos und vis à vis stehen und zwar mit gebeugten Knien und senkrecht gehaltenem Gewehr, in dessen abwärts gerichtetem Lauf statt des Gewehrfeuers bunte Stoffstreifen erkennbar werden. Auf ein weiteres Kommando «wibbeln» die Funken, d.h. sie schwenken im Takt einer Musik das rückwärts herausgestreckte Gesäss seitlich hin und her (Abb.1). Ein abermaliges Kommando beendet diesen «Tanz».

Auf dem Fossum-Felsen begegnet uns neben anderen Darstellungen eine in der äusseren Form dem rheinischen Stippeföttche ähnliche Scene, soweit man bei einer Zeitdifferenz von rund 3 000 Jahren von einer solchen Ähnlichkeit sprechen kann. Es handelt sich bei dieser Gruppe um drei Männer, die so angeordnet sind, dass der linke Mann Gesicht zu Gesicht zu dem mittleren, der rechte Rücken an Rücken zu ihm steht. Alle drei sind nackt, haben die Knie leicht gebeugt und tragen einen senkrecht gehaltenen Gegenstand, vermut-

Fig. 1. Kölner «Stippeföttche» (nach einem Foto von A. Koch).

Fig. 2. Darstellung auf dem Felsen von Fossum (nach Fredsjö 1960).

lich einen Stock, in der Hand (Abb. 2). Man hat den Eindruck, dass es bei den Fossum-Männern um eine beschwörende Handlung geht.

Die Darstellung von einer Gesicht zu Gesicht und Rücken zu Rücken gewandten Menschenreihe findet sich auch bei einigen Felsbildern in Valcamonica. Bei der einen Gravur von Seradina scheint es sich nach Anati um einen Kulttanz (oder eine kultisch-kämpferische Auseindersetzung?) zu handeln. Die Darstellung von Naquane lässt Anati an eine homophile Darstellung denken.

Nach dem Sinngehalt des rheinischen Stippeföttche befragt, vertrat der mit dem Kölner Karnevalsbrauchtum befasste Historiker Schwering (1972) in Übereinstimmung mit Wrede (1965) die Auffassung, dass es sich bei dieser Darstellung um eine Persiflage allzustreng gehandhabter Bräuche im Militärdienst handle. In Anbetracht der 1794 aufgezwungenen Besetzung der Rheinlande durch Frankreich erscheint nach deren Beendigung eine solch volkstümlichdrastische Geste plausibel. Bei der Wiedereinführung des bis dahin verboten gewesenen rheinischen Karnevals im Jahre 1823 wurden die Besatzungs-Verordnungen nachträglich dem Spott preisgegeben und durch das Stippeföttche karnevalistisch persifliert.

Von einer Absage an den Militärdienst, die an die Stippeföttche-Darstellung anklingt, weiss Bächthold-Stäubli (1931/32) aus Flandern zu berichten. Wenn ein Rekrut einberufen wurde und sich, um vom Militärdienst freizukommen, eine hohe Losnummer wünschte, dann musste er in eine bestimmte Kapelle gehen und dem dort befindlichen Heiligenbild (!) das entblösste Gesäss entgegenstrecken. Er erhalte dann die gewünschte hohe Losnummer. Dass Zeigen des nackten Gesässes war offenbar verschiedenenorts als Abwehrmittel gegen den unbeliebten Militärdienst bekannt. Im jetzigen rheinischen Stippeföttche erscheint dieser Abwehrzauber neuzeitlich und städtisch «verfeinert», im flandrischen recht urtümlich dargestellt. Der Geste als solcher scheint ein alter apotropäischer Sinn zu Grunde zu liegen.

In einem persönlichen Gespräch mit dem Linzer Volkskundler, Prof. Dr. Burgstaller, vertrat dieser die Meinung, dass das Zeremoniell des Stippeföttche nicht nur eine nachträglich persiflierende Absage an das französische Regime darstelle, dass es vielmehr noch andere Dinge ausdrücke, die an die für Naquane von Anati vermuteten anklingen. Da jedoch das moderne rheinische Stippeföttche hier nur einen Aufhänger für die Betrachtung des Problems um die drei Männer von Fossum abgibt, soll nicht weiter darauf eingegangen werden. Auszuschliessen ist allerdings eine homophile Darstellung für Fossum nicht, doch ist es wohl fraglich, ob solche Auffassungen in dem Rahmen der schwedischen Felsbilder und in der Mentalität der damals an der stürmischen Nordseeküste Schwedens lebenden Bauern Raum hatten.

Die Volskunde kennt nach Bächthold- Stäubli (1931/32) das Entgegenstrecken des Gesässes in mehreren Versionen, so als Absage, Herausforderung oder Verhöhnung und als allgemeines Apotropäum, das in Sonderheit auch als Abwehr gegen den bösen Blick wirksam sein solle. Weiter ist es aus Fruchtbarkeitsriten bekannt, wie es auch als Mittel in der Handhabung von Windmagie Bedeutung hatte. Im ganzen also eine reiche Palette.

Der Volkskunde ist nach Eckstein (1934/35) auch der Begriff der zauberischen Nacktheit, die die Ausstrahlung magischer Kräfte ausdrücken soll, bekannt. Für die Darstellung der drei in halbhockender Stellung befindlichen Fossum-Männer könnte sich aus den genanten Aspekten eine Erklärung und Sinndeutung ergeben.

Überlickt man die schwedischen Felsbilder ihrem Sinnengehalt nach, so schält sich neben anderem vor allem der Gedanke der Fruchtbarkeitsmagie als im Mittelpunkt stehend heraus. Fruchtbarkeit und Gedeihen für Mensch, Tier und Feldflur. Man geht wohl nicht fehl in der Annahme, dass die Vorstellung von Vegetationsgottheiten oder -dämonen bei den Felsbildern eine nicht unwesentliche Rolle gespielt hat. Die Darstellung zahlreicher kleinerer und grösserer Schiffe auf den Felszeichnungen lässt annehmen, dass schon damals Schiffart betrieben worden ist. Handle es sich nun um Küstenschiffahrt oder um weiterreichende Schiffswege, das Skagerak wird den Schiffern der Bronze- und frühen Eisenzeit nicht selten schwierige und gefährliche Aufgaben gestellt haben, deren Ende keineswegs immer gut verlaufen sein dürfte. Lassen die Felsbilder Bohusläns schon Ausübung von Magie annehmen, so liegt es bei dem häufigen Vorkommen bemannter Schiffsdarstellungen nahe, auch auf eine die Schiffahrt betreffende Wind- und Wettermagie zu schliessen.

Das Wetter wurde als von Göttern oder Dämonen gemacht oder gar als deren Offenbarung aufgefasst. Erinnert sei an den skandinavischen Windriesen Fasolt, an Wotan, an den litauschen Windgott Wejopatis, den griechischen Gott der Winde, Äolus, und viele andere imaginäre Gestalten des Luftreiches. Auffallend ist es, dass bei einigen von ihnen Doppelgesichtigkeit genannt wird, so verweist Zimmermann (1938/41) auf den zweigesichtigen Wejopatis der Litauer und auf den gelegentlich ebenfalls zweigesichtig dargestellten Boreas, dem die griechische Sage 2 Söhne, Kalais und den gegensätzlichen Zetes zuspricht. Was nun die Windmagie anlangt, unterscheidet man nach Zimmermann einen postiven und einen negativen Zauber, wobei der positive bei Flaute einen kräftigeren Wind herbeizaubern, der negative dagegen bei Sturm eine Abwehr-

massnahme darstellen und eine Abschwächung des Sturmes bewir-
ken soll. Windzauber verschiedener Art ist aus Schweden, Finnland,
Estland, Litauen, Ostpreussen, der ganzen südlichen Osteeküste und
vielen anderen Landschaften, Windzauber durch Zeigen des
nackten Gesässes vor allem aus den Küstengebieten Italiens und
Frankreichs, aber auch aus dem alpinen Wallis und der Oberpfalz
Bayerns bekannt. In Italien war dieser drastische Zauber insbesondere Brauch der Seeleute und Fischer. So berichten Bächthold-Stäubli
(1931/32) von italienischen Fischern, die auf offenem Meer in Seenot
gerieten und sich dadurch gerettet haben sollen, dass der an Bord
befindliche erstgeborene Sohn des Fischers schnell die Hosen
fallen liess und unter gleichzeitigem Anrufen christlicher Heiliger
(!) seitens seiner Kameraden dem Sturm das nackte Gesäss präsentier-
te, worauf dieser sogleich innehielt. Bei französischen Seeleuten, insbesondere in der Bretagne, ist ebenfalls die Nacktheit als Apotropäum und speziell die Zauberwirkung des nackten Gesässes als Abwehrmittel gegen Sturm bekannt. Im alpinen Wallis gilt die gleiche
Geste als Abwehrzauber gegen einen dort gefürchteten Wirbelwind.
Aus der Oberpfalz wird ähnliches berichtet. Ferner ist nach Bächthold-
Stäubli überliefert, dass Wettermacher das nackte Gesäss dreimal
in Wasser zu tauchen pflegten, woraufhin ein Rauch aufsteige,
der rasch zur schwarzen Wolke werde. Auch von Frauen ist aus
den östlichen Karpaten, Serbien und der Lausitz bekannt, dass
sie durch Zeigen des nackten Gesässes Wetterzauber ausübten,
doch handelt es sich in diesem Fall um Abwehr von Hagel und
Gewitter. Alle diese Praktiken des Wetterzaubers, insbesondere ein
positiver Windzauber aus Estland, über den Bargheer (1931/32, Spalte
336) zu berichten weiss, tragen auffallend archaische Züge und lassen auf tief in die Vergangenheit zurückreichende Wurzeln schliessen. Von besonderem Interesse ist hier eine lappische Sage. Eckstein
(1929/30) berichtet, dass darin von einer Lappenfrau erzählt wird,
die bei Herannahen einer Tschudenflotte dieser unter Absingen
von Zauberliedern ihr Hinterteil gezeigt habe, worauf ein Sturm
losbrach, der die feindlichen Schiffe vernichtete. — Im skandinavischen Norden ist also der Gesässzauber als Mittel der Wettermagie
bekannt gewesen.

Vergegenwärtigen wir uns, dass das Zeigen des nackten Gesässes
als Windzauber vor allem von Küstenstrichen Italiens und Frankreichs
bekannt geworden ist, dann erhebt sich die Frage, ob ein solcher magischer Brauch nicht möglicherweise aus dem Mittelmeergebiet nach
Nordeuropa gelangt sein könnte. Sieht man die drei Männer von
Fossum an, von denen je zwei ein einander zugewandtes oder einander abgewandtes Paar bilden, dann denkt man unwillkürlich an

andere Doppelgestalten der Antike. Ihnen haftet etwas Zwiespältiges, Gegensätzlichen an, sie blicken quasi in entgegengesetzte Richtungen. Ihnen obliegt die Entscheidung über den Ausgang eines Kampfes oder einer Situation, wenn diese auf des Messers Schneide stehen. Sie sind die von den Schiffern in höchster Seenot angerufenen «Schirmherren», die «Retter der Menschen», denen die Winde gehorchen. Sie lassen sich wohl auch als Sterne auf den Schiffsschnäbeln nieder oder erscheinen als St. Elmsfeuer. Solche Lichtsymbole dauten nach Schadewaldt (1956) auf Züge einer alten Naturdoppelgottheit hin. Die Sage von den beiden Söhnen des Boreas, dem Gott der kalten Nordwinde, Kalais und Zetes (dem «Schönweher» und dem «Stürmer») bringt zwei göttliche Brüder unmittelbar mit dem Wind in Beziehung. Sie trägt deutlich naturmythische Züge. Die Darstellung von dem Fossum-Felsen könnte eine Abwandlung alter Vorstellungen sein, die ihre Wurzeln im Vegetationskult hatten, und die schon frühzeitig aus dem Mittelmeergebiet nach Nordeuropa gelangten. Zeugnisse für Beziehungen kultureller Art treten in immer stärkerem Mass zu Tage.

Fasst man die hier genannten aus der Volkskunde belegten und als zauberwirksam angesehenen Praktiken zusammen, dann kann man sich des Eindruckes nicht erwehren, dass es sich bei der Darstellung auf dem Fossum-Felsen um Praktizierung eines Windzaubers gehandelt haben könnte. Die in unmittelbarer Nähe der drei Männer befindlichen Schiffe verstärken noch diese Annahme.

Bei dem Windzauber spielen nach Zimmermann (1938/41) u.a. Pfeifen (Heranpfeifen des Windes), Spucken gegen den Wind, Beschimpfungen des Windes, allgemeiner Lärm, Prügeleien, Schlagen mit Stöcken, Werfen von Steinen oder Hölzern ins Wasser oder Moor — in neuere Zeit auch scharfes Schiessen — eine Rolle. Dieses Imponiergehabe wird im Sinn des positiven Windzaubers als Herausforderung des Windes aufgefasst, während das Zeigen des nackten Gesässes in gebeugter Stellung den Wind besänftigen soll. In dieser letzgenannten Geste liesse sich im Gegensatz zu dem lärmenden und herausfordernden Verhalten eine Demuts- oder Unterwerfungsgeste gegenüber den Windgöttern oder -dämonen erblicken.

Der Charakter des bei gebeugten Knien herausgestreckten Gesässes als Devotionsgeste klingt noch in einem alten Kölner Kinderspiel an. Wrede (1965) berichtet von einem 1840 bekannten und beliebten, heute anscheinend vergessen Ballspiel von Knaben, das als «urkölnisch» bezeichnet wird. Es trägt ebenfalls den Namen «Stippeföttche». Wrede schreibt auf S. 132: «Bei diesem Spiel muss der Ball mehrmals aufgefangen werden, wem dies nicht gelingt, der muss sich an die Wand oder Mauer stellen und das

Hinterteil *erusstippe,* herausstrecken. Dies darf dann der Gegenspieler bombardieren». In diesem Kinderspiel wird das vorgestreckte Gesäss als «Demutsgeste» noch erkennbar.

Betrachtet man die Fossum-Darstellung unter diesem speziellen Gesichtspunkt, dann erhebt sich die Frage, ob hier ein Windzauber dargestellt ist, bei dem die Gesicht zu Gesicht und Rücken zu Rücken stehenden Männer Phasen des positiven und negativen Windzaubers ausdrücken, und ob die senkrecht gehaltenen Stecken in ihren Händen Requisiten dieses Zaubers sind.

Im Zusammenhang mit den hier dargelegten Erwägungen um den Windzauber sind auch die «Windheiligen» nicht ohne Interesse. Sie dürften ein Zeugnis dafür sein, dass dem Windzauber in vorchristlicher Zeit eine nicht geringe Bedeutung zukam, die es in christlicher Zeit zu überwinden galt. Die Windheiligen stellen eine christliche Assimilierung der Windgötter oder -dämonen dar. So ist einem dieser Windheiligen, dem hl. Clemens, in Deutz, einer Köln rechtsrheinisch gegenüberliegenden ehemals bedeutenden Schiffer- und Schiffbauerstadt, eine unmittelbar am Rhein gelegene alte Kirche geweiht. Von Clemens wird berichtet, er habe die Schiffer das Herbeipfeifen des Windes gelehrt, eine Aussage, aus der sich sehr alte Beziehungen herleiten lassen dürften.

Zwischen der Fossum-Darstellung und dem kölnischen «Stippeföttche» ist kein eindeutiger Zusammenhang auszumachen. Dennoch scheint das Moment der Abwehr eines Ungemaches durch Herausstrecken des Gesässes beiden Darstellungen gemeinsam zu sein. Im ersteren Fall handelt es sich höchstwahrscheinlich um eine persiflierende Abwehr des Militärdienstes, im zweiten Fall möglicherweise um Abwehr unheilvoller Wetterdämonen, wobei Wettermagie mit im Spiel gewesen sein mag.

SCHRIFTTUM

Almgren, O. (1934): Nordische Felszeichnungen als religiöse Urkunden, Frankfurt.

Althin (1945): Studien zu den Felszeichnungen von Skåne, Lund und Kopenhagen.

Anati (1960): La grande Roche de Naquane. Arch. de l'Instit. de paléontogie humaine. Mem. 31, Paris.

ders. (1963): La datazione dell-arte preistorica Camunica. Studi Camuni, vol. 2, Brescia.

ders. (1964): Camonica Valley, London.

Bächthold — Stäubli (1931/32): Artikel «Hinterer» in: Bächthold — Stäubli; Handwörterbuch des Deutschen Aberglaubens, B. 4, Berlin u. Leipzig.

Bargheer (1932/33): Artikel «Kot» in: Bächthold — Stäubli, Handwörterbuch des Deutschen Aberglaubens, B. 5, Berlin u. Leipzig.

Bröndsted (1962): Nordische Vorzeit, B. 2, Neumünster.

Eckstein (1929/30): Artikel «Entblössung» in: Bächthold-Stäubli, Handwörterbuch des Deutschen Aberglaubens, Bd. 2, Berlin u. Leipzig.

Eckstein (1934/35): Artikel «Nackt, Nacktheit» in: Bächthold — Stäubli, Handwörterbuch des Deutschen Aberglaubens, B. 6, Berlin u. Leipzig.

Fuchs — Schwering (1972): Kölner Karneval, Köln.

Glob (1969): Helleristninger i Danmark, Odense.

Schadewaldt (1956): Die Sternsagen der Griechen. Fischer — Bücherei, B. 129.

Schwering (1972): s. Fuchs und Schwering.

Wrede (1965): Neuer Kölnischer Sprachschatz. 3 Bde., Köln.

Zimmermann (1938/41): Artikel «Wind» in: Handwörterbuch des Deutschen Aberglaubens, B. 9, Berlin und Leipzig.

The problem of European impulses in the Nordic area of agrarian rock art

BY SVERRE MARSTRANDER

Most archaeologists emphasize the importance of impulses from the east concerning the group of rock carvings which has its background in the milieux of hunters and fishermen. Most recently it has been stressed in Gutorm Gjessing's lecture at this symposium. But the views held about the factors responsible for the origin of the agrarian rock art in the North are more controversial. It seems necessary to distinguish here between the underlying ideas and their formal expression. This group of Northern rock art seem to have developed on the basis of a «Symbolgut» of various origins, — a world of thought and conceptions partly of homely origin, partly transplanted to Nordic soil. But this «Symbolgut» has found its formal expression in symbols and figures conformable to Nordic perception. It has been nearly a dogma to interpret this group as formally rather independent in relation to other European rock art areas. It is really difficult to give indisputable proofs of foreign models to northern motifs on the usual rock carvings of agrarian type. Some motifs can appear in similar forms within separated European rock carving areas i.a. the four-wheeled waggon, which is to be found both on the Scandinavian penninsula and in the Camonica valley in North Italy (Anati 1961, p. 144; Marstrander 1963, fig. 44,6.) But in most cases there appearant conformities must be interpreted as convergence phenomena, not as proofs of real cultural connections.

The difficult problems of origin have been vividly discussed ever since the time of Montelius, who himself found the models of the Nordic figures of ships and axes among the engravings of West-European Megalith monuments (Montelius 1976 p. 473). His opinions have later on been shared by several scholars i.a. Ekholm (1916 p. 292 ff, 1935 p. 160—61) and Nordén, who especially has set off the probability of a connection between NW-Iberian and Swedish rock carvings. (Nordén 1925, p. 152—61).

But other areas have also been involved in the discussion of the archetypes of our rock carvings. According to one theory they should have clear presuppositions in the figurative scenes in the Greek geometric style of the 8th cent. B.C. (Hansen 1908) or they could partly have been influenced by decorative motives on imported bronze vessels from the area of the Hallstadt culture. (Althin 1945, p. 235–36).

Recently Glob has tried to separate some elements of possible foreign origin in the Danish rock carving material (Glob 1969, p. 131–33). Glob pays attention to the group of «cup and ring» carvings in the north-western part of the Iberian peninsula which MacWhite termed the Galician series (MacWhite 1946, p. 59). This group spread, according to MacWhite, to Ireland and North Britain and the motif consisting of one or more rings around a cup in the center and with another cup on one of the rings, should at last have travelled across the North Sea. But the very few parallels MacWhite refers to in Scandinavia (1946 p. 72) are, as also Glob maintains, not convincing and cannot be taken as proof of the existence of West-European elements in the Nordic spectre of rock carving motifs. On the other hand Glob (1969, p. 135) seems to be of the opinion that the eldest rock carvings in the Danish area, especially cups, grooves and concentric rings around a cup could be explained by assuming inpulses from West-European bronze-smiths, who may have been working in South Scandinavia. But it is dubious if we have the right to draw any conclusions concerning a possible connection between the group of Irish-English objects in the eldest Danish bronze material and the hewing of the eldest Danish rock carvings. This theory can hardly represent more than a rather hypothetical possibility.

There is, however, in the Norwegian material a small group of decorated slabs from Bronze Age graves which seems to give us more real indications of foreign elements in Nordic rock carving, and which deserve more attention than they have received up to date.

The slabs which for the most part were published by de Lange (1912) and later more completely described by the Fetts (1941) were used as gables in, or as a cover over stone cists, but some of them were found lying among the material of earth and stones of which the mound over the cist was built. The drawings of the decorative patterns published here are based on the author's investigations.

1. Slab from Skjølingstad, Karmøy, Rogaland (Fig. 1). Found in a burial mound as capstone covering a clay vessel containing charred bones. Decoration consisting of two elements: transverse panels forming a rather irregular herring-bone pattern and a group of concentric arcs with an interrupted line through their centre.

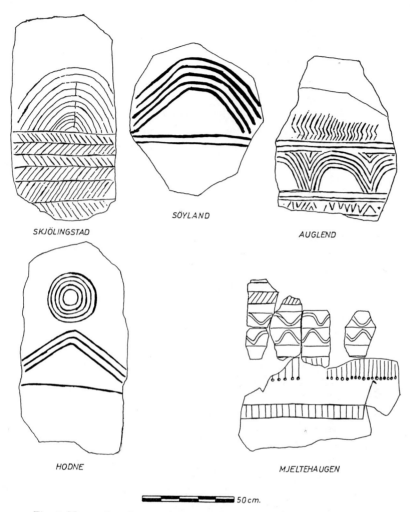

SKJÖLINGSTAD   SÖYLAND   AUGLEND

HODNE   MJELTEHAUGEN

50 cm.

Fig. 1. Norwegian decorated grave slabs from Rogaland and Sunnmøre.

2. Slab from Søyland, Jæren, Rogaland (Fig. 1). Originally forming one of the gable walls of a stone cist where only som few sherds of pottery and fragments of charcoal were found. Decoration on the inside: two transverse parallel lines, surmounted by a group of concentric arcs.

3. Slab from Auglend, Jæren, Rogaland, said to have been found in a burial mound (Fig. 1).

47

Two decorative elements: at bottom a panel of groups of concentric arcs in a row, bordered by parallel lines; above vertical parallel lines forming a sort of vertical chevron pattern. The furrows are now partly very difficult to follow, but analyses with the aid of modern methods have in the main affirmed the correctness of the old drawing in de Lange's paper (1912 fig.2).

4. Slab from Hodne, Jæren, Rogaland, said originally to have belonged to a stone cist (Fig. 1). At bottom a horizontal line surmounted by three angular parallels, perhaps part of a chevron pattern and appearing in very distinct furrows. The concentric group of circles above is now difficult to discern, but new investigations have made it clear that it consists of 5 circles.

5. Most remarkable are the numerous fragments of decorated slabs from a big stone cist which formed the central grave of a large burial mound called Mjeltehaugen at Giske, Sunnmøre (Fig. 1). The scheme of decoration comprises several elements; the division into narrow horizontal panels as on the Skjølingstad slab is a characteristic feature. The linear patterns consist of chevroned or undulating lines as well as rows of oblique furrows often placed beside each other so as to form a herringbone pattern. One of the fragments shows defective concentric circles with a radial groove as on the Skjølingstad slab. Without parallels on the other slabs is a decorative pattern consisting of small, rectangular cavities in two rows beside each other, each cavity in the one row placed opposite the interspaces in the other row (Fig. 3, 5). Of particular interest is the border of tassels at the bottom of several of the fragments. It conveys the impression that the entire decoration of the wall is intended to represent textile hangings adorning the walls of the tomb. Important is, finally, the occurrence of ship figures which do not at all conform with the usual types of the agrarian rock carvings but in all cases seem to be related.

6. Slab from Austrheim, Karmøy, Rogaland (Fig. 2). Human figure with disc-formed body consisting of four very distinct concentric circles.

7. Fragment of a slab from Steine, Byneset, Trøndelag, decorated on both sides (Steine A and B). The slab served as capstone covering a burial chamber which proved empty on excavation. On the one side (Steine A, Fig. 2) decoration consisting of two elements: a border of tassels somewhat different from the form of the motif on the Mjeltehaugen fragments (No.5) and a group of concentric arcs of rather clumsy design, with a radius through their centre.

8. Decoration on the other side of the slab from Steine, Byneset, Trøndelag (Steine B) showing a fragmentary panel of groups of concentric arcs (Fig. 2). The best preserved of the groups has a radial line through the centre.

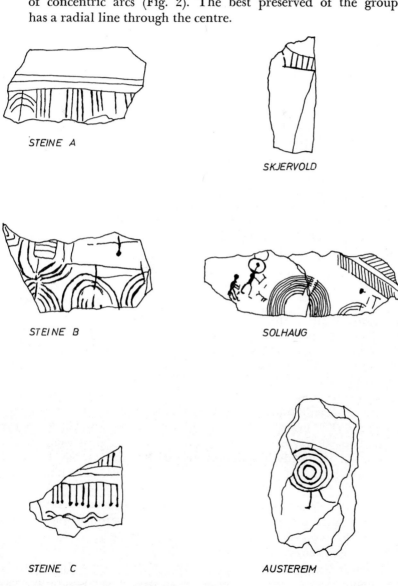

STEINE A

SKJERVOLD

STEINE B

SOLHAUG

STEINE C

AUSTEREIM

50cm.

Fig. 2. Norwegian decorated slabs from West-Norway and Trøndelag.

9. Another fragment of a slab from the same burial chamber at Steine, Byneset, Trøndelag (Steine C Fig. 2) It is decorated with a border of tassels of exact same type as on the Mjeltehaugen slabs.
10. The most recent addition to this group of ornamented grave slaps comes from Solhaug, Ørlandet, Trøndelag (Fig. 2). The decoration consists of three elements: a fragmentary herring-bone pattern; two human figures, one of them with a circle around the head, holding a weapon in the outstretched arm; a fragmentary group of concentric circles with two radial lines which connect the circles and mark an opening into the centre.
11. Fragmentary slab from Skjervoll, Skatval, Trøndelag, with part of a ship figure clearly of the same type as on the Mjeltehaugen slab (Fig.2).

The slabs which we have described here have rather a differenciated spectre of motifs. (Fig. 3). Eight of the graves to which they belong were decorated with groups of concentric arcs or — in two cases — concentric circles; three of the arc groups show the interesting variant with radials crossing the arcs through their centre (1, 7, 8). Three of the stone cists (1, 5, 10) had a decoration of narrow panels with oblique lines often combined to herringbone patterns; especially in the Mjeltehaugen tomb this element was as the fragments display a most characteristic feature. A variant of this linear decoration were panels with chevron or undulating patterns (4, 5); one of the slabs (3) has a vertical chevron-like group of parallel lines. The slabs from Steine and Mjeltehaugen (5, 7, 9) are exceptional in that they shows borders of textile-like tassels at the bottom of the ornamentation as to give an impression of decorative wall hangings. There are several examples of the tassels motifs on the Mjeltehaugen fragments. Finally, in two of the graves (5, 11) the decoration included ship figures related to the double furrowed types which form a so common feature of the rock carvings in the open field.

The Mjeltehaugen slabs with their wealth of decorative elements naturally form the most important item of the group and a discussion of the problems of origin which these elements raise, seems to be an appropriate starting-point.

After the first publication by de Lange (1912), the Mjeltehaugen fragments hav only been sporadically treated. Their decoration was at first rather superficially characterized as the result of West-European impulses (Hoernes-Menglin 1925, p. 242), but K. Willvonseder has later rightly pointed out that the horizontal panels with

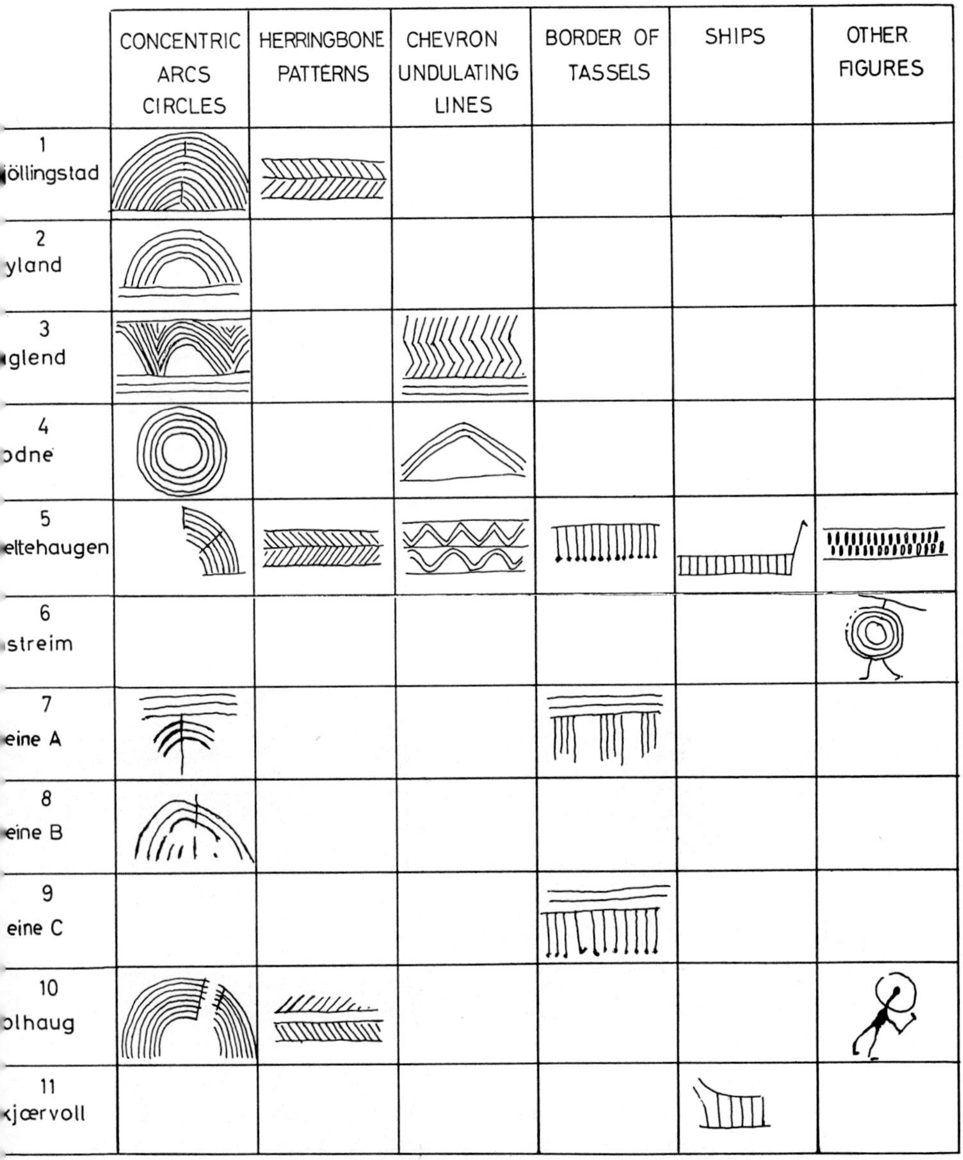

	CONCENTRIC ARCS CIRCLES	HERRINGBONE PATTERNS	CHEVRON UNDULATING LINES	BORDER OF TASSELS	SHIPS	OTHER FIGURES
1 öllingstad	◿	◿				
2 yland	◿					
3 glend	◿		◿			
4 odne	◿		◿			
5 eltehaugen	◿	◿	◿	◿	◿	◿
6 streim						◿
7 eine A	◿			◿		
8 eine B	◿					
9 eine C				◿		
10 olhaug	◿	◿				◿
11 kjærvoll					◿	

Fig. 3. Spectre of motifs on the decorated grave slabs.

chevron and herring-bone patterns have close parallels in the Göh-litzsch grave in the Halle district (Willvonseder 1937, p. 121). The grave furniture consisting of i.a. corded ware amphoras and a facet-ted stone axe, has generally been accepted as a reliable reason for the cultural attribution. A comparison between the decorative schemes of the northern slab in the Göhlitzsch cist and one of the Mjeltehaugen fragments displays congruences which could hardly be explained as coincidences. (Fig.4).

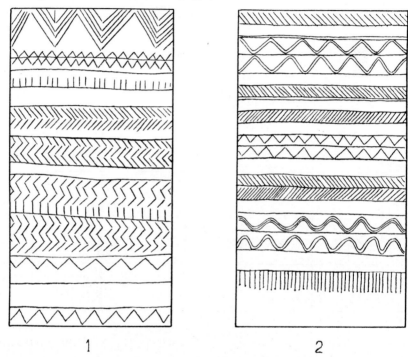

1   2

Fig. 4. Schemes of decoration on: 1. slab of the northern wall of the Göhlitzsch cist, Merseburg; 2. slab from the Mjeltehaugen, Giske, Sunnmøre.

The Göhlitzsch grave belongs to a group of tombs in Central Ger-many with engravings on the stone walling slabs which have been the object of new studies in recent years. Important discoveries have been made in connection with a reexcavation of the Züschen cist near Fritzlar (Uenze 1958) and through the investigation of a mound covering a stone cist with decorated slabs on the Dölauer Heide near Halle a.d. Saale. This last grave lies only some 20 kms away from the Göhlitzsch cist. (Behrens 1958).

It is perhaps astonishing that the Züschen grave is mentioned in this context as it is usually classified as a construction of Megalithic character with collective burials, where a port-hole slab divides the grave into a long chamber and a short antechamber. The well-known designs of horned animals drawing some kind of vehicle and perhaps representing connections with rock art in the Ligurian Alps, belong to the Megalithic milieu, but the fine chevron patterns executed in deep pick technique near the upper edge of two of the slabs have a different background. Uenze has rightly emphasized the close connection of the chevron style both in pottery and grave decoration with the Single Grave/Cord Ware culture. During the re-excavation, sherds of the Cord Ware pottery came to light and they occured only in the deposits immediately below the roof. The most probably explanation, as indicated by Uenze, is the supposition of a secondary use of the tomb by Single Grave people at a time when only the upper portions of the walling stones were free. Such intrusive burials in elder tombs by groups of Single Grave people have, as we know, many parallels. The chevroning must be the work of the intruders.

The new Dölau grave shares the chevron and herring-bone patterns with the Züschen and Göhlitzsch cists and gives us perhaps the best instances of this decoration style in Neolithic tomb art. The

Fig. 5. 1. Stone 9, Dölauer Heide. After Powell. — 2. Menhir von Ellenberg in Hesse. After Uenze.

cist is bigger than usual in the Single Grave/Cord Ware culture, approximately 4 m long, and a third of the floor had been occupied by a wooden platform. 7 of the 11 stones were highly decorated; 5 had patterns executed by the use of a deep cutting pick; on one stone the decoration had been effected by colouring in white and on another both picking and painting had been used. Slab 9 (Fig. 5, 1) shows a straightforward pattern with rows of close-set chevrons, almost identical with the secondary zig-zags of the Züschen grave. The other slabs are decorated with related designs, vertical or horizontal rows of oblique lines forming chevrons.

Exceptional is the painted scheme of one of the gable stones (slab 5), consisting of hatched triangles forming reserved vertical zigzags — a «Wolfzahnmuster».

In conclusion we may say that this group of Central German stone cists displays closely related examples of a linear decorative art which seem to have clear connections to burials of Single Grave/ Cord Ware cultures. The peculiar Menhir von Ellenberg in Hesse (Fig. 5, 2), with its close-set vertical chevrons, seems to be a clear proof of this connection. (Uenze 1958, p. 105).

The analyses of the designs of this decorative style has in many cases led to a search for parallels in the incised art of the Megalithic graves in Atlantic Europe. The papers of Waldtraut Schriekel can be seen as representative of this tendency. (Schriekel 1957, 1962). But the assumption of West-European elements in the decorative art of Neolithic tombs of Central Germany cannot in any case be characterized as based on convincing parallels. In my opinion T.G.E. Powell is right in rejecting these attemps to search for comparisons in the west in his important paper «Megalithic art and other art, Centre and West.» (1960). The art of the Halle tombs is quite different in execution, content and arrangement. The connections, are as already pointed out by A. Tallgren in a famous paper from 1934 and later verified by Marta Gimbutas (1956), to be found in the opposite direction, eastwards.

It has long been recognized that the Halle tombs belong to a tradition of house-graves of long endurance, known thoughout the grasslands North of the Caucasus and extending into the Pontic region north of the Black Sea. The house-graves in this area were often built of wood, but in the Globular Amphora and Cord Ware cultures there are examples of graves built by slabs which provide reasonable prototypes for the Halle graves (Powell 1960, p. 186-7).

But it is the dolmens to the south of the river Kuban in the western Caucasus which primarily give clear evidences for painted and incised wall decoration. Already Tallgren noticed the textile

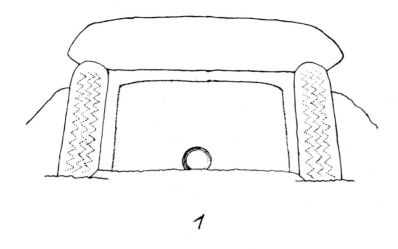

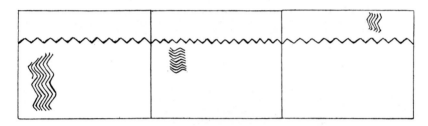

Fig. 6. 1. The dolmen at Zhana with chevroned patterns on the projecting side walls. — 2. Chevroned patterns on the walls of the dolmen at Aderba, Guelend-zhik. — After Tallgren.

character of some of the linear patterns of the dolmens (Fig. 6) and suggested a connection between these decorative elements of the Caucasian graves and those of the Göhlitzsch tomb. (Tallgren 1934, p. 38-39).

Maria Gimbutas has later carried on the ideas of Tallgren, pointing out the importance of the Kurgan culture in Ukraina as the medium of impulses concerning grave-forms from the Kuban area to the Globular Amphora and Single Grave/Cord Ware cultures in Central and Northern Europe. The Hut-grave phase of the Kurgan culture provides the closest analogies for the Central European graves showing direct evidence for wall hangings in the form of patterned rugs. (Gimbutas 1956, p. 74-80).

From a number of prehistoric settlements in central and eastern Europe we know examples of wall plaster surfaces which as counterparts of the disappeated wall tapestries can give us an impression of Neolithic and Bronze Age wall decoration (Chile 1929, p. 88 and 99; Piggott 1965, p. 89, Fig. 79 and p. 147). Of special interest in connection with our investigation is the wall plaster, belonging to the Tumulus Bronze Age, painted in bands of rose-red, whitish-yellow and grey, found in a settlement of Jurikowice in Moravia. As Powell emphasizes, the cultural milieu of this settlement had clear Single Grave/Cord ware antecedents. (Powell 1960, p. 187).

This and other finds indicate that the Bronze Age Cultures of Central Europe inherited elements of that linear art which the decorated cists of the Halle area display.

Fig. 7. Decorated grave slab from Illmitz in Burgenland, Austria. — After Willvonsender.

That linear patterns of similar character as in the Halle graves really have survived into the Bronze Age is perhaps best illustrated by the slab from Illmitz im Burgenland, Austria (Willvonseder 1938; Gimbutas 1965, p. 307, Pl.60). The rather thin slab (Fig. 7), 63 cm long, comes from a cemetery of the Early Urnfield period, and formed one of the walls in a stone cist. It has a large hole (Seelenloch) in the middle; the upper part has a decoration of chevrons arranged in five panels separated by incised horizontal lines. Above the hole is a secondary group of concentric circles crossing the original chevron pattern. How the circles should be explained is unclear. There are, as Wollvonseder maintains, no parallels in the Urnfield Culture. But the panels with their chevron must without doubt represent an inheritance from that linear art which characterizes the decorated stone cists of the Single Grave/Cord Ware Culture, especially the Göhlitzsch grave.

The grave furniture of the Illmitz cist, which i.a. included fragments of two Spindlerfeld fibulas and sherds of a channelled vessel, affirms the dating to Early Urnfield period, most probably Hallstat A, roughly corresponding to Montelius Per. IV.

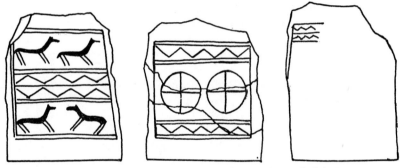

Fig. 8. Slabs 3, 4 and 5 of the Kivik grave. The carvings of slab 5 seem not to be quite certain. — After Nordén.

From Bronze Age Central Europe impulses must have found their way to the North, where we on three of the slabs in the famous Kivik grave meet the same chevron pattern arranged in horizontal panels bordered by incised lines (Fig. 8). Already Willvonseder mentions the chevron of the Kivik grave as a parallel to the decoration of the Illmitz slab.

According to usual dating to Mont. Per. III, the Kivik grave should be a little older than the Illmitz slab (Althin 1945, I, p. 66-71, Marstrander 1963, p. 329-33).

But similar impulses, only following other routes, seem also to have reached the western coasts of Norway. The slabs from Skjølingstad, Augland, Hodne, Mjeltehaugen and Solhaug (Nos. 1, 3, 4, 5 and 10 described above) are decorated with rows of alternating oblique lines, and chevrons usually arranged in horizontal panels. Their lineal patterns seem to be related to the wall decorations of the Cord Ware cists in the Halle region and the Bronze Age slab from Illmitz in Burgenland. It seems reasonable to explain the characteristic borders of tassels in the graves of Mjeltehaugen and Steine (No. 5 or 7-9) in the same way.

It is temptating to imagine how these impulses could have come from Central Europe to our country by the important highway which followed the Elbe and continued along the west-coast of Jutland to SW-Norway. (Marstrander 1950, p. 77). This highway was of special importance during the Early Nordic Bronze Age, but was without doubt also used later.

We have very few clues for a more exact dating of the Norwegian slabs. The Mjeltehaugen slabs belonged to a big cist in a mound, and probably covered an inhumation burial of Early Nordic Bronze Age type, possibly from the beginning of the period, because the ship figures seem to represent an earlier type than those of the usual rock carvings. Concerning the other slabs, we only know that the Skjølingstad slabs was lying as capstone over a cist containing a vessel filled with charred bone, which seems to indicate that it probably is not older than the Late Nordic Bronze Age. The same conclusion can be drawn concerning the Søyland slab, from a cist with sherds and charcoal, which now unhappily are lost. The other slabs are throughout small, and seem to have belonged to small stone cists with cremation burials of Late Bronze Age type. But it must be confessed that the dating is connected with several uncertainties within the range of the Bronze Age.

But not all motifs on our slabs can be explained by impulses from Central Europe. The groups of multiple, roughly semicircular arcs, which decorate some of them, have no analogies at all in the decorated graves of Central Europe. They appear single as on the slabs of Skjølingstad, Søyland and Steine A (Nos. 1, 2, 7) or in groups arranged in a horizontal panel as on the slabs of Augland and Steine B. (Nos, 3 and 8). In some cases the arcs are supplied with a vertical radial through the midst of the figure. (Skjølingstad, Steine A and B). The only comparable figure in the Nordic Area outside Norway is found on the fragmentary Tibirke stone from the northern

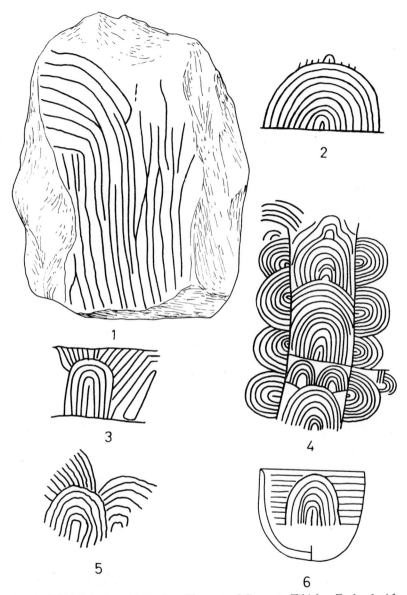

Fig. 9. Multiple arcs or horseshoe-like curved lines. 1. Tibirke, Zealand. After Glob. — 2-4. Gaurinis, Brittany. After Crawford. — 5. Lough Crew, Ireland. After Crawford. — 6. Vase from dolmen of Conguel, Quiberon, Brittany. After L'Helgouach.

part of Zealand (Fig. 9,1). (Glob 1969, p. 106-7). It is quite clear that the Tibirke carving originally consisted of multiple, approximately parallel, carved lines which, however, were more horseshoe-like than semicircular. Perhaps there was another group of the same type beside it.

It is worth mentioning that already Sophus Müller referred to parallels in West-European Megalithic art when he first published the carving (Müller 1918, p. 83 og 274) and consequently considered it as being of foreign origin. Brøndsted has later rightly classified it as belonging to the Bronze Age milieu in connection with his treatise of Danish rock carvings. (Brøndsted 1958, p. 292).

It is difficult to join Glob in his sceptisism concerning the true Bronze Age character of the Tibirke carving. The West-European parallels, especially in the Megalithic art of Brittany (Fig. 9,2-6), seem to represent a near and reasonable model to the peculiar construction of the Nordic figure.

The motif and the question of its wandering from West-Europe to the North have been discussed anew in some more recent papers. O.I.S. Crawford interprets the stones with the carvings of multiple arcs as blurred images of the Mother goddess (the Eye goddess) put into the tomb to look after the dead person. These images, which mainly give the impression of a face cult, are assumed to have spread westwards in the Mediterranean and reached the Atlantic coasts. As the eyes are the dominating feature in the rendering of the goodess, the vertical sets of multiple arcs in the passage grave of Gavrinis are i.a. explained as dublicated simple eyes surrounded by multiple lines which represent the orbits and are sometimes confused with eyebrows. But Crawford adds cautiously: here and elsewhere there is an obvious confusion of motifs and we must not press the identification too hard (Crawford 1957, p. 68-72). To Crawford the Tibirke stone appears as evidence in support of his rather questionable theory of an immigration to Denmark from West-Europe of passage-grave builders, where one point of departure should be Brittany (Crawford 1957, p. 110).

Peter Gelling has concentrated his studies on the religious rites and symbols which the engravings of the Northern Bronze Age embody and has, following lines similar to those of Crawford, tried to give more general interpretations of some of the curvilineal patterns which could be of interest in connection with our investigations.

Gelling, who has accepted Crawford's idea of how the series of eye-goddess representations could be traced from the Mediterranean to the Atlantic coasts and Denmark, follows the motif further to

SW-Norway and Östergötland (Gelling 1967, 106-11). The «Leitmotif» figures with multiple curves of approximate horseshoe or semicircular form are interpreted as a degenerated figuration of the eye-goddess's face. The vertical, discontinuous line through the centre of the concentric arcs of the Skjølingstad slab is by Gelling denoted as a lingering reference to a nose, and the multiple arcs of the Søyland slab could represent further stages of degeneration. (The zigzag carvings of thes lab from Hodne, which Gelling also mentions in this connection, has in my opinion nothing to do with our curvilineal patterns.)

Regarding the various interpretations of the group of multiple arcs or curves which are listed above, it seems convenient to quote some wise words by Stuart Piggott: «and here we enter very dangerous ground, none other than the fabled realm of the Mother goddess whose existence is as unsubstantiated in the chambered tombs of the west as among the figurines of the east.» The apprehension of what ideas the symbols are intended to express will always be hypothetical and is of secondary inportance for our investigation. Essential in this connection is a discussion of the probability of relationship between the groups of carved multiple arcs in the North and in West-Europe based on comparisons without any regard to their meaning.

The few and rather featureless items Gelling mentions as evidence of the theory that elements of West-European Megalithic art had also reached Sweden seems to me quite inadequate for drawing such far-reaching conclusions (Gelling 1967, p. 106, Fig. 48). But regarding the slabs from SW-Norway and Zealand, their position seems in my opinion to be rather different.

Could, for instance, the conformity between the concentric semicircles of the Gavrinis grave and the similar pattern on the Skjølingstad slab be explained as merely a coincidence? (Fig. 1 and 9, 2-4). Or is the correspondence between the multiple horseshoe curves of Gavrinis and the carving of the Tibirke Stone only a convergence phenomenon? (Fig. 9,1 and 9,3-4). It seems to me that the curvilineal patterns with which we are here dealing, do not at all belong to those elementary abstract designs which are found widespread all over the world. Their rather restricted distribution in Europe indicates that they have their roots in a special cultural milieu from which they may have wandered to other areas.

There are no parallels in the Galician or other groups on the Iberian peninsula, (Sobrino Buhigas 1935; Anati 1968) and the ornamental alphabet of the Irish passage graves can only offer a few items of multiple arcs on some of the Lough Crew tombs. (Fig. 9,5;. Herity 1974, fig.s. 37, 39, 46, 81).

In Brittany the occurence of multiple arcs is, as we know, consentrated to the Gavrinis passage grave, where almost every support is decorated with concentric semicircles or horseshoe carvings arranged in elaborate compositions. In some passage graves and gallery graves there are also a few plain items which must be classified as belonging to the same category. (Pequart et Le Rouzic 1927, Pl. 17, 38, 71, 84, 99-134). In the rest of Europe outside the Nordic area there are, as far as I know, no parallels. In some few cases the motif appears as part of the decoration of passage grave pottery (Fig. 9,6).

The problem of possible relations between West-Europe and West and Southwest Norway in the period corresponding to the Nordic Bronze Age has never been subjected to systematic research. But some points of interest could be mentioned, indicating that the theory of a connection between late Megalithic art in Western Europe and the Bronze Age decorated grave slabs in Norway does not deal with as isolated phenomena as perhaps generally believed.

In the county of Rogaland, Southwest Norway, our attention has been directed to a group of big earth mounds from Per. II-III covering graves, man-size cists, most careful built with small stones. This type of cist seems inexplicable as a result of local development, but could have been introduced to Southwest-Norway in connection with impulses from Western Europe, where graves of similar construction are found in the Armorican area (Möllerop 1962, p. 42 ff.)

Another feature of great interest in this connection is the marked terraces which distinguish a certain group of big mounds in Rogaland. Terraced mounds appear as a foreign element in the Nordic Bronze Age, but could perhaps be explained as offshoots of the

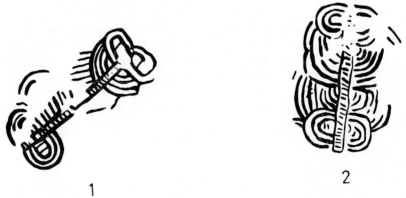

1

2

Fig. 10. Geometric patterns from the rock carving at Ausevik, Flora, West-Norway. After Hagen.

terraced «bell barrows» which characterize the Wessex culture (Möllerop 1962, p. 34).

But perhaps more conspicuous as an indication of relations between Atlantic and Norwegian coasts are some peculiar figures of the rock carving at Ausevik, West-Norway, briefly published by Hagen (1969). Between carved figures of human beings and numerous animals, there are a number of spirals, circles, frames with inner decoration, net-formed figures and other geometric patterns which extensively could have their origin in the agrarian rock art. But this can not be maintained for all figures. The one true labyrinth and the labyrinth-like figures of Ausevik cannot have their models among the motifs of the agrarian carvings where mazes are unknown. It is more probable that the labyrinth-motif was introduced from West-Europe, where labyrinths are well known both in Megalithic grave art (New Grange) and on rocks (Pontevedra, NW-Spain). Further patterns like Fig. 10 are without parallels in the Nordic area. But the panels of semicircular concentric arcs on both sides of a central axis seem in a remarcable way to be paraphrases of the theme well-known from the decorated supports of the Gaurinis grave (Fig. 9,4). It is difficult to believe that the conformity of these extraordinary line constructions in Brittany and West Norway is to be explained only as convergence. I would like to add that also our colleagues Eva and Per Fett have expressed similar opinions concerning the West-European background of the Ausevik figures.

In his conclusion Peter Gelling evades a discussion of the chronological problems which the pointing out of these possible West-European Late Neolithic elements in a Nordic Bronze Age milieu raise (1969, p. 106). All accessible information about the Norwegian slabs indicates that they belonged to stone cists of Bronze Age types. It seem quite clear that they have no relation whatsoever to any late Neolithic milieu in Scandinavia. Could, then, the impulses from the Atlantic coast have reached the North during the final stages of Megalithic grave art, corresponding to the transition to or the beginning of the Nordic Bronze Age — roughly the centuries of the first half of the second millennium B.C.?

This seems to be within the borders of the possible. In varied forms collective chambers tombs (passage and gallery graves) continued to be used and, indeed, in some regions to be built up to and perhaps beyond the mid-second millennium B.C. (Piggott 1965, p.61, Pl. VII). The Gaurinis tomb has often been considered as rather late; Piggott dates it roughly to the early second millennium B.C. Recent studies in Brittany seem to affirm the theory of longliving Megalithic traditions in the West (L'Helgouach 1973).

Fig. 11. Boat-like symbols of megalithic art in West-Europe. 1. Kervéresse, Brittany. — 2-5. Mané Crud, Brittany. — 6-8. Lough Crew, Ireland. — 9. Sowth, Ireland. — 10. New Grange, Ireland. — 11. Ri Cruin, Kilmartin Valley, Scotland. Arrows at 6, 9 and 10 indicates upper edge.
— After the author's drawings.

The so-called *sépultures Mégalithiques à entrée laterale* are a further development of the usual passage graves, where the elongated chamber lies on the left side of the gradually shortened passage. This group of graves, which for the most part is concentrated on the northern coast area of Brittany, seems according to the C^{14} dates to belong to a period of roughly 500 years, starting about 2300 B.C. The C^{14} date of the tomb of Crech Quillé on the northern coast has provisionally given the youngest limit for the use of a Megalithic grave of this type: 1810 B.C.

The gallery-graves *(les allées couvertes)* seem roughly to belong to the same period as the graves with elongated chambers. The youngest of them seem to have been erected after the phase of Armorican Barrow culture, probably shortly after 2000 B.C. In some marginal areas groups of Megalithic graves such as the *dolmens Angevins à portique* were in use for rather a long time. The big dolmen complex of Barnenez on the north coast was still in use in the Early Bronze Age (l'Helgouach 1973).

New investigations will without doubt give us more comprehensive information about the survivals of Megalithic traditions in the early phases of the West-European Bronze Age. But already now it seems possible that the curvilineal patterns on the Danish-Norwegian group of slabs could be explained by impulses from Megalithic art in its last, lingering phases.

There is still one element in the decorative scheme of the Norwegian slabs which must be discussed: the ship figures seen in the Mjeltehaugen and Skjervoll slabs (Nos. 5 and 11 Fig. 3). It is superfluous to say that this motif has no analogies in the decorative patterns of the tombs in Central Germany, neither is there any convincing parallel in the Megalithic art of West-Europe. In some of the Morbihan passage graves there is among the carvings a design resembling a boat with a high prow and poop, with vertical lines representing the masts or the crew (Fig. 11), but the interpretation of these and other similar figures in West-Europe is doubtful and not generally accepted. (Giot 1962, p. 52, Fig. 10). The ship figures of the Mjeltehaugen and Skjervoll cists are all of the same type, with straight, almost vertical stems ascending high up directly from the bottom of the hull (Fig.3). This type, which also has parallels in other parts of the country (Trøndelag, Rogaland, Østfold) is different from the usual ship figures on the Bronze Age rock carvings, with their characteristic double-prow construction and curved stem and stern. It seems to represent an earlier phase of the art of shipbuilding, probably of Neolithic ancestry. It is generally supposed that it was still in use at the beginning of the Bronze Age, as already indicated by our collegues Eva and Per Fett in their book on rock carvings in South-West Norway (Fetts 1941, p. 137).

A *terminus antequem* is represented by the observation that a ship of this type on the carving at Unneset, Askvoll, Sunnfjord, is cut by a shipfigure of Late Bronze Age type.

If our suppositions hold good, we have reason to conclude that the carvings of our slabs seem to combine Central — as well as West-European impulses with homely traditions represented by the ship-figures of Mjeltehaug type.

REFERENCES

Althin (1945): Carl-Axel Althin. Studien zu den bronzezeitlichen Felszeichnungen von Skåne, I, II, Lund.

Anati (1961): Emmanuel Anati. Camonica Valley, N.Y. 1961.

Behrens (1958): Hermann Behrens. Ein neolithischer Grabhügel mit darunterliegendem Hausgrundriss bei Halle (Saale). Neue Ausgrabungen in Deutschland, Hamburg, pp. 93—98.

Brøndsted (1958: Johs. Brøndsted. Danmarks oldtid, 2. Bronzealderen, Kbh.

Childe (1929): V.G. Gordon Childe. The Danube in Prehistory, Oxford.

Crawford (1957): O.G.S. Crawford. The Eye Goddess, London.

Ekholm (1916): Gunnar Ekholm. De skandinaviska hällristningarna och deras betydelse. Ymer 36, pp. 275—308.

Ekholm (1935): Gunnar Ekholm, Forntid og Fornforskning i Skandinavia, Sth.

Fetts (1941): Eva og Per Fett. Sydvestnorske helleristninger, Stavanger.

Gelling (1967): Peter Gelling and Hilda Ellis Davidson. The Chariot of the Sun, London.

Gimbutas (1956): Maria Gimbutas. The Prehistory of Eastern Europe, I, p. 140—57.

Gimbutas (1965): Marija Gimbutas. Bronze Age cultures in Central and Eastern Europe, The Hague.

Giot (1962): P.R. Giot. Britanny, London.

Glob (1969): P.V. Glob. Helleristninger i Danmark. Jutland Archaeological Society Publications, Vol. VII, Odense.

Hagen (1969): Anders Hagen. Studier i vestnorsk bergkunst. Årbok for Universitetet i Bergen.

Hansen (1908): Andreas M. Hansen. Om helleristningene. Aarsberetning fra Foreningen til norske fortidsmindesmærkers bevaring, pp. 1—61.

L.'Helgouach (1965): Jean L'Helgouach. Les sépultures mégalithiques en Armargue, Alencon.

L'Helgouach (1973): Jean L'Helgouach. Les sépultures de l'ouest de la France. Évalution et chronologie — Megalithic Graves and Burial. Papers pres. at the III Atlantic Colloquium, Moesgård 1969, pp. 203—19, Kbh.

Herity (1974): Michel Herity. Irish Passage Graves, Dublin.

Hoernes — Menghin (1925): Moritz Hoernes. Urgeschichte der bildenden Kunst in Europa. 3. Aufl. erg. v. Oswald Menghein, Wien.

de Lange (1912): Eyvind de Lange. Ornerte heller i norske bronsealdersgraver. Bergens Museums Årbok, nr. 4.

MacWhite (1946): Eoin MacWhite. A New View on Irish Bronze Age Rock Scribings. The Journal of the Royal Society of Antiquaries of Ireland, Vol. LXXVI.

Marstrander (1950): Sverre Marstrander. Jylland-hista. Viking 14, pp. 63—85.

Marstrander (1963): Sverre Marstrander. Østfolds jordbruksristninger (The Agrarian Rock Carvings of the County of Østfold, SE-Norway). Institute f. Comparative Research in Human Culture, Ser. B, Vol. LIII, Oslo.

Montelius (1876): Oscar Montelius. Sur les sculptures de roches de la Suède. Congrès int. d'anthropologie et d'archeologie Préhist. Compte rendul, Stockholm.

Møllerop (1962): Gudmund Møllerop. Fra Rogalands eldre bronsealder. Stav. Museums årb., Stavanger.

Müller (1918): Sophus Müller. Stenalderens kunst, Kbh.

Nordén (1925): Arthur Nordén, Östergötlands bronsålder, Linköping.

Pequart et le Rouzic (1927): Marthe et Saint Just Pequart et Zach. Le Rouzic. Corpus des signes gravés des monuments megalithiques du Morbihan, Paris.

Piggott (1965): Stuart Piggott. Ancient Europe, Edinburgh.

Piggott (1973): Stuart Piggott. Problems in the Interpretation of Chambered Tombs. — Megalithic Graves and Burial. Papers, pres. at the III Atlantic Colloquium, Moesgård 1969, p. 203—19, Kbh.

Powell (1960): T.G.E. Powell. Megalithic and Other Art: Centre and West. Antiquity XXXIV, pp. 180—90.

Schriekel (1957): Waldtraut Schriekel. Westeuropäische Elemente im Neolithikum und in der früheren Bronzezeit Mitteldeutschlands. Veröffentl. d. Landesmus. f. Vorgesch. B. 5, Dresden.

Schriekel (1962): Waldtraut Schriekel. Westeuropäische Einflüsse im neolithischen Grabbau Mitteldeutschlands. Germania 40, p. 22—32.

Sobrina Buhigas (1935): R. Sobrina Buhigas. Corpus petroglyphorum Gallaeciae. Compostella.

Tallgren (1934): A.M. Tallgren. Sur les monuments mégalithiques du Caucase occidental. ESA LX, p. 1—46.

Uenze (1958): Otto Uenze. Neue Zeichensteine aus dem Kammergrab von Züschen. Neue Ausgrabungen in Deutschland, Hamburg, pp. 99—106.

Willvonseder (1938): Karl Willvonseder. Das Steinkistengrab der älteren Urnenfelderzeit von Illmitz im Burgenland. Wiener Prehist. Zeitschr., B. 24, pp. 109—28.

Forschungsstand der alten Felskunst in Bulgarien

BY GEORGI ILIEV GEORGIEV

In den Gebieten Bulgariens kommen nur wenige Denkmäler der prähistorischen Felskunst vor. Daher bestand bisher ein verhältnismäzig schwaches Interesse für die Werke dieser Kunst. Nur die Zeichnungen in der Höhle Magura beim Dorf Rabiša, Bezirk Vidin, und die Ritzungen bei Gortalovo (Karaguj), Bezirk Pleven, haben die Aufmerksamkeit bulgarischer und ausländischer Wissenschaftler erweckt. Darüber sind auch die meisten Veröffentlichungen erschienen.

In der letzten Zeit wuchs das Interesse für die Felsritzungen und Felszeichnungen, die in verschiedenen Landesteilen Bulgariens entdeckt wurden. Die Forscher datieren sie meistens in die früheste Zeit. Anderseits werden die natürlichen Risse und Ritzen häufig als figürliche, symbolische oder Buchstabenzeichen betrachtet.

Die Bedeutung der mit authentischen Darstellungen, ungeachtet ihrer Zugehörigkeit zu einem bestimmten historischen Zeitalter, ist längst erkannt. Sie ermöglichen einen Einblick in das geistige Leben und die ästhetischen Ansichten des Menschen.

Die umfangreichen Ausgrabungen prähistorischer Siedlungen aus der Zeit des Neolithikums und Chalkolithikums, die in den letzten Jahren in Bulgarien auf weiten Flächen durchgeführt wurden, ermöglichten eine gute Untersuchung der Bauweise und der inneren Anlage der Wohnstätten. Es wurden auch öffentliche und kultische Bauten entdeckt, deren Wände mit geometrischen Motiven reich verziert sind (Karanovo, Azmak-Siedlungshügel bei Stara Zagora, Russe u.a.)[1]. Diese ersten Wandmalereien aus prähistorischer Zeit sind mit den Darstellungen in Kleinasien (Çatal Hüyük)[2] synchron, unterscheiden sich aber durch ihren Charakter und veranlassen, die ihnen vorausgehenden und nachfolgenden Darstellungen zu ermitteln. Daher wuchs in letzter Zeit das Interesse für die monumentale Wandmalerei in den Gebieten Bulgariens und deren Ursprung. Dieses erhöhte Interesse veranlaßte zur Ermittlung neuer Denkmäler der alten Felskunst sowie zu deren Datierung und Interpretation.

1. Felszeichnungen in der Höhle Magura beim Dorf Rabiša, Bezirk Vidin

Die bedeutendsten bisher in Bulgarien entdeckten alten Zeichnungen, die, wie bereits erwähnt, ständiges wissenschaftliches Interesse erwecken, befinden sich in der 1,5 km vom Dorf Rabiša, Bezirk Vidin (Nordwestbulgarien) entfernten Höhle Magurâ[3] (Abb. 1—4).

In den letzten Jahren wurde die Magura-Höhle durch Beleuchtungs — und andere Anlagen zu einer Sehenswürdigkeit für Touristen ausgebaut. Sie ist in einem nicht hohen, 3 km langen und etwa 800 m breiten Karsthügel ausgebildet, der denselben Namen trägt.

Der nach Süden geöffnete, 2,60 m hohe, an der Basis 6 m breite Höhleneingang führt zu mehreren großen Sälen, von denen der größte (der Triumphsaal) gute Wohnmöglichkeiten geboten hat, sowie zu zwei größeren und mehreren kleineren Gängen.

Die Felszeichnungen von Menschen, Tieren (von 15 bis 150 cm Höhe) und symbolischen Zeichen befinden sich im Innern der Höhle, und zwar in der linken Verzweigung des rechten Ganges. Obwohl sie mehrfach untersucht worden sind, liegen bisher keine stichhaltigen Interpretationen vor, die ihr absolutes Alter und ihren Gehalt bestimmen.

Wir haben nicht die Absicht, die Felszeichnungen ausführlich zu analysieren. Wir möchten nur auf die Datierung der Zeichnungen hinweisen.

In neuester Zeit wurden die Zeichnungen bei verschiedenen Gelegenheiten von Touristen und böswilligen Schatzgräbern mehrfach beschädigt. Dieser Umstand erschwert die Lösung der Hauptfragen und vor allem der Zeitbestimmung.

Mit der Datierung und Auslegung der Zeichnungen hat sich früher V. Mikov eingehend beschäftigt. In letzter Zeit untersuchte E. Anati auf breiterer Grundlage die Zeichnungen[4].

Während V. Mikov die einzelnen Perioden der Chronologie richtig erkannt und den Unterschied zwischen den alten, seines Erachtens prähistorischen und den neueren, im 19. Jahrhundert und später aufgetragenen Zeichnungen ermittelt hat, zählt E. Anati einen größeren Teil der neuesten Zeichnungen von Schatzgräbern und Höhlenbesuchern zur prähistorischen Kunst in Bulgarien.

V. Mikov stützt sich in seinen Untersuchungen auf Stilanalysen, und zwar vor allem auf die Darstellung der Frauengestalt in der Stellung der Adorantin, die in einem großen Teil der Kompositionen eine wichtige Rolle spielt. Er sucht analoge Darstellungen auf Tongefäßen aus dem Bereich der Hallstattkultur und nimmt an, daß die ältesten Zeichnungen aus dem Anfang der Älteren Eisenzeit stammen. Dieselbe Datierung schlagen auch andere Forscher vor, die sich in den letzten Jahren mit den Zeichnungen beschäftigt haben (Z. B. Hänsel, IX^c Congrès UISPP, III, Beograd 1973, 3.112 ff.)

E. Anati zieht ein umfangreiches Vergleichsmaterial aus weiten Gebieten heran und datiert die Felszeichnungen in den Anfang der Bronzezeit, die seines Erachtens in das Ende des 3. Jahrtausends v.u.Z. zu bestimmen ist. Sein Hauptargument für diese Datierung ist die Darstellung von Streitäxten in vielen Kompositionen. Seines Erachtens decken sie sich völlig mit den in der ersten Hälfte der Bronzezeit gefertigten Streitäxten dieses Typs. Dazu ist zu bemerken, daß die Darstellungen, von denen die Rede ist, zu den in neuerer Zeit gezeichneten Kompositionen gehören. Noch wichtiger ist aber, daß keine «Streitäxte», sondern gewöhnliche, aus Eisen gefertigte Hacken dargestellt sind. Daher sind die Argumente bezüglich dieser Einzelheiten der Zeichnungen und, folglich, auf die darauf gegründete Datierung der Wandzeichnungen hinfällig.

Nicht belanglos für die genauere Datierung der Zeichnungen ist auch die Tatsache, in welchem historischen Zeitabschnitt die Höhle bewohnt gewesen ist. Daher teilen wir die Ergebnisse der neuesten, auf einer Fläche von 650 m^2 im ersten Abschnitt des seitligen Ganges und im Triumphsaal von N. Džambazov und R. Katinčarov 1971 durchgeführten Ausgrabungen mit[5]. Es wurden zwei Kulturschichten und in jeder mehrere Wohnniveaus festgestellt, die durch eine sterile Schicht getrennt sind. Die erste (älteste) Schicht enthält Funde (vor allem Keramik und Werkzeuge) aus der ersten Hälfte der Bronzezeit, die zweite aus der Älteren Eisenzeit. Die Schicht aus der frühen Bronzezeit entspricht vielleicht der Kultur Coţofeni und ihrer synchronen Kulturgruppen in Rumänien sowie dem mittleren Zeitabschnitt von Ezero in Südbulgarien.

Die ältesten Lebensspuren des prähistorischen Menschen, die bisher durch archäologische Untersuchungen der Höhle nachgewiesen sind, gehören, folglich, zur Mitte des 3. Jahrtausends v.u.Z. Die Funde aus der Älteren Eisenzeit entsprechen dem 12.–8. Jahrhundert v.u.Z. Die Höhle wurde auch während der Römerzeit und in späteren Zeitaltern besucht. Die neuen Ausgrabungen bestätigen nicht die früher geäusserte Ansicht, wonach die Höhle auch während des Neolithikums bewohnt gewesen sei. Die Entdeckung derartiger Funde ist aber nicht ausgeschlossen.

Unter Berücksichtigung der archäologischen Angaben sind, folglich, die Zeichnungen in die eine der nachgewiesenen Zeitperioden zu datieren. Für welche Zeit sprechen die verschiedenartigen gewonnenen Angaben?

Auf den ersten Blick und beim Vergleich der Zeichnungen sind Unterschiede in der Technik und in der Auftragung der Farbe sowie

Abb. 1. Jagdszene aus der Magura Höhle Wandmalereien.

Abb. 2. Wandmalerien aus der Höhle Magura.

71

Abb. 3. Wandmalereien aus der Höhle Magura.

Abb. 4. Wandmalereien aus der Höhle Magura.

Abb. 5. Tierdarstellungen auf dem Felsmassiv Mečoka in Cortalovo, Bezirk Pleven (nach V. Mikov).

Abb. 6. Die Malereien in Cañon des Flusse Černjalka.

73

Abb. 7. Veliki Preslav, Bezirk Sumen. Zwei Hirschritzungen.

Abb. 8. Felsritzung eines Hirsches beim Dorfe Carevec. Bezirk Vraca.

Abb. 9. Felsblock mit Menschen-und Tierdarstellungen und symbolischen Zeichen beim Dorf Orešak, Bezirk Loveč.

vor allem im Stil der Ausführung und im Sujet festzustellen. Diese Unterschiede zeigen, daß die Zeichnungen aus verschiedenen historischen Perioden stammen. Die ältesten, prähistorischen Zeichnungen sind mit dunkelbraunem Fledermausguano gefertigt. Sie heben sich durch das 1,0 bis 1,5 cm hohe Relief von der Kalksteinoberfläche, infolge der Verwitterung, leicht ab. Die neueren, mit dunkelrotem bis schwarzem Ocker aufgetragenen Zeichnungen treten nicht so deutlich hervor. Sie sind eine offensichtliche Imitation der älteren Zeichnungen mit zahlreichen neuen ergänzenden Elementen, vor allem mit andernorts üblichen Schatzgräberzeichen, die häufig die älteren Zeichnungen überdecken oder als Grund neuer Darstellungen benutzen.

Felszeichnungen mit zum Teil ähnlichen Sujets und vor allem mit verwandten Besonderheiten des Stils und der Zeichentechnik wurden bisher nur in zwei Orten der Balkanhalbinsel, in Lipci (Montenegro)[6], und in Tren (Albanien)[7], entdeckt und in den Zeitabschnitt vom 2. Jahrtausend v.u.Z. bis zum Anfang der Eisenzeit datiert. Das letzte Datum sei, nach der Ansicht der Forscher der erwähnten Zeichnungen, wahrscheinlicher und könnte auch für die älteste Schicht der Zeichnungen (z.B. für die Jagd-, die Phallus- und andere ähnliche Szenen) in der Magura-Höhle beim Dorf Rabiša gelten, obwohl auch diese Datierung nicht befriedigt, da sie nicht ausreichend argumentiert und sicher ist.

Wie bereits erwähnt, ist die Datierung der Zeichnungen in den Anfang der Bronzezeit nach der Darstellung der «Streitäxte» nicht überzeugend. Aus dem gleichen Zeitalter wurden bisher in Südosteuropa weder Höhlenzeichnungen derselben Art entdeckt noch plastische Darstellungen von Adoranten, mit Ausnahme der zwei Knochenplättchen aus Ezero bei Nova Zagora gefunden[8]. Sie gehören aber zum letzten Lebensabschnitt dieses Ortes, der in den Anfang der Mittelbronzezeit und nicht in den Anfang der Frühbronzezeit datiert wird. Außerdem handelt es sich hierbei um Gegenstände für praktische und nicht für kultische Zwecke, die nur scheinbar anthropomorphen oder zoomorphen Darstellungen ähneln.

Alle Forscher verweisen auf den religiösen Charakter der Darstellungen. Manche verbinden sie mit dem Fruchtbarkeitkult.

2. Felsritzungen und -zeichnungen im Tal des Flusses Černjalka beim Dorf Gortalovo (Karaguj), Bezirk Pleven

Ein gewisses wissenschaftliches Interesse erwecken auch die früher von V. Mikov entdeckten und die in letzter Zeit (1969) bekannt gewordenen Felsritzungen und malerischen Darstellungen im Cañon des Flusses Cernjalka beim Dorf Gortalovo, Bezirk Pleven.

Die Tier- und Menschengestalten, Inschriften und Zeichnungen in der Ortschaft Mečoka im Dorf Gortalovo, die V. Mikov veröffentlichte und in das Neolithikum (die Eintiefungen), vielleicht auch in die Bronzezeit (die Menschengestalten) datiert, konnten wir bei einem Besuch im Jahre 1972 des Cañons des Flusses Černjalka nicht sehen, da der Felsblock mit den Ritzungen sich vor einigen Jahren von der Felsmasse losgelöst hat, von den Bauern zerkleinert und für die Mauern der Schafpferche an Fuße des Felsens verwendet wurde (Abb.5).

In den letzten Jahren wurden bei archäologischen Bodenuntersuchungen im Flußtal neue Ritzungen, Zeichen und Felszeichnungen entdeckt, die das bisherige Bild ergänzen. Bei diesen Untersuchungen fand vor allem V. Gergov vom Historichen Museum in Pleven archäologische Fundplätze aus verschiedenen Zeitaltern, einschließlich der prähistorischen Zeit, die die bisherige derartige Forschung ergänzen und eine deutlichere Vorstellung von der ursprünglichen Besiedlung des Tales und seiner Umgebung vermitteln sowie zur Klärung der Datierung der Felsdarstellungen des Cañons beitragen. Die ältesten Überreste der materiellen Kultur der Siedler in diesem

Gebiet gehören zum Ende des Neolithikums — Chalkolithikum, und die spätesten zum Spätmittelalter. Die prähistorische Siedlung aus dem Neolithikum — Chalkolithikum befand sich in der Ortschaft Provartenika auf einer Platte, auf der später, während der Spätantike, und im Mittelalter eine kleine Festung gestanden hat.

Der Name Carevata Dupka, den eine kleine Höhle trägt, deutet darauf hin, daß zur Zeit des in diesem Raum stark entwickelten Einsiedlertums im Spätmittelalter (13.—14. Jh.) ein Felskloster in dieser Höhle untergebracht war. V. Gergov stellte während der Bodenuntersuchungen Felslöcher fest, in die, unseres Erachtens, Holzpfähle eingerammt waren.

Folglich liegen archäologische Angaben vor, die eine deutlichere Vorstellung von der Entstehungszeit der Ritzungen vermitteln.

Der oberflächliche Vergleich der Ritzungen und Zeichen mit ähnlichen Ritzungen an anderen Orten, z.B. beim Dorf Carevec, in Velixi Preslav und Topčika, auf die wir noch zurückkommen werden, zeigt dieselben Besonderheiten der Sujets und des Stils, die zum Mittelalter und nicht zur prähistorischen Zeit führen, obwohl, nach V. Mikov, einige Tierdarstellungen aus Gortalovo einer bronzenen Hirschfigur aus Sevlievo ähneln, die zum Anfang der Eisenzeit gehört. Es besteht aber nur eine äußerliche, scheinbare Ähnlichkeit zwischen den primitiven, in Felsen eingeritzten Darstellungen und dem aus Metall gefertigten Kunstwerk der geometrischen thrakischen Plastik — zwei Größen, die schwer miteinander zu vergleichen sind.

Wenn wir die im Laufe vieler Jahrhunderte, in verschiedener Technik während des Mittelalters und auch später in die Felsoberfläche eingeritzten Darstellungen und Zeichen beiseite lassen, können wir uns schwieriger bezüglich der Datierung der Malerei orientieren.

Was stellen die fraglichen Felsbilder dar und in welcher Zeit sind sie entstanden?

Die interessantesten Darstellungen in der Ortschaft Koncetata sind in eine flache Felsnische eingeritzt, die sich etwa 7 bis 8 m über der gegenwärtigen Oberfläche erhebt. Dies sind zwei Gruppen zu je zwei Pflanzenfressern (Schafe oder Ziegen), die durch einen Spalt getrennt und in entgegengesetzter Richtung angeordnet sind (Abb. 6). Die primitive Zeichnung auf dem Kalkfelsen ist mit demselben Ort entnommen blaßgelben Ton ungeschickt ausgefürt. Anscheinend waren ursprünglich mehr Figuren als heute zu sehen. Die übrigen sind in neuester Zeit beschädigt und vernichtet worden. Am Fuße der Nische mit den Zeichnungen haben Schatzgräber ein tiefes Loch gegraben. An der Oberfläche der Felsnische sind frische Spuren von Schlägen mit einem harten Gegenstand zu sehen.

Die erwähnten Figuren sind nicht die einzigen im Cañon des Cern-jalka-Flusses. Spuren ähnlicher Tierdarstellungen kommen auch an anderen Stellen vor, die wir aber wegen der Unzugänglichkeit nicht untersuchen konnten. Wir haben nur die Spuren ähnlicher Darstell-ungen und vor allem die Zeichentecknik am Felsmassiv an der Ein-biegung des Cernjalka-Flusses, genau gegenüber der Nische mit den Tierdarstellungen einer näheren Betrachtung unterzogen.

Nach Sujet, Stil und Technik ähnliche Felsbilder sind in Bulga-rien außerordentlich selten. Dazu gehören, z.B., einige in der Höh-le Magura beim Dorf Rabiša, die wir bereits besprochen haben. Darunter kommen auch einige Tierdarstellungen vor, die zum Teil denen im Tal des Cernjalka-Flusses weitgehend ähneln. Daher sind wir geneigt, die Felsbilder beim Dorf Gortalovo in die gleiche Zeit wie die ältesten authentischen Zeichnungen der Magura-Höhle, und zwar in die Ältere Eisenzeit zu datieren. Dabei stützen wir uns, unter anderem, auch auf die weitgehende Ähnlichkeit bezüglich der Lage, des Sujets und des Stils der Ausführung mit den Felsbildern bei Lipci (Montenegro), die in das 2. Jahrtausend v.u.Z. (1600—1200) datiert sind, mit größerer Wahrscheinlichkeit aber zur Älteren Ei-senzeit gehören (M. Garašanin) und vor allem auf die Felsbilder bei Tren (Albanien), die von vornherein in das letzte Zeitalter datiert wurden (M. Korkuti).

Die Körper der Tiere bei Gortalovo haben kleine Abmessungen. Sie sind mit dichter Farbe aus Ton gezeichnet, um eine Körperlich-keit zu erreichen. Nach diesem Merkmal ähneln sie den Darstell-ungen in Tren (Albanien), unterscheiden sich aber von den schraf-fierten in Lipci.

Obwohl wir diese Datierung annehmen, sind wir von ihrer Rich-tigkeit nicht vollständig überzeugt. Nicht ausgeschlossen ist die Zugehörigkeit der Zeichnungen bei Gortalovo zu einem späteren Zeitalter, z.B. zum Mittelalter. In letzter Zeit wurde diese Meinung auch über die Zeichnungen in Tren geäußert.

3. Steinritzungen in Veliki Preslav

Sicherere Angaben über die Datierung der alten Steinritzungen in Preslav liefern die von D. Ovčarov im Jahre 1971 entdeckten mehr als 100 Ritzungen auf Steinblöcken, aus denen die östliche Festungs-mauer der Innenstadt von Veliki Preslav, der zweiten Hauptstadt des Ersten Bulgarischen Reiches errichtet ist.[10]

Eingeritzt sind einzelne Menschen- und Tiergestalten, verschiedene symbolische Zeichen, Jagd- und andere Alltagsszenen. Es kommen auch Darstellungen von Hirschen, Rehen, Schafen, Hunden, Raubtieren, eines Adlers, eines Hasen, eines Schiffes und andere vor (Abb. 7).

Die Menschen und Tierfiguren sind mit Konturen umrissen, einige davon, wie die Hirschfiguren im Dorf Carevec, Bezirk Vraca (vgl. weiter unten), schraffiert, um ihnen größere Körperlichkeit zu verleihen.

Der Teil der östlichen Festungsmauer von Veleki Preslav mit den Zeichnungen wurde um das Ende des 9. oder zu Anfang des 10. Jahrhunderts errichtet. Aus demselben Zeitalter stammen, nach D. Ovčarov, auch die Zeichnungen. Diese früheste Datierung der Zeichnungen kann, natürlich, nicht auch die letzte sein. Zeichnungen wurden in die Wand auch nach ihrer Errichtung von den Wachen, die sie beschützten, sowie von den späteren Bewohner der Preslav-Festung eingeritzt. Historischen Angaben zufolge war Veliki Preslav auch in den nachfolgenden Jahrhunderten (13.–14. Jh.) bewohnt, obwohl die Stadt ihre ursprüngliche Bedeutung als Thronstadt eingebüßt hatte. Es ist daher nicht ausgeschlossen, daß einige Zeichnungen, z.B. die Darstellung des Shiffes, in diesen Zeiten entstanden sind.

Wir verzeichnen nur nebenbei die Felszeichnungen in Veliki Preslav, da sie nach Sujet — und Stilementen mit ähnlichen Darstellungen aus anderen Landesteilen Bulgariens, z.B. in Gortalovo (Karaguj), Bezirk Pleven, Carevec, Bezirk Vraca, und anderen engverwandt sind und da sie durch das genauere früheste Datum die Datierungen der übrigen Felszeichnungen erleuchtern. Sie haben, natürlich, eine Bedeutung als historische Quellen zur Untersuchung der Lebensweise und der Lebensverhältnisse der Bevölkerung im mittelalterlichen Bulgarien. Analoge Zeichnungen wurden früher in Madara, Pliska, Červen und anderswo entdeckt.

4. Steinritzungen beim Dorf Carevec, Bezirk Vraca

Die in der Umgebung des Dorfes Carevec, Bezirk Vraca, entdeckten Steinritzungen stellen Menschen und Tiere, Zeichen und kyrillische Inschriften dar. Sie sind in die Wände der kleinen Höhlen und Nischen im Felsmassiv am linken Ufer des Flusses Iskăr, in den Ortschaften Govedarnika und Srednijat kamik in einer Höhe von 7 bis 15 m vom Wasserspiegel des Flusses eingeritzt.

Ein Teil der Zeichnungen und vor allem die Inschriften wurden von M. Mičev im Jahre 1964 entdeckt und zum ersten Mal veröffentlicht.[11] Später haben sich auch andere Forscher für die Felszeichnungen und Inschriften interessiert.

In Begleitung von M. Mičev besichtigten wir das Felsmassiv in den genannten Ortschaften und unterrichteten uns über die Art der entdeckten Zeichnungen und Inschriften. Größere Aufmerksamkeit brachten wir den Tier- und Menschenfiguren sowie den symbolischen Zeichen entgegen, die in groβer Menge vorkommen und nicht nur für dieses Gebiet kennzeichnend sind.

Wie bereits erwähnt, sind vor allem Figuren von Hirschen in verschiedener Gröβe, in der Länge von 6 bis 36 cm mit niedrigen oder hohen verzweigten Geweihnen, glatten oder schraffierten eleganten Körpern dargestellt. Einige Figuren, vor allem die eines Hirsches mit groβem Geweih, sind von ganz schematisch eingeritzten Waldbüschen umgeben (Abb. 8). In der Ortschaft Srednijat kamik ist nur ein einziger, an den Stelzen 8 cm hoher und 10 cm langer Vogel mit langem Hals dargestellt, der den Vögeln aus der Jagdszene der Zeichnungen in der Magura-Höhle beim Dorf Rabiša, Bezirk Vidin, ähnelt. Menschengestalten kommen seltener vor. Auf demselben Felsblock mit dem Vogel und in der Nähe davon ist ein Jäger mit Bogen und Pfeil zu sehen, der mit den Jägern in der Magura-Höhle eine enge Verwandtschaft zeigt. Es sind zahlreiche Reiter eingeritzt, die die Zügel fest in der Hand halten. Die Zeichnung ist stark schematisch. Nach der Darstellung ähneln einige Hirsche weitgehend den verwandten Tierzeichnungen (Fohlen) in der Topčika-Höhle beim Dorf Dobrostan, Bezirk Plovdiv. Die Figuren in den beiden Orten sind in dem gleichen primitiven Stil der Ritzeichnung dargestellt.

Obwohl wir die Möglichkeit hatten, die Ritzeichnungen beim Dorf Carevec ausführlich zu betrachten, werden wir auf sie nicht näher eingehen, da wir uns davon überzeugt haben, daβ sie nicht aus der prähistorischen, sondern aus einer viel späteren Zeit, und zwar nicht früher als aus dem Spätmittelalter (13.–14. Jh.), zum Teil sogar auch aus dem 18. und 19. Jh. stammen, wie die kyrillischen Inschriften zeigen.

M. Mičev verweist darauf, daβ ein Teil der Inschriften im Jahre 1762 zur Zeit einer Pestepidemie eingeritzt worden sind, vor der die örtliche Bevölkerung geflogen ist. Sie stammen seines Erachtens von der Hand von Mönchen aus den Dörfern und Klöstern der Umgebung.

Manche Zeichen, von denen eines dem Monogramm des Zaren Šišman sehr ähnlich sieht, zeigen, daβ einige Zeichnungen und Zeichnen in das Mittelalter, und zwar in das 14. Jh. zu datieren sind und von Einsiedlermönchen in den Höhlen und Felsvorsprüngen eingeritzt wurden, wo sie über aus Holz gefertigte Behausungen verfügten. Spuren derartiger Behausungen, die auch in anderen Landesteilen Bulgariens nachgewiesen wurden, sind in einer Höhle der Ortschaft Govedarnika erhalten. Dies sind die Löcher zur Einführung von Holzbalken. Auch die bereits erwähnte Gestalt des Bogenschützen gehört wohl zum Mittelalter.

Die Darstellung des als heiliges biblisches Tier verehrten Hirsches

80

in zahlreichen Zeichnungen ist verhältnismäßig sehr gut gelungen und wohl mit der Rotwildzucht in diesem Landesteil während der früheren Zeitalter verbunden. Nicht zufällig trägt eine Ortschaft in unmittelbarer Nähe, am gegenüberliegenden Ufer des Iskar-Flusses, den Namen «Košušto pole» (nach einer Mitteilung von M. Mičev). Spuren einer Hirschdarstellung mit roter Farbe sind auch an der Fassade der alten Kirche im Dorf Carevec erhalten, die um das Ende des 18. Jhs. erneuert wurde. Aus dieser Zeit stammen auch die Fels-inschriften. An der Oberfläche von in die Mauern derselben Kirche eingefügten Steinblöcken sind Inschriften eingeritzt, die nach dem Inhalt und den paläographischen Besonderheiten der Buchstaben mit den Ischriften auf dem Felsmassiv in den Ortschaften Govedar-nika und Srednijat kamik übereinstimmen.

Die symbolischen Zeichen wie Sonnen, Treppe, ein wellenförmiges Zeichen, Quadrate und Kreise mit kleinen Punkten, senkrechte Ritze in Gruppen und andere kommen in großer Menge vor und sind eine übliche Erscheinung bei derartigen Darstellungen in Bulgarien, z.B. bei Gortalovo im Bezirk Pleven. Sie begleiten die Zeichnungen und Inschriften, sind mit denselben technischen Mitteln ausgeführt und gehören zum selben Zeitalter.

Zusammenfassend halten wir es für notwendig, darauf hinzuwei-sen, daß die Zeichnungen und Inschriften beim Dorf Carevec, Bezirk Vraca, die einander ergänzen, interessante Angaben über das histo-rische und geistige Leben der einheimischen Bevölkerung im Mit-telalter und in neuerer Zeit liefern. Vorläufig sind keine Beweise für die Bewohnung der Felshöhlennischen durch den prähistorischen Menschen bekannt.

5. *Felsritzungen in der Höhle Topčika beim Dorf Dobrostan, Bezirk Plovdiv*
Die Höhle Topčika befindet sich in dem nörlichen Teil des Rhodo-pen-Gebirgsmassivs etwa 7 km südwestlich des Dorfes Dobrostan, Bezirk Plovdiv, in einer schwer zugänglichen Ortschaft an einem Abhang in südlicher Lage in der Höhe von 1000 m rechts vom Fluß Sušica. Der Eingang ist 5 m hoch und blickt nach Süden. Der 110 m lange, trockene Hauptsaal ist als Höhlenwohnung gut geeignet.

Die 1969 in der Höhle durchgeführten archäologischen Ausgra-bungen bewiesen, daß sie in der Älteren (Hallstatt) und der Jüngeren (La-Tène-Zeit) Eisenzeit bewohnt war.[12] Tierknochen und vor allem zwei Zähne eines Höhlenbären bezeugen, daß die Höhle im Quartär von Tieren bewohnt war. Überreste der materiellen Kultur des pa-läolithischen Menschen wurden bisher nicht entdeckt.

Die Höhle wurde der wissenschaftlichen Literatur vor allem durch die 1967 und 1968 entdeckten Felsritzungen bekannt.

An der Stirn- und Vorderseite eines 1,43 m hohen und 1,50 m breiten Felsblocks in unmittelbarer Nähe der linken Höhlenwand, 85 m vom Eingang sind Tierzeichnungen eingeritzt. Unter einigen davon kommen Inschriften mit kyrillischen Buchstaben vor. An der Stirnseite des Felsblocks sind sehr gut gelungene Umrisse zweier Pflanzenfresser (wahrscheinlich Pferde) eingeritzt. Es kommen auch Fragmente zweier andere Tiere vor, deren Zeichnung in einen in neuester Zeit abgebröckelten Felsteil eingeritzt war. Mehrere Tierfiguren sind auch an der Vorderseite desselben Blocks zu sehen, von denen am besten ein Pferd dargestellt ist. Die Art der übrigen Tiere ist mit Sicherheit nicht zu bestimmen. Es handelt sich offensichtlich um Pflanzenfresser, die die Umgebung der Höhle bewohnten. In diesem Bezirk des Gebirges kommen gute Weideplätze vor. Daher war dort die Tierzucht früher stark entwickelt. Dafür zeugen auch Überreste von Schafpferchen. Am Höhleneingang sind zwei Wohnräume errichtet, die bis vor nicht langer Zeit von den Schäfern als Pferch benutzt wurden.

Zweifellos wichtig ist in diesem Zusammenhang die Datierung der Ritzungen und die Festellung, ob sie zur prähistorischen oder zu einer späteren Zeit gehören. Nach dem Stil der Ausführung, bei der getrennten Betrachtung jeder einzelnen Ritzung, ohne Vergleiche mit anderen in den Gebieten Bulgariens und der Nachbarländer anzustellen, ist auf den ersten Blick anzunehmen, daß sie zum Jungpaläolithikum und damit zur II. Stilgruppe nach dem Schema von A. Leroi Gurhan gehören.[13] Der erste Forscher der Ritzungen, A. Pejkov, datiert sie in das Jungpaläolithikum, da die Zeichnungen, seines Erachtens, vor der Loslösung des Felsblocks eingeritzt worden sind, die am Ende des Paläolithikums erfolgt sei. Wir sind der Ansicht, dass für eine derartige Annahme keine sicheren Beweise vorhanden sind. Die Loslösung ist eher um die Mitte des Pleistozäns eingetreten, das der größten (Riß) Vereisung entspricht, während der sich im Östlichen Mittelmeerraum und, folglich, im Rila-Rhodopenmassiv die größten tektonischen Verschiebungen der Erdrinde ereignet haben.[14] Unseres Erachtens sind die Zeichnungen nach der Loslösung des Felsblocks entstanden. Diese Tatsache, sowie die Inschriften mit kyrillischen Buchstaben an der Vorderseite des Felsblocks, die die vorhandenen Ritzungen berücksichtigen, sowie auch die Ähnlichkeit, sogar die in bestimmten Fällen vollständige Analogie zu ähnlichen Darstellungen an anderen Orten, z.B. beim Dorf Carevec, Bezirk Vraca, in Veliki Preslav, Bezirk Šumen, die nachweislich zum Mittelalter gehören, erwecken Zweifel am jungpaläolitischen Alter dieser

Ritzungen und veranlassen uns, sie in die gleiche Zeit wie die soeben erwähnten Felszeichnungen zu datieren. Die Verbindung der Rıtzungen mit der Eisenzeit, zu der die in der Höhle entdeckten Funde gehören, würde den soeben angestellten Überlegungen offensichtlich widersprechen.

Die Felsritzungen in der Höhle Topčika beim Dorf Dobrostan müssen, unseres Erachtens, aus dem Bereich der prähistorischen Kunst in den Gebieten Bulgariens ausgeschlossen werden.

6. Steinritzungen aus dem Dorf Orešak, Bezirk Loveč

Mit den Steinritzungen von Gortalovo, Carevec, Veliki Preslav und Topcika sind auch die Darstellungen auf der Felsplatte aus dem Dorf Orešak, Bezirk —Loveč, verbunden die das Historische Bezirkmuseum der Stadt Loveč verwahrt und von V. Mikov veröffentlicht wurde (Abb. 9). Unter Berücksichtigung der weiter oben untersuchten Steinritzungen und Malereien gehören diese aus dem Dorf Orešak zweifellos zum Mittelalter.[15]

***

Der flüchtige Überblick über die Untersuchungen der alten Felskunst in den Gebieten Bulgariens zeigt, daß in diesem Bereich sehr wenig geleistet worden ist. Anderseits geht daraus hervor, daß die Forscher über kein sicheres Kriterium für die Datierung und Interpretation der Denkmäler verfügten. Daher müssen die Forscher, die sich künftig mit der Untersuchung der Felskunst beschäftigen werden, die klassischen Denkmäler der prähistorischen Felskunst der entsprechenden Zeitalter in allen Einzelheiten kennen und die Methoden beherrschen, mit denen sie datiert und interpretiert wurden. Es versteht sich von selbst, daß nur mit Hilfe von Stilanalysen und Analogien keine sicheren Ergebnisse zu erwarten sind. Daher müssen auch andere, vollkommenere Untersuchungsmethoden angewendet werden, um in der Untersuchung der alten Felskunst Fortschritte zu verzeichnen.

ANMERKUNGEN

1. *Georgi i. Georgiev:* Das Neolithikum und Chalkolithikum in der Thrakischen Tiefebene (Südbulgarien). Probleme des heutigen Forschungsstandes. Thracia. I. Serdicae. 1972. S. 5 ff.
2. *J. Mellaart:* Çatal Hüyük. Bergisch Gladbach 1967.
3. *U. Mikov:* Risunkite v pesterata Magurata (Die Zeichnungen in der Höhle Magura). Zs. Izkustvo. 1955. V. 3. S. 70 ff.; *G. Markov, N. Džambazov.* Rabiška peštera, grandiozna prirodna zabelezitelnost i pametnik na pǎrvo-

bitnata kultura v Bǎlgarija. (Die Rabiska-Höhle, eine bemerkenswerte sehenswürdigkeit und ein Denkmal der prähistorischen Kultur in Bulgarien.) Sbornok naši rezervati i prirodni zabelzitelnosti. B. 2. Sofia. 1970. S. 127 ff.

4. *E. Anati:* Magurata Cave, Bulgaria. Bolletino del Centro commune di studi preistorici. Vol. VI. 1971. S. 83 ff. und die darin zitierte Literatur.

5. *N. Džambazov, R. Katinčarov:* Razkopki v pešterata Magura. (Ausgrabungen in der Höhle Magura). Bulletin de l'Institut archéologique, Sofia. B. XXXIV. (Im Druck.)

6. *M.U. Garašanin.* Neue prähistorische Felsbilder an der adriatischen Küste der Crna Gora (Montenegro). Germania 46. 1968. 2. Halbband. S. 213 ff.; Vgl. dazu auch *D. Boskovič.* O poreklu kompozicije sa predstavama lova na jelene u Lipcima, Starine Crne Gore. III—IV. Centinje. 1965—1966. S. 13.

7. *M. Kurkuti:* Le pitture di Treni (Albania). Bolletino del Centro communo di studi prestorici. Vol. IV 1969. S. 89 ff.

8. *U. Mikov:* Skalni izobrazenija ot Bǎlgarija. (Felsdarstellungen aus Bulgarien.) Bulletin de l'Institut archéologique bulgare. V. Sofia. 1928/29. S. 291 ff.; *M. Conceva.* Hudozestvenoto nasledstvo po trakijskite zemi. (Das Kunsterbgut in den Gebieten der Thraker.) Sofia. 1971. Tafel 8—9.

9. *D. Boskovič:* Reflexions sur les peintures cynégétiques du rocher de Spile. I er Colloque sur les Illyrienes. 14.—20. septembre 1972, und die darin zitierte Literatur.

10. *D. Ovčarov:* Kamennata kartinna galerija na Veliki Preslav. (Die steinerne Bildergalerie von Veliki Preslav.) Zs. Naša rodina. Nr. 1 (217). XIX. Januar, 1972. S. 24 f.

11. *M. Mičev.* Skalni nadpisi i risunki pri s. Carevec, Vracansko. (Felsinchriften und -zeichnungen beim Dorf Carevec, Bezirk Vraca.) Zs. Archeologija. 1964. 2. S. 34 ff.

12. *A. Pejkov:* Njakoi predvaritelni rezultati ot razkopkite i proucvanijata v pešterata Topčika prez 1969 g. (Einige vorläufige Ergebnisse der Ausgrabungen und Untersuchungen in der Höhle Topčika im Jahre 1969.) Annuaire du Musée national archéologique, Plovdiv. Bd. VII. S. 7 ff.

13. *Z. Florczak:* Sztuka lamie milczenie. Krakow. S. 50.

14. *D. Kanev:* Kvarternerna geologija. Quartärgeologie.) Sofia. 1971. S. 240.

15. *U. Mikov:* Skalni izobrazenja, Abb. 165.

Relationship between the rupestrian art in the Canary Islands and the Atlantic world during the Bronze age

BY ANTONIO BELTRAN

Rupestrian art is inequally distributed in the Canary Islands, as Fuerteventura, Tenerife and La Gomera lack it to date, while the differences in the other islands are so great that at first glance we can distinguish the homogenous group of La Palma, Julan and the «Tifinagh» writing from the Iron Age, the complex group of carvings and paintings from Gran Canaria and the meagre examples of carvings from Zonzamas, in Lanzarote; there is no cultural unity among islands, except for a scanty pan-Canarian background which is scarcely of any value with regard to rupestrian art.

Most of the rupestrian art consists of carvings with thick marks pricked on basalt, fonolita, or lava; only in Gran Canaria there is a group of drawings of human beings painted in red and (Galdar's painted cave) geometric and ornamental paintings in several colours. The subjects are: a) *schematic human figures* (Balos gorge, Agaete Moor's Cave and Majada Alta paintings); b) *equestrian figures* (Balos riverbank); c) *spirals, labyrinths, concentric circles and semi-circles, meanders, serpent-like drawings, small roses and similar figures,* all with many varieties (Zonzamas in Lanzarote, Palma, many other sites; d) *circles, ovals,* and simple figures, some of them with leave out the ornamental paintings of Galdar's Cave and the Iron Age «Tifinagh» alphabetic inscriptions of Hierro, La Palma and diameter and radius/(Julan Hierro, La Palma and Balos). We Gran Canaria. On the other hand we must point out that the Julan group contains most of type b) and many marks of type c).[1]

The main question, which has not been solved yet, concerns the origin and chronology of the rupestrian art of each of the Canary Islands, and the possible ways by which these subjects and techniques may have reached them. There is no doubt that an evolution, which caused some originalities and deformities in relation to the possible models of these marks, went on inside the closed atmosphere of each isle.

We must consider the Atlantic way, unless we think that the Canary culture is an original creation of the natives which seems impossible at the present stage of research.[2] It is evident that any element or influence must have crossed the Atlantic, either from the near African litoral or from the European world which spreads out from the Spanish coast, especially the Galician, to that of Northern Europe, mainly Ireland.[3] Neither can we forget that the Mediterranean Sea, Central Europe, Scandinavia and North Germany are other points of origin and contact. A connection with America and other islands, for such as the neighbouring islands of Madeira, seem hardly possible.

E. Serra Rafols, J. Martinez Santa-Olalla and L. Pericot thought the Atlantic element to be the origin of the Canarian petroglyphs, even though, at the time of writing, they knew only a very small group on the Isle de la Palma, with little accuracy, the group in Bales and some of the motives in Julan.[4] They followed the comparative theory and some of the evident similatities of Belmaco and Fuente de la Zarza (Isla de la Palma) with several Galician, Breton, Irish and Scottish patterns, working out a cultural background necessarily common to all of them. Together with the Atlantic influences came Mediterranean and African impulses, and they stressed the specific areas in the North of Europe, such as Gavrinis, New Grange and Lough Crew. Pericot insisted on the close contact of the Canarian cultures with prehistoric groups on the Continent, in three stages none of these occurred before the second millennium B.C.

These vague comparisons were not convincing enough, and diverse researches on how and when these influences from the Old Continent came to the Islands have been carried out. Wölfel tried to find the starting point in Crete, finding a direct relation with the Canary Islands; but he confined his work to only some of the Julan carvings and the neglected versions from Balos. His hypothesis has been accepted by his disciples who now publish «Almogarén» magazine.[5]

An interesting hypothesis comes from Eoin MacWhite supported by some «petroglyphs» from La Palma, though «the possibility that the west European spiral, instead of coming from the Aegaean, by way of Malta, had a predynastic Egyptian origin, and that it expanded along North Africa and from there to the Canary Islands, thus reaching the European Atlantic province».[6] Though the first part of this hypothesis may be possible, this is not true of the second, since the roughness of the La Palma and Hierro carvings shows an avolution *in situ* which by no means approaches the purity of the Irish examples.

Obviously, the majority of the spirals and labyrinths in the Eastern Mediterranean, Babylonia, Crete and Mycenae can superficially be put in touch with the analogous symbols from the Canary Islands

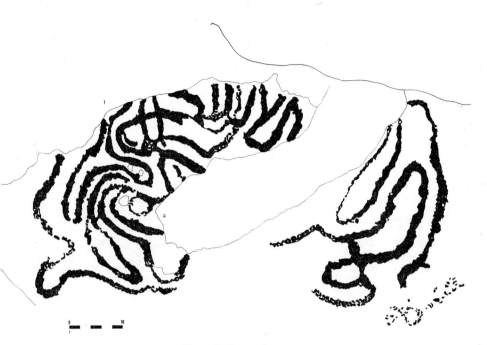

Fig. 1. Belmaco I.

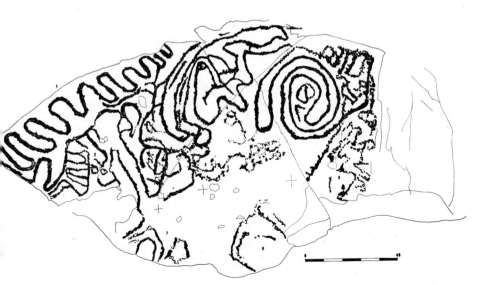

Fig. 2. Belmaco II.

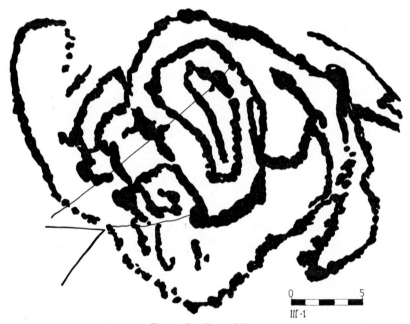

Fig. 3. La Zarza III, 1.

and some other places. This can be explained only through some spreading, very difficult to follow, since the typological similarities can be disturbed by the universality and simplicity of some subjects, such as some unadorned circles, or circles crossed by radii or diameters, some concentric ones, etc. For this reason we must be very careful when using the comparative, simple method which we shall apply when dealing with carvings from some relatively closed and well contacted areas.[7]

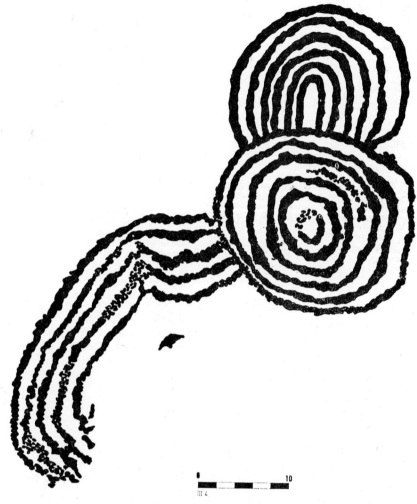

Fig. 3. La Zarza III, 4.

Before discussing the different paths of diffusion of the subjects and techniques of the engravings, we must consider the problem of the Atlantic sailings at which the inhabitants of the Canary Islands were not especially good, not even at sailing to or from Africa; it seems that the sailing were sporadic, made by chance and relatively late. Moreover, non-Canary sailors could have taken advantage of favourable winds and currents, coming from the Mediterranean and from different places in Europe and Africa, as early at the Neolithic

Fig. 4. Zarza VI.

90

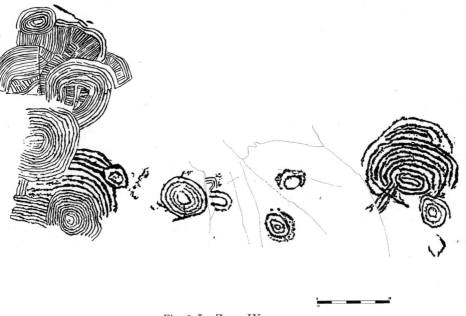

Fig. 5. La Zarza IX.

period. Some transatlantic sailings in the Bronze Age have even been exposed, on the basis of the Mexican «pintaderas» (baker's tools), trepanation, and some other examples of cultural contacts, which are certainly very difficult to test.[8]

Crawford, looking for the origin and significance of the petroglyphs of La Palma, which he defines as an Garafia type, maintains that they have a community of cult with other regions where there are similar drawings from the European Bronze Age, probably through contact with Mediterranean sailors, in the second millennium, an assumption which is confirmed by the Hercules legend; these affinities may be traced in Morocco, England, Ireland and Denmark.[9]

Doubtless there are close resemblances with Irish models, though the petroglyphs of La Palma are rougher. We must note the concentric circles with a radial line at Mevagh (Donegal) and Youghal (Cork); the closed labyrinth at Hollywood (Wicklow); the linked circles and semicircles at Seskilgreen and New Grange; the linked spirals at this last station; the concentric circles with a radius crossing all the lines or coming from the outermost, at Auchnabreach (Scot-

91

land); the parallel of the concentric semicircles of Zonzamas with Knowth.[10]

There are evident and close parallels with Galicia, in spite of the great differences in some types of marks. Apart from the closed labyrinth in Mogor, we may cite the concentric circles with radius Villar de Mateos, Figueirido o Salcedo, the labyrinth with radius and the cluster of concentric of Lombo da Costa and some others that repeat Irish or Palma types. Sobrino Lorenzo Ruza defends the independence of what he calls the Galician-Atlantic petroglyphs, and considers them the origin of those in Ireland, Scotland, North of England and Scandinavia, and even, in some way, of the megalithic symbols of the Boyne Valley (Ireland) and of Morbihan (Bretagne). But in any case, as Sobrino thinks, the Galician-Atlantic petroglyphs must come from the Mediterranean area. It is not clear how the above petroglyphs compare with those in the Canary Islands, the Atlas mountains, West-Sahara and Algeria which, nevertheless, show strong affinities with the Galician ones, and must have spread towards the South, as it is shown by that found in Tchitundo — Hulo in Angola, and those discussed below.[11]

The great number of similarities which the Canary petroglyphs — especially those on La Palma — show with the Irish regions and Galicia do not preclude the similarities with some Central-European models. We may here specify the stelas of the Valtellina, with circles provided with elongations, linked spirals and other elements of the stones in Gayen, Valgella, Ossimo, Borno and Sonico, which Anati dates between 2200 and 1000 and which have close parallels with the petroglyphs of Belmaco and La Zarze: we must bear in mind, too, the close resemblance with the circular labyrinth and the ornamentation of the big stone at Luine.[12] We must also refer to the circles at Carschenna in Switzerland, the sun-stelas near Bremen, and less obviously, the presence of some Mediteranean nucleii with the spiral line of the «oinochoe» of Tragliatella 7th century B.C., as well as the independent material from Malta, all these from the Eastern Mediterranean.[13]

There are many reasons for believing that the influence of the African elements in the Canary petroglyphs is important; the relationship between the archipelago and the African coast seems unquestionable, though it is thought to have been late and fragmentary, that is to say later than the Neolithic period of Capsiensis tradition and the period of El Kiffin in Atlantic Morocco, which is dated to the third millenium. On the other hand, according to Balout, it must have been the first sailors who spread the campaniform vases, and we have noe traces of them in the Canary Island;

in any case, there must have been occasional sailings, made by chance, and most of them with no return.[14]

The parallels with the Marakech area (Ukaimedes) and the Sahara are connected with the fact that in these regions we can find the origin of the veramics at the Cosmological Museum in Santa Cruz de la Palma, which are unique in the Archipelago, and which surely come from these regions. Nevertheless, those in Lanzarote and Fuerteventura, to which not much attention has been devoted as yet, can provide many surprises. We must not forget the three stelas in the Rabat Muséum, which have meanders with parallel round marks, like those in Gavrinis, Pola de Allende (Oviedo Museum) or the petroglyphs in Belmaco and some other places.

In Talat N'Isk, in the Atlas mountains, there are engravings on slab of stone, consisting of a ring which enclosed signs, approximately semicircular, formed by some parallel lines, while in Aougdal N. Quegona, the internal part of the ring is replaced by very complicated labyrinths; we must observe that in both cases we can see small lines emanating from the circle, which might represent sunbeams.[15]

The agreement of signs is not confined to the Mogreb or Sahara area, since there are circles, concentrics, spirals, arboreal marks and some labyrinths in the shape of meanders in the whole African South East.[16]

The relationship with the megalithic schematic art, probably contemporary, is much more doubtful and difficult to prove, although there are some similarities due, perhaps, to cultural parallelisms in which the community of religious and obscure ideas could have had an influence which is partly valid in any great measure, at least as regards the Canary Islands. We may mention the dolmen of Buzy, the «allées couvertes» of Boury, Oise, the dolmen of Areny, Dampmesnils and the destroyed one in the Forêt de Meudon (Seine). Some similarities may be traced back to the elements common to the Canary engravings and the schematic megalithic ones. A very peculiar contact between the flat and many-figured stones in Barranco de Balos and some of the zones in the South West of Anatolia is established.[17]

It is even more difficult to establish the direct relationship with the Scandinavian Atlantic world, although there are some similarities, mainly in the most simple and general figures, such as circles, concentries, simple or with radius or diameter, simple ovals, footprints and some spirals.[18]

Finally, we may conclude that there is a certain basic community between the petroglyphs of the Canary Islands, specially those of the Isle of La Palma, and other engravings of the Atlantic world. It is impossible to know precisely when these contacts were made and by which route, though it seems that the engravings of the Canary Islands reflect the atmosphere of the European Bronze Age, and the routes associated with the nuclei in Ireland, Galicia and North Eastern Africa, without forgetting the basic identity with the primeval elements of the Eastern Mediterranean. It does not seem as if we were dealing with a model of continous diffusion, but rather with multiple routes enclosing the above examples of Central Europe, and the spreading to the furthest points, either to Scandinavia or the Central Africa or South Africa, leaving aside those that reach the South or South East of Asia, Australia or South America.

The chronological mystery is still unsolved. Since the petroglyphs of the Canary Islands show an aspect of the Bronze Age, the European influence could have reached them by that time or a little later and undergone an independent evolution in the closed circle of each of the islands.

NOTES

1. *Antonio Beltran*, Los grabados del Barranco de Balos, Gran Canaria, Las Palmas 1971. Cfs. the bibliographical information can be found in the conclusions, pg. 142—155. *L. Diego Cuscoy*, Paletnologia de las Islas Canarias, Sta. Cruz de Tenerife, 1963, p. 45—48. We are preparing the publication of the groups of La Palma, El Hierro and minor stations of Lanzarote and Gran Canarian, in collaboration with *L. Diego Cuscoy*. Mauro *Hernandes Perez*, Grabados Rupestres de Santo Domingo (Garafia, La Pala). «Revista de Historia» 165—168, La Laguna 1970, pg. 90—106.

2. *Antonio Beltran*, El arte rupestre canario y las relaciones atlanticas, «Anuario del Instituto de Estudios Atlanticas», Madrid 1972, number 17, pg. 281—306. *L Balout*, Reflexions sur le probléme du peuplement préhistorique de l'archipel canarian, «Anuario de Estudios Atlanticos», 15, Madrid, 1969, pg. 133.

3. In 1970 the first International Symposium on the possible precolombian Atlantic relationships was held in Tenerife and Gran Canaria, and its lectures are compiled by the «Anuario de Estudios Atlanticos», 17, 1971, Madrid, 1972, 578 pages.

4. *Avelina Mata y Elias Serra Rafols*, Los nuevas grabados de la Isla de la Palma, «Revista de Historia», VII, 1940-1, pg. 352. *Bernardo Saenz Martin*, Las Trabajos del Seminario de Historia Primitiva del Hombre en Canarias, en 1948. «Cuadernos del S. de H. P. del H.», III Madrid, 1948. *Luis Pericot*, Algunos nuevos aspectos de los problemas de la Prehistoria Canaria, «Anuario de estudios Atlanticos» I, 1959, p. 697, ss.; on page 601 he deals with the problem of the prehistorical sailings and with the function of the Canary Islands in the transatlantic sailings, referring to the «pintaderas», the trepanation, pumpkins, cotton and writing.

5. *D. Wölfel* and *Leonardo Torriani:* Die Kanarischen Inseln und Ihre

Urbewohner, Leipzig, 1940 and references to the comparisons with the «almogarenes» of Cuatro Puertas, and Roque Bentaiga of the Crete altars. *Sebastian Jimenez Sanchez*, Exponentes megaliticos culturales de los aborigenes canarios, «Actas del V Congreso Panafricano», II, 1966, p. 156. *Hans Biedermann*, Altkreta und die Kanarischen Inseln, «Almogaren» in volume 9, 1966 of «Mitteilungen der Akademischen Druck- und Verlagsanstalt», Graz.

6. *Eoin Macwhite*, Estudias sabre las relaciones atlanticas de la Peninsula Hispánica en la edad del Bronce, Madrid, 1951, p. 24. He based his hypothesis on the work of *R. Vaufrey*, L'art rupestre nord-africain 1939 and on a paper by *L. Martinez Santa Olalla*, announced in the «Museo Canaria» to be published in 1947 but which did not appear.

7. Among the large bibliography on the subject, of very different value, we may select: *Karl Kereny*, Labyrinth Studies, 1st ed., Amsterdam — Leipzig, 2nd ed. Leyden 1950. *Reinhold Wurz*, Spirale und Voluten von der Vorgeschichtlichen Zeit bis zum Ausgang der Altertums, München, 1914, evaluating Neolithic samples of spirals in the ceramic of Butmir (Yugoslavia), Jordansmith (Silesia) and Mycene and its development in Egyptian scarabs of the XII to XVIII dynasties, in Cyprus and in Trojan ceramics of the II to V levels. *Oswald A. Menghin*, Estudios del arte rupestre de Patagonia, Acta Prehistorica», I, Buenos Aires, 1957, p. 121 and Labyrinte, Vulvenbilder und Figurenrapporte in der Alten und Neuen Welt. «Beiträge zur Interpretation Prähistorischer Felsgraphik», Beiträge zur Alten Geschichte und deren Nachleben. Festschrift für Altheim zum 6. 10. 1968, I, Berlin, 1969, p. I. Menghin would accept a way from Europe to Indonesia and Oceania. Spirals in the ceramic of Ban Chieng Thailandia, cf. *Chin-You-Oi, Pisit Charoenwongsa*, Ban Chieng «Archaeology», University of Silpekern, 4, I, 1972, pp. 16 pp.; The dates of these ceramics, by thermoluminescence are from 4630 to 3570.
One the Babylonian ornaments, vid.: *Robert Koldewey*, Das wiedererstehende Babylon, Leipzig 1913, fig. 158. On the Mycenean spiral, Colin Renfrew, The Cyclades and the Aegean in the Third Millenium B.C., London 1972. *Jose Alcina Franch*, Las pintaderas mejicanas y sus relaciones, Madrid, 1958.

8. *Elias Serra Rafols*, La navegación primitiva en el Atlántico africano, «Anuario de Estudios Atlanticos», 17, Madrid 1971, p. 391, *J. Alvarez Delgado*, La navegación entre los canarios prehispánicos, «Archivo Espanol de Arqeologia» XXIII, 1950, p. 164. *Raymond Mauny*, Les navigations médiévales sur les côtes sahariennes antérieures á la découverte portugaise, 1434, Lisboa 1960 and Hypothéses concernant les relations precolombiennes entre l'Afrique et l'Amerique, «Anuario de Estudios Atlánticos» cit. p. 369. *Luis Pericot*, El problema del Atlántico en la Prehistoria, «Anuario de Est. Atlánticos» cit. p. 21.

9. *O.G.S. Crawford*, The Eye Godess, London s. a., p. 125—129.

10. *E. Macwhite*, A new view on the Irish Bronze Age rock scribing, Dublin 1946. *Coffey*, New Grange and other inscribed tumuli in Ireland, Dublin 1912. *Stuart Pigott*, Neolithic cultures of the British Isles, Cambridge 1954, (set of motives based on Breuil) p. 211, fig. 33). *Sean O'Riordain*, Antiquities of the Irish Countryside, 3rd Ed. London, 1956, p. 56. *V. Gordon Childe:* The prehistory of Scotland, London 1936. *Pericot* et al., Prehistoric and Primitive Art, London, 1969, p. 106. *Sean O'Riordian* and *Glyn Daniel*, New Grange, London 1954. *Claire O'Kelly*, Illustrated Guide to New

Grange, 2nd ed., Wexford, 1971. *Macalister,* A preliminar Report on the excavation of Knowth, «Proceedings of the Royal Irish Academy» XLIX, 1948, pp. 131—166. *Ronald W.S. Morris,* the cup and ring marks and similar sculptures of South West Scotland. «Transactions of Ancient Monuments Society, vol 14, 1966-7 and Part II, «Proceedings of the Society of Antiquaries of Scotland», 100, 1967-8.

11. *R. Sobrino Buhigas,* Corpus Petroglyphorum Gallaeciae, Santiago 1935. *R. Sobrino Lorenzo Ruza,* Los Motivos de laberintos y su influencia en los petroligos gallego-atlánticos, «Revista de G. Guimaraes», 1963 y Ensayo de los laberintos grabados del tipo de Tragliatella, Ibidem 1956. *E. Anati,* Arte Rupestre nelle regioni occidentali della Penisola Iberica, Valcamonica, 1968.

12. *E. Anati,* Arte preistorica in Valtelinna, 1968.

13. *Christian Zindel,* Felszeichnungen auf Carschenna, Gemeinde Sils in Domschleg. «Ur Schweiz» XXXII, 1, 1968. *Wolfgang Asmus,* Zur westdeutschen Sonnensteine, «Symposium on Rock Art», Hankø, Norway, 1972.

14. *L. Balout,* Canarias y Africa en los tiempos prehistóricos, «Anuario del Instituto de Estudios Atlánticos», 17, 1971, p. 101.

15. *R. Vaufrey,* L'age des spirals de l'art rupestre nord-africain, «Societé Préhistorique Française» 33, 1936, p. 624, *Jean Malhomme,* Corpus des gravures rupestres du Grand Atlas, Rabat I, 1959 and II, 1961. *R. Pyto y J.C. Musso,* Corpus des peintures et gravures rupestres de Grand Kabylie, Paris 1969. *Magín Berenguer,* Arte en Asturias, Ovideo 1969, p. 106, fig. 48. *Souville,* Stéles gravées du Maroc Occidental, «Bolletino del Centro Camuno di Studi Preistorici», VII, 1971, p. 77.

16. *Ernst R. Scherz,* Felsbilder in Südwest-Afrika ohne den Nord-western des Landes, Köln 1970.

17. *Crawford,* loc.cit. p. 129. *Bernhard Duhourceau,* Un sanctuaire megalithique pyrenéen: Le dolmen de Buzy, son pétroglyphe et sa pierre álegende, «Archaelogia», 49, Paris 1972, p. 72. *Antonio Beltran,* Réligion préhispanique aux Canaires. Lüapport des gravures rupestres, «Symposium International sur les Réligions de la Préhistorie», Valcamonica 1972. *Susanne Haas* and *Irmgard Grüninger,* Felsgravierungen inSüdosta natolien, Basel, 1971.

18. *Sverre Marstrander,* Østfolds Jordbruksristninger, Oslo 1963. *Gro Mandt Larsen,* Bergbilder i Hordaland, Bergen 1972. *Åke Fredsjö,* et al., Hällristningar i Sverige, Stockholm 1956. *Carl-Axel Althin,* Studien zu den bronzezeitlichen Felszeichnungen von Skåne, Lund 1945. *P.V. Glob,* Bornholms Helleristninger, 1948. *Peter Gelling* and *Hilda Ellis Davidson,* The Chariot of the Sun and other Rites and Symbols of the Northern Bronze Age, London 1949.

Medicine men and spirit animals in rock art of western North America

BY DALE W. RITTER AND ERIC W. RITTER

Introduction

At numerous petroglyph and pictograph sites in western North America special anthropomorphs are portrayed which suggest gods, supernatural beings, medicine men, sorcerers, or shamans. In some cases they may be portraits of personal spirits, supernatural intermediaries, guardian spirits, or self-portraits. Often nearby on the same panel, or occurring separately, are special zoomorphs which also appear to be associated with the sacred and supernatural. Less often objects and phytomorphs occur which appear to have similar meaning and relationship. Many symbols or signs possibly have similar significance, may represent abstract concepts (e.g. magic control, transmigration, trans states, totemism, etc.) and *per se* be examples of creativity or inventiveness. Here theory, explanation, and identity become more speculative and inferential.

It is proposed that often these portrayals and relationships to the sacred or supernatural are of medical importance, the term «medical» referring mainly to the primitive, more inclusive concept of universal, societal, cultural and personal order and disorder, but also to the more restrictive modern concept of disease prevention and cure. It is also proposed that many of these sites were selected and made by or under the influence of prehistoric medical practitioners.

Method and Material

The interpretive approach will stress functional analysis, will use both direct historical and inferential or analogous evidence, both hypothetico-deductive and processual-inductive forms of reasoning. For example, from the premise that some rock art is medically oriented and shamanistically derived it can be deduced that particular motifs or themes illustrate medical concepts or events. On the other hand ethnographic analogy and comparison of prehistoric rock art with contemporary rock art and related media such as sandpaintings of the Navajo, birch bark records of the Ojibway Grand Medicine Society, the buffalo robe winter counts of the Sioux, or totem art of the Northwest Coast Tribes allow certain inductions. In some instances a continuum of practice and content, even trends can be noted projecting from the prehistoric through the historic. A study of *Kokopelli* for instance reveals his associations with hunting in earlier cultures, later with crop production, and in both instances with fertility or increase, dancing, ritual, music (flute), and pictorial art.

Whether or not it be independent invention or diffusion the plumed serpent *(Quetzalcoatl* in Mexico, *Awanyu* in the southwestern United States, and *Sisiutl* along the northwest coast of America) is a commonly portrayed mythical or composite animal associated with the likes of *Kokopelli,* healing, fertility, and increase. His provenience is remote, his domain extensive, he is still being portrayed on various media in the southwestern United States with the same meaning as in Mexico almost 500 years ago. It seems logical to induce the same modern functional associations for his prehistoric appearance in rock art.

The Medicine Man, Shaman or Religious Formulator

Since the proposal has been advanced that a portion of rock art is made by medical practitioners such as the American medicine man, the Siberian shaman, and the African witch doctor, an outline of their role and behavior should be productive of some understanding of this portion of rock art (see Table I).

The association between magico-religious practitioners and pictographic art has been recorded by several authors. One of the earliest such observations was by John Tanner in the early part of the 19th century (James 1956, pp. 179–180, pp. 341 ff). Schoolcraft (1851, p. 112) used *Chingwauk,* an Algonquin *Meda'* to help him interpret the prehistoric inscriptions on Dighton Rock. Schoolcraft also noted the medicine men and the medical societies of the Chippewa (Ojibway or Ojibwa), Dakotah (Sioux), Menomini, Winnebago, Potawatomi, and Ottawa employed a system of picture writing which was familiar to all (1851, p. 338, Pl. 48). He also compared these pictographic records with those in Siberia, even quoting an earlier such observation by Sheffer in Lapland (1851, pp. 64, 65, 425). A recent and more convincing presentation regarding these associations is given by Lommel (1967, p. 25).

Medicine Art and Magic

Recognition of the art of aboriginal medical practitioners depends on certain proposed criteria such as site selection, special associations, site use, and content (see Table 2). Site selection may be made at localities which already serve medical, ceremonial or ritual functions such as Kivas (e.g. *Kuaua* Kiva near Bernalillo, New Mexico), (Dutton 1963, pp. 41, 47, 72, 73, 84, 112, 166, 199, 200), or at spas where hot or mineral springs were used in curing (e.g. Ojo Caliente, New Mexico; Fig. 1). Contrariwise sites originally having another use may be secondarily used as healing shrines. Seal Rocks, Vancouver Island, Canada, may serve as an example (Fig. 2). This site, probably originally representing sympathetic magic of the hunt to attract seal, was used by the local Indians to cure smallpox through contagious magic. Diseased members of the tribe were placed near this petroglyph with 3 or 4 days' food supply during an epidemic in 1877 (Smith 1962, personal communication). Traditionally the rock shelters about a pictograph site known as «Hospital Rock» (Fig. 3) in Sequoia National Forest, California were used by the Potwisha, later by Euro-american pioneers, to house the ill or injured (Farquhar 1926, p. 43). Not infrequently sites are found near natural resources (pipestone, flint quarries, obsidian, silver, turquoise, ochre, water, game and plant foods, etc.) in areas of great natural beauty, or at prominent landmarks. Some of the reasons for this might be secular, however. Occasionally an association such as pictographs and jimson weed (*Datura meteloides*), a psychodelic plant, strongly suggests not only a medicinal use but supernatural associations (Dutton 1963, p. 59, Fig. 96; Barrett and Gifford 1933, p. 169; Kroeber 1925, p. 938; Steward 1929, p. 227).

Even more revealing than special site selection, use, and association is the pictographic content and the spatial or temporal relationships of this content within the site. Special themes, topics, motifs, and graphic inventions can be recognized and correlated with similar pictography on other media and with their historic utilization. (Lommel 1967, p. 25; Mallery 1893, p. 237, pp. 463—467; Maringer 1960, p. 195; Ritter 1970, p. 399; p. 402; Strong 1959, p. 120) (Tables 3,4).

Special enclosures or spatial restriction may suggest consecration or magic power (Figs. 4, 5). Ojibway animals connected with certain sacred ceremonies were represented as encircled (Mallery 1893, pp. 773, 774). Thus, the underground wildcat (*Gitche-a-nah-mi-e-be-zhew*), who derives his power from medicinal roots and herbs, is shown encircled by his tail.

This spirit or mythical animal also illustrates another motif commonly found in supernatural art, namely the *composite animal*. This animal is shown with the body of a panther, but with antlers or horns, sometimes a sawtooth or dentate back or serpent-like tail

99

(Figs. 6, 7). Other examples of composite animals would be the *Awanyll* (Fig. 8) already mentioned, the *Piasa Monster* (Squier 1851, p. 110, p. 136, figs. 20, 24), the two-headed sheep in Big Petroglyph Canyon, Inyo Co., California (Fig. 9), two-headed bear hunting fetishes of the Zuni (Fig. 10), the plumed monster along the Solomon River in Kansas (Fig. 11), a sheep with a serpent tail in Nine Mile Canyon, Utah (Fig. 12), the «water devil» from the Dalles on the Columbia River, water monsters shown at Kulleet Bay, Sproat Lake, and Nanaimo, Vancouver Island (Fig. 13), totem pole animals, *Kleetso, Kolowisi,* and *Palulukon* (Sims 1950, Pl. VIII, XI, XIII, XVI; Dutton 1963, p. 41. Fig. 55, 72-76; Fewkes 1897, pp. 2, 3; Smith and Ewing 1952, pp. 212-216, Fig. 8, 14). A horned serpent is noted above *Kokopelli* (a Puebloan god who will be discussed more later) at the Cienagillos Site, Santa Fe Co., New Mexico (Fig. 15). Another most interesting great crested serpent with mammae, *Baho-li-kong-ya,* is found on the cliffs of Segi Canyon, Arizona. According to 19th-century Moki priests who worshipped it, the mammae were the source of the blood of all animals, and the waters of the land (Mallery 1893, p. 476, Fig. 661). Analogous horned serpents related also to the *Water Snake* of Acoma and *Kolowisi* of Zuni, are found painted on layer I-33 at *Kuaua* Kiva. On its underbelly are symbols of fructification representing blood from the snakes' heart and rain (Dutton 1963, pp. 97-104, Figs. 72, 73, 76).

Eskimos often show the serpent *Pal-rai-yuk* and a two-headed serpent in their decorative art (Covarrubius 1954, p. 155). Among the Ojibway the water monster serpent played a significant role in their Grand Medicine Society (Emerson 1965, p. 43, p. 45; Hoffman 1891, p. 291; Landes 1968, p. 48). A footed serpent, probably *Unk-ta-he,* the same or similar mythic serpent of the Innuits, is painted beneath the night panther or underground wildcat at the *Agawa* site (Mallery 1893, p. 475, Fig. 662; Emerson 1965, p. 41, Fig. 6). The mythical serpent *Sisiutl* is known among the Kwakiutl, Nootka, and Tsimshian. It has been found on the ivory charm of a Tsimshian sorcerer. Also found among rock pictographs of the Coast Salish is a horned serpent and serpent-like double-headed animal (Gjessing 1958, p. 259, p. 260).

Crow medicine bundles were considered to hold various mythical creatures and their power, including the chief of the underwater animals called the «*Long Bug*». This creature was thought to possess the body of a huge snake and is double-headed (Wildschut 1960, p.11, p.12). Many other examples of these spirits or mythical composite animals can be shown in North America and certainly a large number have been documented in other parts of the world. (Spinden

1957, pp. 53-57, 246-247; Okladnikov 1969, Pl. 15; Lommel 1967, p. 128).

Spirit or supernatural animals including human or human-like creatures may be identified in pictography by several other motifs. A listing of these are found in Table 2, under E2 and more fully considered in Table 4. *Projections* of various types can indicate a supernatural state or power (perhaps only mortal superiority). Hoffman (1891, p. 174) mentions the presence of horns attached to the head as a common symbol of superior power. A *heart to mouth line* indicates inspiration (p. 186); a circle about the head denotes more than the ordinary amount of knowledge (p. 255). Cadzow (1934, p. 40) also felt the portrayal of a face, head, or horns indicated a superior being such as a chief or shaman. Symbols representing a probable shaman which are pictured by Mallery (1893, p. 474, Fig. 653d) show rays, feathers, horns, and other symbols about the head. Hoffman (1891, figs. 6 ff) also portrays many anthropomorphs with cephalic projections of various sorts. See his Fig. 6 (no. 1, 4, 7), Fig. 7 (no. 1, 5, 12, 13), and Fig. 8 (no. 1, 5, 12, 13). The headgear of the *Yei* and *Kachinas* of the southwestern United States found in petroglyphs, pictographs, sandpaintings, wall paintings, textiles, and on pottery are good examples. The Fremont pictographs and petroglyphs of the Colorado Plateau are other good examples (Fig.16). Many figures with cephalic projections are noted also in Big and Little Petroglyph Canyons, Inyo Co., California (Fig. 17).

Among the Ojibway and Dakota, spirals or wavy lines indicate «spirit» or «wakan» and animals shown with these are considered supernatural (Mallery 1893, pp. 773, 774). This author describes some of these *spiral* or *wakan lines* in some pictographs of the Dakota, which indicate the act or power of a medicine man or shaman to «shoot» objects into a victim and cause injury, disease or death. He also illustrates the Dakota symbols for a medicine man which include wavy or zig-zag lines (pp. 463, 464, 467). Such lines among the Ojibway also meant magic influence (Mallery 1893, p. 237, Pl. XVIII).

Two unusual Ojibwa pictographic records show medicine men or shamans treating patients. One depicts the practitioner (*a Jessakkid,* specialist of the Grand Medicine Society) using a rattle and treating a man. A wavy line from his eye to the patient's abdomen indicates he has located the demon causing the illness. The other record shows a medicine man treating a woman using a bone tube and rattle. This pictograph was on a piece of birch bark, carried in the medicine sack of a shaman and was intended to record a healing event of importance (Hoffman 1891, Figs. 31, 32).

The heart to mouth line, *heart line,* or life line referred to briefly above is mentioned by many authors and occurs widely in pictography. Animals shown with the heart line are considered supernatural by the Ojibway and Zuni. The heart line is a common motif among the Ojibway bark pictographs (James 1956, p. 181, p. 345), the medicine tipis of the Blackfeet (McClintock 1936, p. 123), the Sioux Winter Counts, the Kiva walls of the Pueblos (Dutton 1963, p. 74), and is found among petroglyphs and pictographs of similar, yet wider distribution (Connor 1962, p. 29; Erwin 1930, Pl. 12, p. 65; Renaud 1938, Pl 12) (see Figs. 18, 19).

Maringer (1960, p. 195) states that the magical character of circumpolar art is indicated by the «life line» (heart line). He notes that this practice was observed among the Ojibway as late as the 1890's; their sorcerer drew exactly the same sort of line. It is also found on modern pottery, in sandpaintings and among the rock art of the Puebloan and Navajo cultures in Arizona and New Mexico, on other rock pictures in North America, Siberian engravings, and Lapp art (Schaafsma 1963, pp. 41, 60).

Lommel (1967, p. 57 ff. p. 109, pp. 130-133) includes the heart line and the *exposed rib* depictions as forms of the X-ray motif. He shows many examples from Siberia, Lappland, Australia, and in Eskimo art. Black (1964, p. 16) describes the X-ray type portrayal from Arnhem Land in Australia. Along the Columbia River in Oregon and Washington, Strong (1959, p. 120) identifies this common stylistic element as the exposed rib motif. Cheng Te-K'un (1966, Pl. 24) presents an anthropomorph with the exposed rib motif found painted on Yang-shao pottery from China. The same bowl is illustrated by Covarrubius (1954, p.61) and compared with a pottery bowl (Pueblo II-III) from the southwestern United States. In North America the X-ray style or motif is more commonly seen in the prehistoric and historic aboriginal art of the Great Plains and Northwest Coast region (Ritter 1961, p. 4), (Figs. 13, 20, 21).

Consanguinity lines or lines joining zoomorphs and anthropomorphs, occasionally phytomorphs, inanimate objects, and personified (anthropomorphized) objects are proposed as another motif used by the medicine men, shamans, or their intermediaries. These might be called kinship or blood lines intended to show a natural relationship such as mother and offspring or a supernatural relationship such as a person to his totem animal. A number of instances where such lines occur are noted in rock art (Figs. 22, 23). An ethnographic corollary is noted in the pictographic autobiographies or tribal roster of the Ogalala, the census of Red Cloud's band (Mallery 1886, pp. 165-187), and in pre-Columbian Mexican genealogic tables (Spinden 1957, Pl. XLVII). Although this type of line probably is a secular device in this instance, it can also be of shamanistic derivation and use.

At several sites lines are noted to run through the site or part of the site joining component parts. Such lines are proposed as a shamanistic device perhaps to indicate a temporal, spatial, natural, or supernatural relationship of the components or to indicate that the panel is to be considered as a composition or whole. These lines could properly be called *continuity lines* or site lines (Figs. 24, 25). The *ground line* may be a special type of continuity line or an artistic device to show composition, perhaps perspective (Figs. 26, 27).

Motifs showing the eye in various ways and relationships are more common in the southeastern United States where rock art is less common (Howard 1968, p. 9, p. 26, p. 34). Here the aboriginal art on shells, stone discs, pottery, etc. shows the eye and hand, open eye, and forked eye. In the West, the eye and joint, the open eye, and weeping eye are common. The former occurs primarily in the *split* or *splayed animal* depictions of the Northwest Coast on media other than rock surfaces, although the *wide open eye* is common in rock art of this region (Fig. 28) and the *weeping eye* or *forked eye* is occasionally seen (Fig. 29).

Genital depictions are common in rock art throughout western North America and vary from groove or cupule to realistic portrayal (Figs. 30, 31). They usually indicate a concern for human procreation or crop and animal increase. Sometimes a *tagged* or *labelled animal* will have a genital sign placed upon it (Fig. 4, 30a).

«Conception Rock» located near Ukiah, California, was used by the Pomo Indian women to promote and protect pregnancy. Those desiring pregnancy used to sit on this boulder and swallow minute portions scraped from it. The surface is covered with depressions and grooves suggestive of the generative organs. There are in the region several other rocks used for this purpose (Curtis 1924, p. 66).

Gifford (1937, p. 186) describes two baby shaped rocks visited secretly by a Pomo couple wanting offspring. Both would run uphill to it, then the woman would scratch a line on one of the rocks and they would copulate there. At a similar rock in Pomo territory a husband and wife, accompanied by the chief, would mark it with steatite used like chalk — «V» for a desired male child, «X» for a female, then they lay on the design. Later the chief came to them, they arose, and he pecked the design they had marked on the rock.

«Mother Rock», on the west side of Corn Mountain, Zuni, New Mexico, is covered with cupules and vulvaforms (Stevenson 1904, Pl XII, Fig. 15, Fig. 31). Pregnant Zuni women, especially those

Table 1

PROFILE, PROVINCE, PSYCHODYNAMICS, AND PRACTICE OF THE MEDICINE MAN
(proposed outline including witch doctoring and shamanism)

I. ATTRIBUTES, ASSETS, QUALIFICATIONS, MODALITIES

A. Spiritual, supernatural, magic, religious
1. recovery from death
   - a.) resurrection
   - b.) reincarnation
   - c.) rebirth
2. recovery from illness (especially self-cure)
3. revival
4. altered or trans states*
   - a.) transformation
   - b.) transfiguration
   - c.) possession states
   - d.) transcendentalism
   - e.) consecration
   - f.) personification
   - g.) narcosis
   - h.) trance, dissociation
   - i.) self-hypnosis
   - j.) other(hysteria, amnesia, faint, fugue, coma, siezures, sleep, somnambulism, somniloquy, etc.)
5. transmigration*
   - a.) visitation
   - b.) transcend
   - c.) ascend
   - d.) descend
6. supernatural communication and liaison*
   - a.) by 1, 4, & 5
   - b.) pictography, magic symbols (including rock art)
   - c.) visions, portent
   - d.) divination, augury
   - e.) dreams, oneiromancy
   - f.) hallucination
   - g.) totem relationships
   - h.) communion
   - i.) incantation
   - j.) conjure
   - k.) prayer, worship
   - l.) hypnosis
   - m.) coitus, bestiality
   - n.) omens, oracles, astrology
   - o.) necromancy
   - p.) other(plastromancy scapulomancy, etc.)
7. supernatural skills*
   - a.) exorcise
   - b.) charm
   - c.) hypnotize, induce
   - d.) sorcery, voodoo
   - e.) cast spells, hex
   - f.) other (e.g. 4I, 6b-f, 6i-p)
8. personal spirits and spirit control*

B. Natural, real
1. physical
   - a.) certain imperfections deformities, epilepsy
   - b.) recovery from illness
   - c.) immunity to illness
   - d.) dexterity, coordination
   - e.) other
   - f.) stamina
   - g.) male (preferred)
   - h.) other
2. mental, emotional
   - a.) motivation
   - b.) intelligence
   - c.) wisdom, sagacity
   - d.) insight
   - e.) observant*
   - f.) intuition
   - g.) creativity*
   - h.) artistry*
   - i.) drive
   - j.) persuasiveness
   - k.) compassion
   - l.) psychoneurosis(sometimes)
   - m.) psychosis(seldom)
   - n.) other(clairvoyance, etc.)
3. social
   - a.) training, education*
     - preceptorship*
     - initiation
     - restitution, fee
     - knowledge
     - ventriloquism
     - legerdemain
     - other skills*
     - histrionics
   - b.) reputation, raport
   - c.) selection
     - kinship
     - inheritance
     - circumstance, chance
     - custom
   - d.) interrelationships (patient, student, group, audience, kin, to practitioner)
     - credibility
     - confidence
     - conditioning
     - fear
     - faith
     - love
     - hysteria
     - awe
     - other
   - e.) experience

II. FUNCTIONS*

A. Maintain order (correct disorders)*
   1. individuals
   2. society
   3. universe, nature
B. Assure success
C. Assure good luck
D. Avert evil, bad luck (or cause them)
E. Propitiation
F. Spiritual guidance
G. Absolution
H. Prophesy, interpretation
I. Communication, liaison
   1. supernatural
   2. dead
   3. living
   4. nature
J. Cure and prevent illness
K. Inspiration, leadership
L. Training, teaching, advice
M. Custodial care (sacred materials, beliefs)
N. Officiate, consecrate

III. MEDIA, VEHICLES, AIDS

A. Arts*
   1. picture art, "3D" art (including rock art)
   2. drama
      - a.) ceremony
      - b.) ritual
   3. dance
   4. music
   5. architecture(kivas, etc.)
B. Science, pseudoscience
   1. pharmacy, alchemy
   2. surgery
   3. psychology*
   4. physical sciences
   5. natural*
   6. palmistry, phrenology*
   7. astrology*
   8. other(logic, philosophy, etc.)
C. Intermediaries, mediums
   1. supernatural*
   2. real
D. Accoutrements*
   1. charms, talismans, fetishes, idols, figurines
   2. sucking tubes, knives, needles
   3. musical instruments
      - a.) rattle
      - b.) drum
      - c.) flute
      - d.) other
   5. medicine, drugs, herbs
   6. medicine bundles
   7. baton, mace, staff
   8. weapons
   9. various paraphernalia
E. Dress*-animal parts & disguise, allegoric symbols, magic adornments

IV. CONCEPTS OF DISEASE**

A. Etiology, Pathology
1. supernatural
   - a.) soul loss
   - b.) intrusion
   - c.) trans states*
   - d.) spell, hex, curse*
   - e.) breach, sin, transgression
     - taboo law principles
     - custom moral other
2. real
   - a.) stress, psychic, physical
   - b.) injury
   - c.) genetic
   - d.) poisoning
   - e.) allergy
   - f.) infection
   - g.) malnutrition
   - h.) other
B. Diagnosis
   1. supernatural communication*, ESP
   2. observation, experience, logic
   3. testing, trial & error, analysis*
   4. hypnoanalysis, psychoanalysis
C. Treatment
1. correct etiology*
   - a.) recapture the soul (may use soul catcher)
   - b.) remove intrusive objects (sucking, legerdemain)
   - c.) remove curse, hex
   - d.) spirit control
   - e.) other
2. physical therapy
   - a.) exercise or rest
   - b.) heat, cold, sweats*
   - c.) massage, flagellation
   - d.) acupuncture, tattoo*(also act as magic, psychotherapy)
3. medicine, drugs, herbs*
   - a.) emetics
   - b.) cathartics
   - c.) counterirritants
   - d.) hallucinogens
   - e.) narcotics
   - f.) other
4. surgery*
5. midwifery, obstetrics*
6. set and splint fractures
7. hypnotherapy, suggestion
8. psychotherapy, sociatry*
9. ritual and ceremony*
   - a.) curing
   - b.) maturation
   - c.) fertility
   - d.) hunting
   - e.) crop
   - f.) mortuary
   - g.) other
   - h.) other
10. magic(sympathetic, contagious)*
11. offerings, sacrifice, atonement*
12. prayer, incantation, worship*

*rock art and other pictography may be instrumental or associated   **emphasis on personal disease (vs. societal, universal)

© 1972 Ritter and Sons

Table 1 (condensed)

PROFILE, PROVINCE, PSYCHODYNAMICS, AND PRACTICE OF THE MEDICINE MAN
(proposed outline including witch doctoring and shamanism)

I. ATTRIBUTES, ASSETS, QUALIFICATIONS
   A. Spiritual, supernatural, magic
      1. recovery from death
      2.   "   " illness
      3. revival
      4. altered or trans states*
      5. transmigration*
      6. supernatural communication*
      7.   "   skills*
      8. personal spirits, spirit control*
   B. Natural, real
      1. physical
      2. mental, emotional*
      3. social*

II. FUNCTIONS*
   A. Maintain order (correct disorders)
   B. Assure success
   C.   " good luck
   D. Avert evil, bad luck (or cause them)
   E. Propitiation
   F. Spiritual guidance
   G. Absolution
   H. Prophesy, interpret
   I. Communication, liaison
   J. Cure and prevent illness
   K. Inspiration, leadership
   L. Training, teaching, advice
   M. Custodial care (sacred materials and beliefs)
   N. Officiate, consecrate

III. MEDIA, VEHICLES, AIDS
   A. Arts*
      1. pictorial art, "3D" art (including rock art)
      2. drama
      3. dance
      4. music
      5. architecture
   B. Science, pseudoscience
      1. pharmacy, alchemy
      2. surgery
      3. psychology*
      4. physical sciences
      5. natural " *
      6. astrology*
      7. palmistry, phrenology
      8. other (logic, etc.)
   C. Intermediaries, mediums
      1. supernatural*
      2. real
   D. Accouterments*
      1. charms, talismans
      2. fetishes, idols, figurines
      3. sucking tubes, knives, needles
      4. musical instruments
      5. medicines, drugs, herbs
      6. medicine bundles
      7. baton, mace, staff
      8. weapons
      9. other paraphernalia
   E. Dress*
      1. animal parts and disguise
      2. magic adornments
      3. allegoric symbols

IV. CONCEPTS OF DISEASE**
   A. Etiology, pathology*
      1. supernatural
      2. real
   B. Diagnosis
      1. supernatural communication*
      2. ESP
      3. observation, experience, logic
      4. testing, trial & error, analysis*
      5. hypnoanalysis, psychoanalysis
   C. Treatment
      1. correct etiology*
      2. physical therapy*
      3. medicine, drugs, herbs*
      4. surgery*
      5. midwifery, obstetrics*
      6. set and splint fractures
      7. hypnotherapy
      8. psychotherapy, sociatry*
      9. ritual and ceremony*
      10. magic (sympathetic, contagious)*
      11. offerings, sacrifice, atonement*
      12. prayer, incantations, worship*
      13. other

*rock art and other pictography
 may be instrumental or associated

**emphasis on personal disease
 (vs. societal, universal)

© 1972 Ritter and Sons

Table 2

ROCK ART OF THE MEDICINE MAN, WITCH DOCTOR, OR SHAMAN
(proposed characteristics)*

ite Selection
1. associations
   a.) ceremonial   d.) habitations
   b.) hunting   e.) routes
   c.) crops   f.) spas
2. areas of natural attributes
   a.) scenic
   b.) resources
      water   pipestone
      food   wood
      minerals   etc.
3. physical properties
   a.) visibility f.) accessibility
   b.) vantage   g.) rock type
   c.) shelter   h.) " size
   d.) caves   i.) surfaces, cliffs
   e.) facings   j.) rock alignments
4. previous site
5. present   "

ite Use
1. special function
2.   "   communication
3. secondary uses
   a.) shrine   e.) burial
      (including healing) f.) cache
   b.) meeting place   g.) other
   c.) refuge
   d.) ritual, ceremony

*not exclusive and may be
associated with secular art.

C. Spatial Relationships
   1. resriction   8. enclosures
   2. condensation   9. superimposition
   3. composition   10. revamping
   4. grouping
   5. incorporation of rock features
   6.   "   "   prior art
   7. directional orientation

D. Temporal Relationships
   1. superimposition 4. evolution
   2. reuse, revamping 5. negation
   3. continuum of use

E. Special Content
   1. themes, topics
      a.) cosmology
      b.) mythology
      c.) dichotomy
      d.) altered, spirit, trans states
      e.) supernatural communication
      f.) sympathetic magic
      g.) other magic
   2. motifs
      a.) projections   l.) eye motifs
      b.) life or heart lines m.) genital
      c.) consanguinity   " n.) receptive female
      d.) continuity   " o.) phytomorphs
      e.) ground   " p.) sacred object
      f.) x-ray (exposed rib) q.) weapon
      g.) composite animals   r.) sun circle
      h.) bipolar   " s.) cross
      i.) distorted   " t.) celestial
      j.) labelled   " u.) combinations
      k.) totems   v.) other

3. miscellaneous (other artistic,
   graphic devices)
   a.) perspective   h.) impressionism
   b.) 3D   i.) representation
   c.) motion   j.) pictograms
   d.) esthetics   k.) ideograms
   e.) scenes   l.) rebus?
   f.) abstractions m.) other
   g.) conventionalization
4. typical examples**
   a.) supernatural anthropomorphs
      medicine men gods, Kachinas
      shamans   ancestors
      sorcerers   spirits
   b.) hunting magic (imitative)
      wounded animals weapons
      spirit   "   hunt scenes
   c.) healing magic
      fertility rocks serpents
      sandpaintings   ritual art

F. Color Significance
   1. red
      a.) used most
      b.) associations with the
         supernatural noted
      c.) associated with ceremony, ritual
   2. black - 2nd most common
   3. white - 3rd   "   "
   4. study is needed

**combination of:
   a.) A1a A3b C4 E1a E2a E2p & q E3g
   b.) A1b A2b C6 D1 E1f E2b E2q E3e F1b
   c.) A1a B3a C1 D3 E1f or g E2g or m E3g

THEMES, TOPICS

Table 3

A. Cosmology
   1. origin   6. space concepts
   2. creation   7. time   "
   3. cosmos   8. seasons
   4. celestial arch 9. world order
   5.   "   bodies 10. other

B. Mythology
   (also legend)
   1. pantheon   8. migrations
   2. deification   9. contests
   3. heroes   10. conquests
   4. totemism   11. quests
   5. ancestors   12. roles
   6. spirits   13. interaction
      a.) beneficent, guardian
      b.) evil destructive
      c.) personal
   7. medicine men, shamans, sorcerers

C. Dichotomy
   1. evil vs. good   5. conflict of supernaturals
   2. male : female   6. twin relationships
   3. death : life   7. natural : supernatural
   4. heaven : hell   8. negation

D. Altered, Spirit and Trans States
   1. transmigration   7. animism
      a.) ascendency   8. possession
      b.) descendency   9. resurrection
      c.) transcendency 10. reincarnation
   2. transfiguration   11. consecration
   3. transcendentalism 12. illness
   4. transformation   13. death
   5. personification   14. other
   6. animation

E. Supernatural Communication
   (also liaison, raport)
   1. divination, portent 6. coitus
   2. vision portrayal   7. bestiality
   3. dream   "   8. prayer
   4. visitation records   9. incantation
   5. intermediaries, messengers

F. Sympathetic Magic
   (mainly imitative) (see G,H)
   1. hunt   5. fertility, increase
   2. curing   6. love, sex
   3. crop   7. hate, hex 9. war
   4. rain   8. stealing 10. other

G. Other Magic
   1. symbolism and signs
      a.) good luck h. genital o.) maze
      b.) bad   "   i. coital   p.) other
      c.) death   j.) parturition
      d.) life   k.) parent with young
      e.) illness   l.) nursing
      f.) rain, water m.) magic objects
      g.) cupules   n.) sacred   "
   2. spirit control and influence
   3. exorcism   6. contagious magic
   4. sorcery   a.) curing shrines c.) dress
   5. legerdemain b.) accouterments   d.) other

H. Ritual, Ceremony
   1. see F   5. worship   9. supplication
   2. maturation 6. sacrifice 10. consecration
   3. apotropaic 7. offering
   4. mortuary   8. quest

I. Combined, Merging, and Other Themes

© 1972 Ritter and Sons

Table 4 MOTIFS

A. Projections
  1. extracorporeal, external
     a.) cephalic   c.) caudal
         coronal   tail
         orbital   anus
         oral   genital
     b.) corpus   d.) pedal
         navel   e.) manual
         nipple
         back, etc.
  2. juxtaposed
  3. trajectory, protruding missiles
  4. types
     a.) straight line h.) dots
     b.) broken   "   i.) halo
     c.) zig zag   "   j.) involute
     d.) wakan   "   k.) rays
     e.) spiral   l.) arrows
     f.) circle   m.) feathers
     g.) curve   n.) horns
                        o.) other
  5. significance
     a.) supernatural qualities
     b.)   "   power
     c.)   "   status
     d.) transfer of
         power
         information
         spirits
         disease, etc.
     e.) illness, wounds
     f.) exorcism
     g.) other relationships

B. Life or Heart Lines

C. Consanguinity Lines

D. Continuity Lines

E. Ground Lines

F. X-ray or Exposed Ribs
   , 1. skeletal   3. fetus
     2. internal organs 4. involute

G. Composite Animals
   1. part human, part animal
   2. parts of various animals
   3. pregnant

H. Bipolar Cephalic Animals

I. Distorted Animals
   1. absent parts   8. wounded
   2. added   "   9. dead
   3. head or mask only 10. split
   4. size distortions 11. unfolded
   5. shape   "   12. other
   6. common or shared parts
   7. incongruous parts
      botanical
      inanimate, etc.

J. Tagged or Labelled Animals
   1. geometric   4. genital signs
   2. symbols   5. other
   3. magic signs

K. Totems

L. Eye Motifs
   1. weeping eye 4. eye and hand
   2. open   "   5. "   " joint
   3. forked "

M. Genital
   1. cupules   3. phallic
   2. vulvaforms   4. ithyphallic

N. Receptive Female

O. Phytomorphs
   1. medicines   4. corn
   2. tree of life 5. pollen
   3. sacred plants

P. Sacred Objects
   1. drum, rattle, flute 6. feather
   2. mace, club, staff   7. pottery
   3. prayer stick   8. gourd
   4. medicine bag   9. shell
   5.   "   bundle   10. other

Q. Weapons
   1. atlatl   4. bow and arrow
   2. axes   5. knife
   3. spears   6. shield

R. Sun Circle

S. Cross

T. Celestial

U. Combinations of Motifs

V. Other Motifs

Table 5   Natural Content of Rock Art
                              (functional aspects)

A. Identification
   1. personal (idiographs)*
   2. group
      a.)residency f.)socio-economy
      b.)culture   g.)politics
      c.)totem   h.)status
      d.)kinship   i.)religion
      e.)nature   j.)other
   3. geographic
      a.)territory e.)trails
      b.)boundary   f.)maps
      c.)ownership f.)graves
      d.)natural resources
   4. celestial
      a.)stars   e.)constellations
      b.)planets   f.)planetariums
      c.)sun   g.)celestial maps
      d.)moon

B. Records*
   1. visits   7. myths
   2. events   8. tallies
   3. exploits   9. testimonials
   4. messages   10. memorials
      (semiotica) 11. calendars
   5. stories   12. objects
   6. legends   13. conditions
C. Mnemonic devices
D. Visual, teaching aids
E. Practice, experiment
F. Pastime
   1. doodling
   2. games, puzzles
   3. occupational therapy
   4. decoration
G. Art alone
H. Multifunctional

*Dermatoglyphics and fingerprints shown in
handprints may be useful records of prehistoric
illness or physical anthropology.

5. Chidago Canyon (Chalk Bluff) site near Bishop, California. Repeated use with concentrated glyphs, superimposition, and restriction to the central large boulder suggests consecration or localization of magic power. Suitable rock surfaces nearby were not used.

1. Ojo Caliente, New Mexico. This petroglyph is located in the proximity of a former habitation site and hot springs. The scale indicated in this illustration and others to follow is approximately 10 cm. Where a scale is not shown it is not known.
2. Seal Rocks, southern tip of Vancouver Island, British Columbia, Canada. Members of .he Coast Salish plased members ill with smallpox at this site in hopes of a magic cure. Probably this large seal was placed here originally to attract seal or assist in the hunt through sympathetic magic.
3. Hospital Rock, Sequoia National Park, California. The Potwisha, later pioneers, placed their ill or injured in the rock shelter beneath these red pictographs.
4. Castle Gardens, central Wyoming. Restriction of content within special enclosures is shown here within «shields» or circles. Various techniques are also shown such as rubbing, incising, possible pecking, and color addition. Note also the genital sign placed on the antelope.
6. Awaga site, eastern shore of Lake Superior, Michigan. The large figure represents a composite or spirit animal, probably the night panther or underground wildcat of the Ojibwa.
7. Blackbird Hill, Omaha Indian Reservation, Macy, Nebraska. This petroglyph has similiarities to the night panther at the Agawa site and other depictions on birchbark, wood, and quill work of Indians of the Mississippi or Great Lakes region.
8. Awanyu, the horned or plumed serpent, a widespread composite animal occurring on many media including rock art panels.
   a. San Cristobal. b. Pueblo Clanco — both in New Mexico.
9. Big Petroglyph Canyon, Coso Range, California. Many examples of two headed sheep or deer can be found in this region.

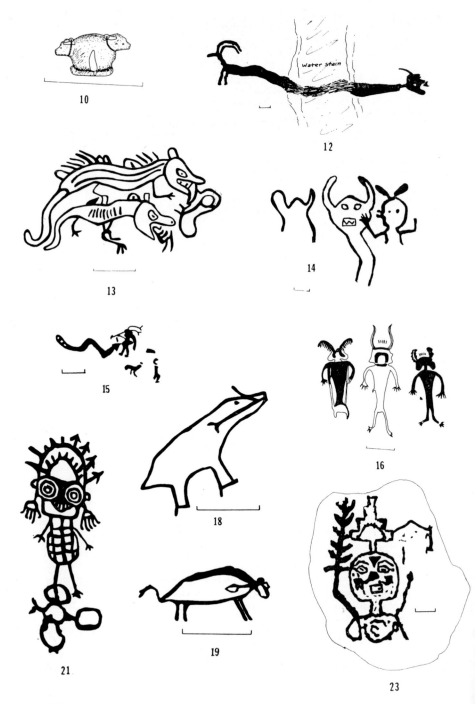

10

12

water stain

13

14

15

16

18

19

21

23

11. Solomon Monster, Solomon River, Kansas. This composite animal has some of the characteristics of both the night panther of the Great Lakes region and the Awanyu of the Southwest.

10. Zuni fetish. Occasionally the Zuni hunters will use a double-headed fetish for hunting luck because «it has twice the power».
12. Nine Mile Canyon, Utah. This interesting sheep-serpent is found pecked where it is crossed by a water seep. Speculation is aroused as to whether this is an intentional or accidental location, and if intentional does it relate to water supply?
13. Nanaimo, Vancouver Island, British Columbia. Throughout the Northwest Coast region mythical water serpent or monsters not only occur in rock art but on totem poles, other carvings and paintings.
14. San Cristobal, New Mexico. The two figures on the right have tentatively been identified as Palulukon (Awanyu) and a mudhead clown.
15. Cienagillos, near Santa Fe, New Mexico. This panel shows Kokopelli in association with serpents (including one above which is horned), birds. other anthropomorphs, a handprint, and a wavy line, possibly frogs.
16. Glen Canyon, Utah. These anthropomorphs identified as Fremont now lie beneath Lake Powell.
18. This Montana bear figure, studied by Stuart Connor of Billings, portrays the heart line.
19. Blue Dome, Idaho. Included in an elaborate pictograph panel is this buffalo figure with a heart line.
21. This anthropomorph formerly located about ten miles above The Dalles on the Columbia River has been destroyed by vandals.
23. Three Rivers, New Mexico. A cloud symbol crowns this figure who appears to hold a phytomorph in one hand. Of particular note is a line from the head to a small zoomorph.

107

17. Little Petroglyph Canyon, Coso Range, California. A large number of anthropomorphs shown in the Coso Range portray cephalic projections of various sorts.

20. Massacre Lakes, Nevada. Located near dry pluvial lake beds on the rim of the Great Basin is this magnificent five foot petroglyph of a primitive sucker type fish done in x-ray style. Its location also represents a peripheral extension of this style from the Colombia River Plateau.

22. Minnie Maud Canyon, Utah. Not only are consanguinity lines shown connecting members of this herd of sheep, but a hunting scene is also portrayed which may represent hunting magic.

24. Near the junction of West Canyon with Glen Canyon, Utah. A few sites in the western United States show lines running through the sites such as is shown here. These lines suggest composition, scenes, or ideographs.

25. Indian Creek, Canyonlands National Park, Utah. Site or continuity lines may be wavy. They may run through the entire site, single panels or various parts of a site.

26. Windy Pictograph, Canyonlands National Park, Utah. A ground or base line is occasionally noted in western rock art, possibly associated with a scene or ideograph.

27. The Lagomarsino petroglyph site near Virginia City, Nevada includes this probable example of a ground or base line.

29. At Cape Alava within the Olympic National Park and facing the Pacific Ocean, several whales and masks are depicted which show the forked and weeping eye motif.

30. Castle Gardens, central Wyoming. Genital depictions are numerous in this panel, including male and female at antomical locations. One placed on the stylized deer probably represents increase magic, (a). Similar depiction of both male and female genitalia is found at Newspaper Rock, Petrified National Forest, Arizona, (b).

32. On White Mountain, near Rock Springs, Wyoming, female anthropomorphs are carved on sandstone cliffs and show various types of genital portrayal including the cupule.

26

27

29

32

30a

30b

28. Tsagalalal, «the goddess who watches all who come and go», found at The Dalles on the Columbia River illustrates the wide open eye motif and the mask of face portrayal of a supernatural being.

31. Mother Rock, on the southwest face of sacred Corn Mountain near Zuni, New Mexico, is covered with genital signs made by pregnant Zuni women.

112

36. This panel in Nine Mile Canyon, Utah, shows several petroglyphs which may symbolically represent unknown objects; e.g., target shapes, grids, and various animals. A consanguinity line and plumed serpent can be identifiedalso.

37. McConkie Ranch near Vernal, Utah. Several panels of large, elaborate anthropomorphs occur at this impressive site.

33

34

35

38

39

40

41

42 a

42 b

33. The spread-eagle, «hocker», or receptive female motif is found at several rock art sites. This one is located at El Morro, New Mexico.

34. Near Taos, New Mexico, site of a pueblo and catholic mission, the Christian cross is found among other aboriginal petroglyphs.

35. Located at the entrance to Sun Temple at Mesa Verde National Park, Colorado, is a carved sun symbol shown here in diagramatic form.

38. McKee Springs, Dinosaur National Monument, Utah. Large anthrophomorphs related to those at the McConkie Ranch also accur here.

39. Cape Alava, Olympic National Park, Washington. This dog-like quadruped pecked on a rock surface facing the sea, may be the mythical god, Sea Dog of the local Northwest Coast tribes.

40. Near Oraibi, Arizona these modern (*circa* 1962) white pictographs probably represent *Ahola*, the Hopi Germ God, who is usually shown with an upturned nose. Perhaps one is his female counterpart and their portrayal memorializes a love tryst between Tico and Liz. Kokopelli and Kokopelli *Mana* are the only other pueblo gods or kachinas shown with an upturned nose, and their portrayal would also have similar implications.

41. *Tunwup*, the flogger kachina, whose floggings of ceremonial participants produced therapeutic value or healing is pictured in the lower right hand side of this panel found at Comanche Cap, New Mexico.

42. *Sayathlia* (also called *Hututu*), another god or kachina of the pueblo pantheon also has a healing role. He is identified at San Cristobal(a). and Pueblo Blanco (b).

who have been unfortunate with previous babies, visit shrines at the base of the rock pillars at this site. Their husbands and a priest accompany them. They deposit prayer sticks and she scrapes a bit of dust from the rock and swallows it, from one side if she desires a boy, from the other if she desires a girl (Bunzel 1932, p. 536). Because of the similarity of these customs of the Pomo of California, the Zuni of New Mexico, and other groups, the possibility arises that these may have been widespread practices in western North America.

Many sites scattered throughout western North America are probably fertility rocks, sometimes associated with human fertility, but also animal or crop fertility. In the latter capacity they are often used in sun worship or for rain production. Cup rocks, cup and groove rocks, genital symbolism (especially female), and occasionally coital scenes are found among the symbolism on fertility rocks. The association of the cup or pit and groove style with human fertility is documented in California through the above ethnographic data regarding the Pomo and by Payen (1959, p. 80; and 1968, p. 37) who has found a female anthropomorphic figure in the Sierra Nevada mountains at Hawley Lake with the sexual parts represented in cupule form. The authors have noted similar anthropomorphs with cupules in the pudendal area at sites in Montana,

Wyoming, Utah, Oklahoma, Kansas, and among the «Danzantes» at Monte Alban in Mexico (Fig. 32).

A motif occasionally noted and related to or part of the genital depiction motif, is the *receptive female* or «hocker» type portrayal of the female (Fig. 33).

Frequently, recognizable objects appear which may be *sacred objects* or *weapons*. Because of ethnographic analogy and archaeological associations, or because they are noted to be grouped in a rock art panel with other supernatural content, they may be inferred as sacred. Such depictions likely would be the work of the medicine man. Examples would be the weapons held or shown near *Kokopelli*, the water gourds and prayer sticks painted on the wall at *Kuaua* Kiva, or the «medicine bundles» held in the hand of a supernatural anthropomorph (Renaud 1948, p. 26; Dutton 1963, pp. 98-103, Figs. 55, 72-76, 95) (Figs. 15, 17, 23).

Sometimes spirit animals such as totem animals or shamans in animal disguise or form, may be represented in a normal or naturalistic way. In these instances they may be indistinguishable from records, art alone, and other secular art. An association with a certain symbol, supernatural anthropomorph, select site, superimposition, retouching or other presumptive evidence of supernatural indication, may then aid in its identification as having more than secular importance. For instance, snakes or birds placed in close association with *Kokopelli*, a known god of the hunt, fertility and medicine, are more apt to have supernatural significance serving as intermediaries or messengers to the underworld and the spirit world above. Some of these groupings might even represent an ideograph. This is speculative, but several instances of this multiple relationship are found at the Cienagillos site (Fig. 15). Still more speculative is the study of conventionalized symbols which in this grouping might be shown as a wavy line (snake), bird footprint (bird), and flute or bow *(Kokopelli)*.

The *use of symbols* could be considered another motif or device of the medicine man or shaman. The use of *certain symbols* which appear in rock art and on other media can be related to sacred ceremonies, rituals or places, and be considered a motif of the medicine man. The accurate assignment of meaning and function to symbols occurring on rock art is highly speculative. Some instances of the Christian *crosses,* that occur near missions such as Taos in New Mexico (Fig. 34) and in La Cueva Pintada near San Antonio Mission, California, or the sun symbol at Sun Temple, Mesa Verde, Colorado, (Fig. 35) are exceptions. Symbols which appear to represent other worlds, the heavens, or the underworld, such as the *sun circle,* other *celestial bodies, birds, snakes, water monsters,* etc. can have supernatural status and may be considered as shamanistic motifs (Howard 1968, p. 9; Grant 1967, pp. 54-67) (Figs. 15, 36).

A number of anthropomorphs found in rock art in North America appear to be medicine men, shamans, sorcerers, their assistants or intermediaries. When found at select sites associated with ceremony or ritual and when they are shown with one or more of the above motifs this appears more likely. Sometimes special stance, animal disguise, distortion (or just a mask; e.g. Fig. 28) and an association with indications of transcendency (birds, clouds, celestial bodies, psychedelics, etc.) are inferential evidence of supernatural status.

In a study of sympathetic magic of the hunt some of these personages can be identified as hunt shamans, gods of the hunt, guardian spirits or keepers of the game (Ritter 1970, p. 397, p. 403; Dutton 1963, p. 75, Fig. 88; Lommel 1967, pp. 16, 28, 78). However, differentiating the medicine man or shaman from other mythical beings, ceremonial participants, culture heroes, venerated ancestors, gods or even ordinary personages is often impossible.

In the Pecos River country of southern Texas, Kirkland and Newcomb (1967, pp. 43, 45, 65) identify the many special anthropomorphs occurring there as shamans with atlatls, darts, stylized projectile points, and medicine pouches. For examples from Baja California, see Ritter (1971).

Among petroglyphs and pictographs along the Angara River in Siberia, Okladnikov (1969, Pl. 8, Pl. 21) found several anthropomorphs he believes are shamans or sorcerers. He compares their headgear with such diverse temporal examples as the sorcerer at Trois Frere, a prehistoric Siberian shaman crowned with elk horns, and present day shamanistic headgear. A very similar type of proposed shaman headgear has been found at Hopewell Mound, Ohio (Wilson 1896, Pl. 13). The above criteria used by Okladnikov in identifying a shaman would fit within the motif of special projections, in these instances cephalic horns.

A few outstanding examples in this study which should be considered as supernatural anthropomorphs are noted in Figs. 15, 16, 17, 21, 23, 28, 37, and 38. (Also see Ritter 1965, pp. 1-4).

Other types of animal forms which could be of shamanistic origin are *distorted animals,* including anthropomorphs. Several varieties of distortion are listed in Table 4 under I. It would be suitable to include the *bipolar cephalic animal* in either this category or the composite category. These forms seem to appear more commonly in sympathetic magic of the hunt.

The fact that a majority (87%) of 900 field-studied petroglyph and pictograph sites with hunting content are found in or near present historic or prehistoric hunting areas (also game trails, hunting blinds, box canyons, water holes, buffalo jumps, etc.) is supportive of the postulate they were used as hunting medicine or magic (Heizer and Baumhoff 1962, p. 281; Schaafsma 1965, pp. 7, 9; Ritter 1970, p. 397). The occasional graphic tricks of placing an animal facing the sun, a trap, an obstacle, or maze; his tracks facing in the opposite direction from the way he is facing, or placing him in association with signs that may stand for supernatural or magic powers, confusion, or peril (e.g. snake, heart line, maze, or spiral) also infers hunting medicine or magic (Ritter 1970, pp. 397, 399, Figs. 195, 198, 200, 201, 202) (see Figs. 9, 10). In a study of the Zuni, Stevenson 1904, p. 439) documents the relationship of pictographs to medicine hunts. «There is a good drawing in blue-gray of a deer on the face of a mesa 30 miles southwest of Zuni, which is shot at by all the hunters who pass that way, and success is inevitable for the one whose arrow strikes the mark».

Among many tribes of the American Indians, *totem animals* were considered biologically and spiritually related to the individual or clan and could be invoked in disease or other need (Gunn 1966, p. 701). Petroglyphs or pictographs of animals in certain instances might then represent such assignment. How these can be differentieted in rock art from hunting magic, hunting records, animal mythology, and the like, is at present impossible to know. Certain inferences from mythology are helpful such as the «underwater panther» or «underground wildcat» of the Midwest (Fig. 6) or «*Sea Dog*» of the Northwest Coast (Fig. 39).

In the Northwest, Gunn (1966, front cover) illustrates a totem pole upon which *Medicine Man* and *Sea Dog* are carved. The former helps man overcome disease and evil spirits. *Sea Dog* symbolizes the evolution or origin of life from the sea to land forms; she is also a symbol of fertility. A petroglyph possibly representing this mythical goddess of life and fertility is found pecked on a seaside boulder at Cape Alava (within Olympic National Park, Washington). She faces the vast expanse of the Pacific Ocean, her mythical domain and origin.

Male fertility gods of the Pueblo Indians can be identified in rock art and on Kiva walls of the Southwest. (Fewkes 1903, p. 67, Pl. VII; Colton 1949, pp. 20, 35; Sims 1950, p. 5, Pl. IV, V, IV: Smith and Ewing 1952, pp. 63, 299). Near Oraibi as modern white pictographs and at San Cristobal as petroglyphs, the chief *Kachina* or Germ God and giver of life, *Ahola (Ahul, Aholi, Alosaka, Alosoka, Muiyinwu)* can be found (Fig. 40). Smith and Ewing (1952, pp. 97,

304) report this particular god in the Puebloan pantheon and in Kiva murals at Awatovi. This Germ God and chief *Kachina* is important enough to appear in six of the regular Hopi ceremonials, including the Winter Solstice, Water Serpent, and Flute ceremonies; also the Snake Dance. These are concerned with crop fertility, but a concern for human fertility is also inferred since his turned-up nose is said to represent an erect phallus. Regardless, his association with crop fertility has medical significance through assurance of good nutrition.

Another Pueblo *Kachina* and god associated with fertility of man, animals, and crops and who is also considered a powerful medicine man, shaman, healer, seducer of young girls, and hunter, is *Kokopelli* (Fewkes 1903, p. 86, Pl. XXV; Renaud 1948, pp. 25-40; Schaafsma 1963, p. 35). He is a participant in modern Hopi, Zuni and other Pueblo ceremonies; e.g. the Blue Flute and Drab Flute Fraternity rituals. During these ceremonies his flute is played over springs and in preparation of certain magical medicines (Renaud 1948, p. 27). His image among petroglyphs is identical with the Hopi *Kachina* and related to a female counterpart, *Kokopelli Mana* who carries food in corn husks (Renaud 1948, p. 37; Smith and Ewing 1952, p. 299). *Kokopelli* or his ancestral analog can be traced back to the 11th century on pottery (Renaud 1948, p. 33; Gladwin, *et.al.* 1965, p. 227, Pl. CLVIII, CLXVI: Grant 1967, p. 60; Lambert 1967, p. 398). His provenience can be identified as far north as Utah and as far south as Costa Rica (Mason 1945, Pl. 43, F), possibly even to the Andes of South America (Smith and Ewing 1952, p. 302). Among petroglyphs and pictographs he is most often depicted in Arizona, New Mexico and Utah. At the Cienagillos site, Santa Fe Co., New Mexico, he is portrayed more than at any other location, in many poses and whith various associations (Renaud 1938, p. 55). His humpback, flute, plumed headdress, and ithyphallacism assure his identification. There is speculation that his hump or gibbous in some instances may not be kyphosis, nor Potts disease, but a bag to carry gifts for maidens whom he seduces. He is shown dancing, playing the flute, hunting sheep, deer, or mountain lion, sometimes on his back in a recumbent pose. Sometimes he is found in association with water or rainfall symbols such as the cloud, rain, lightning, or netted gourds. Snakes, including the rattlesnake and plumed serpent *(Awanyu, Palulukon, Kleetso, Kolowisi)*, birds, lizards, frogs, insects, and other animals which frequently represent fecundity are often pecked nearby (Fig. 15). Similar depictions occur throughout much of the southwestern United States.

Kokopelli figures have been found on pottery from Aztec Ruin,

Chaco Canyon, Arizona, the Great Kiva Ruins near Zuni, New Mexico, Hohokam sites in southeast Arizona and sites in Chihuahua, Mexico (Renaud 1948, p. 33). His most common accouterment is the flute. Although there may be no relationship it is interesting to note that among Indians of the southeastern part of the United States, Jones (1873, p. 29) found that the medicine man was known to suck the painful area of a patient with a «kind of shepherd's flute». Perhaps the same or at least a closely related god or *yei* of the Navajo is the hunchbacked anthropomorph sometimes shown with a head-dress, who carries seeds in his feathered hump (Newcomb *et al.* 1956, p. 40, Fig. 78; Schaafsma 1965, pp. 6, 9, 12 and 1966, pp. 14, 15). This *yei* is associated with animal tracks, rain cloud and corn symbols, and may carry a wand or weapon.

Among the Puebloans of the Southwest there are several other gods or societies whose major domain may or may not be medicine but who do have a medical role. Often a medicine society may recruit members from those who are cured. The clown societies of the Keres Pueblos (the *Koshare)* and of the Tewa *(Kossa)* are able to cure certain diseases and the society membership is increased by those whom they cure (Fergusson 1957, pp. 31, 45). The curing societies of the Keresans are similarly structured (Fox 1967, p. 261). *Koshare* can be identified on Kiva paintings at Acoma made prior to curing ceremonies and possibly among cliff paintings and carvings southeast of the pueblo (White 1932, pp. 113, 131, Pl. 22). A carved painting of *KoBictaiya,* a *Kachina* who treats the ill and gives strength, is found at another cliff site near Acoma (White 1932, pp. 86, 131, Pl. 10). A stone figurine of *KoBictaiya* is used in the curing ceremony of the Flint society of the Cochiti (and other Keresans). It is believed that the spirit of this *Kachina* invests the figurine and aids in healing (Fox 1967, p. 267).

Petroglyphs of Koshare or his archetype are also found at San Cristobal, New Mexico, (Sims 1950, Pl. VIII). The mudhead *(Koyemshi)* and Galaxy *(Newewe) Kachina* of the Zuni are also clowns. Possible mudheads struggling with *Palulukon* the feathered serpent, are also portrayed at San Crisobal and Comanche Gap, New Mexico (Sims 1950, p. 7, Pl. VIII, Fig. 14).

Fergusson (1957, pp. 74, 128) mentions a Hopi god, *Tunwup,* the Flogger *Kachina,* who during the *Powamu* (bean planting ceremony) may whip adults, which is thought to have healing properties; she also states that the Zuni Wood Fraternity sword swallowers have medicine especially good for sore throats. They use a sandpainting during their ceremonies. A cured patient may request admission to this fraternity. *Sayathlia* and *Hututu* who have healing roles, as well as

Tunwup can be tenuously identified at San Cristobal (Sims 1950, p. 6, Pl. V), possibly at Comanche Gap, Pueblo Blanco, New Mexico, Hueco Tanks, Texas (Kirkland 1940, pp. 19, 23); and other sites in the Southwest (Figs. 41, 42).

No doubt other personages of medical import in the pantheon of Puebloan cultures will eventually be identified among rock art anthropomorphs. At present the subject is somewhat confusing, for each Pueblo and language group has pictorial and nomenclature variations for essentially the same *Kachina*. Color characteristics are absent in petroglyphs. Portrayals of *Kachinas* are sometimes sketchy in rock pictographs, on wall art, pottery, textile, and sand-paintings used for such depictions, which makes identification difficult.

Conclusions

A number of hypotheses have been presented in this sketch. It is postulated that a good many portrayals of supernatural themes, topics, motifs and graphic devices are probably inventions of the medicine man, shaman of other medical practitioners. Such handi-work can be recognized in both rock art and related media. Many of these portrayals show a continuity in form and content which transcends temporal, geographic, and cultural boundaries.

These hypotheses have been induced from more restrictive pub-lished hypotheses in North America and other areas, from ethno-graphic accounts, and a knowledge of modern or recent medical practitioners, their methods and armamentarium.

From these hypotheses we have deduced that a significant pro-portion of rock art in western North America is derived directly or indirectly from medical or magico-religious activity. Test implications for this generality — in application to prehistoric sites — include use of ethnographic analogy (historic sites or practices with confir-med interpretation and explanation), the direct historic approach, and/or association of a number of themes and motifs-symbols, with their environment. While we cannot always verify our hypotheses *(vis-à-vis* generality) we can not always disprove them either. We can fail to verify the hypotheses at only a few petroglyph and pictograph sites or parts of sites using similar testing procedures, however. It is difficult — and may always remain so — to determine empirically the statistical validity of this generality. However, we feel verifica-tion to be the case in the majority of the 900 sites studied. This is not to say that other interpretations are not possible, or that our generality would fit a high proportion of the other less verified exam-ples. Since archaeologists deal in probabilities and inferences derived from logical hypotheses, then our generality as presented is probably correct a majority of the times. Further confirmation and testing is certainly needed along with more rigid statistical handling of associations and site content. (Table 5).

This generality and associated hypotheses — to have real meaning — must be integrated with associated cultural events; i.e., the subsistence and economic subsystems, the local culture history, culture processes, and other associations found in the archaeological and environmental record. We have hinted at the possibilities of tracing stylistic drift, population movements, culture change and so on. Through rock art we may be able to delve into the realm of the magico-religious subsystem and integrate this with the total culture and achieve a better understanding of human behavior.

ACKNOWLEDGMENTS

The manuscript received comment and evaluation from Dr. Martin A. Baumhoff and Peter Schulz of the Department of Anthropology, University of California, Davis. Their assistance is gratefully acknowledged. The authors, however, take full responsibility for the contents herein.

BIBLIOGRAPHY

Barrett, S.A., and *E.W. Gifford* (1933): Miwok Material Culture. Bulletin of the Milwaukee Public Museum, Vol. 2, no. 4, p. 169, Milwaukee.

Black, Roman (1964): Old and New Australian Aboriginal Art, p. 16, Sidney.

Bunzel, Ruth (1932): Introduction to Zuni Ceremonialism. Forty-Seventh Annual Report of the Bureau of American Ethnology, p. 536, Washington.

Cadzow, Dinald A. (1934): Petroglyphs (Rock Carvings) in the Susquehanna River Near Safe Harbor, Pennsylvania. Publications of the Pennsylvania Historical Commission, Vol. III, Safe Harbor Report no. 1, p. 40, Harrisbug.

Cheng, Te-K'un (1966): Prehistoric China. Archaeology in China, Vol. 1, Pl. 24, Cambridge.

Colton, Harold S. (1949): Hopi Kachina Dolls, pp. 20, 35. University of New Mexico Press, Albuquerque.

Connor, Stuart W. (1962): A Preliminary Survey of Prehistoric Picture Writing on Rock Surfaces in Central and South Central Montana. Anthropological Paper No. 2, Billings Archaeological Society, p. 29, Billings.

Covarrubius, Miguel (1954): The Eagle, The Jaguar, and The Serpent, pp. 61, 155, New York.

Curtis, Edward S. (1924): The Pomo. The North American Indian, Vol. 14, p. 66, photograph opposite p. 66, Norwood.

Dutton, Bertha P. (1963): Sun Fathers Way, pp. 41, 47, 59, 72—75, 84, 98—104, 112, 166, 199, 200, figs. 55, 72—76, 88, 95, 96. University of New Mexico Press, Albuquerque.

Erwin, Richard P. (1930): Indian Rock Writings in Idaho. Twelfth Biennial Report, State Historical Society of Idaho, p. 65, Pl. 12, Boise.

Emerson, Ellen Russell (1965): Indian Myths, pp. 41, 43, 45, Minneapolis.

Farquhar, F.P. (1926): Place Names of the High Sierra, p. 43. The Sierra Club, San Francisco.

Fergusson, Erna (1957): Dancing Gods, pp. 31, 45, 74, 128. University of New Mexico Press, Albuquerque.

Fewkes, J. Walter (1897): Tusayan Totemic Signatures. American Anthropologist (O.S.), Vol. 10, no. 1, pp. 2,3, Washington.

Fewkes, J. Walter (1903): Hopi Katcinas. Twenty-First Annual Report of the Bureau of American Ethnology, pp. 67, 86, Pl. VII, Pl. XXV, Washington.

Fox, Robin J. (1967): Witchcraft and Clanship in Cochiti Therapy. Magic Witchcraft, and Curing, pp. 261, 267, Garden City.

Gifford, E.W., and A.L. Kroeber (1937): Cultural Element Distribution: IV Pomo. University of California Publications in American Archaeology and Ethnology, Vol. 37, no. 4, p. 186, Berkeley.

Gjessing, Gutorm (1958): Petroglyphs and Pictographs in the Coast Salishan Area of Canada. Miscellanea Paul Rivet Octogenario Dicata, pp. 259, 260, Mexico City.

Gladwin, H.S., E.W. Haury, E.B. Sayles, and N. Gladwin (1965): Excavations at Snaketown Material Culture, p. 227, Pl. CLVIII, Pl. CLXVII, Tucson.

Grant, Campbell (1967): Rock Art of the American Indian, pp. 54—67, New York.

Gunn, Sisvan, W.A. (1966): Totemic Medicine and Shamanism Among the Northwest American Indians. Journal of the American Medical Association, Vol. 196, no. 8, front cover, Chicago.

Heizer, Robert F., and Martin A. Baumhoff (1962): Prehistoric Rock Art of Nevada and Eastern California, p. 281, Berkeley.

Hoffman, W.J. (1891): The Mide'wiwin or «Grand Medicine Society» of the Ojibwa. Seventh Annual Report of the Bureau of American Ethnology, pp. 174, 186, 255, 291, Figs. 6 (no. 1, 4, 7), 7 (no. 1, 5, 12, 12,), 8 (no. 1, 5, 12, 13), 31, 32, Washington.

Howard, James (1968): The Southeastern Ceremonial Complex and Its Interpretation. Memoir Missouri Archaeological Society, no. 6, pp. 9, 26, 34, Columbia.

James, Edwin (1956): A Narrative of the Captivity and Adventures of John Tanner, pp. 175, 179—181, 341—345, Minneapolis.

Jones, Charles C., Jr. (1873): Antiquities of the Southern Indians, p. 29, New York.

Kirkland, Forrest (1940): Pictographs of Indian Masks at Hueco Tanks. Bulletin of the Texas Archaeological and Paleontological Society, Vol. 12, pp. 19, 23, Abilene.

Kirkland, Forrest and W.W. Newcomb Jr. (1967): The Rock Art of the Texas Indians, pp. 43, 45, 65, Austin.

Kroeber, A.L. (1925): Handbook of the Indians of California. Bulletin of the Bureau of American Ethnology, no. 78, p. 938, Washington.

Lambert, Marjorie F. (1967): A Kokopelli Effigy Pitcher From Northwestern New Mexico. American Antiquity, Vol. 32, no. 3, p. 398, Salt Lake City.

Landes, Ruth (1968): Ojibwa Religion and the Midewiwin, p. 48, Madison.

Lommel, Andreas (1967): Shamanism: The Beginnings of Art, pp. 16, 25, 28, 57, ff., 78, 109, 128, 130—133, New York.

Mallery, Garrick (1886): Pictographs of the North American Indians. Fourth Annual Report of the Bureau of American Ethnology, pp. 165—187, Washington.

Mallery, Garrick (1893): Picture Writing of the American Indians. Tenth Annual Report of the Bureau of American Ethnology, pp. 237, 463—467, 475, 476, 773, 774, figs. 474, 662, 653d, Pl. XVIII, Washington.

Maringer, Johannes (1960): The Gods of Prehistoric Man, p. 195, New York.
Mason, J. Alden (1945): Costa Rican Stonework (The Minor C. Kieth Collection). Anthropological Papers of the American Museum of Natural History, Vol 39: part 3, Pl. 43, Pl. F., New York.
McClintock, Walter (1936): Painted Tipis and Picture Writing of the Blackfoot Indians. Masterkey, Vol. X, no. 4, p. 123, Los Angeles.
Newcomb, F.J., S. Fishler and Mary C. Wheelwright (1956): A Study of Navajo Symbolism. Papers of the Peabody Museum of Archaeology and Ethnology, Vol. 32, no. 3, p. 40, fig. 78, Cambridge.
Okladnikov, A.P. (1969): Die Felsbilder Am Angara — Fluss Bei Irkutsk, Siberian. Jahrbuch für prähistorische und ethnographische Kunst, 22 Band, Pl. 8, Pl. 15, Pl. 21, Berlin.
Payen, Louis A. (1959): Petroglyphs of Sacramento and Adjoining Counties, California. University of California Archaeological Survey, Reports, 48, paper 73, p. 80, Berkeley.
Payen, Louis A. (1968): A Note on Cupule Sculptures in Exogene Caves from the Sierra Nevada, California. Caves and Karst, Vol. 10, no. 4, p. 37, Castro Valley.
Renaud, Etienne B. (1938): Petroglyphs of North Central New Mexico. Archaeological Survey Series, Eleventh Report, University of Denver p. 55, Pl. 12, Denver.
Renaud, Etienne B. (1948): Kokopelli, A Study in Puebli Mythology. Southwestern Lore, Vol. XIV, no. 2, pp. 25—40 Gunnison.
Ritter, Dale W. (1961): X-ray Petroglyph in Nevada. Screenings, Vol. 10, no. 2, p. 4, Portland.
Ritter, Dale W. (1965): Petroglyphs, A Few Outstanding Sites. Screenings, Vol. 14, no. 8, pp. 1—4, Portland.
Ritter, Dale W. (1970): Sympathetic Magic of the Hunt as Suggested by Petroglyphs and Pictographs of the Western United States. Valcamonica Symposium, Acts of the International Symposium on Prehistoric Art, pp. 397, 399, 402, 403, Figs. 195, 198, 200—202. Centro Camuno di Studi Preistorici, Capo di Ponte.
Ritter, Eric W. (1971): Review: Indian Art and History, The Testimony of Prehispanic Rock Paintings, by Clement W. Meighan. Caves and Karst Vol. 13, no. 6, pp. 45—47, Castro Valley.
Schaafsma, Polly (1963): Rock Art in the Navajo Reservois District. Museum of New Mexico Papers in Anthropology, no. 7, pp. 35, 41, 60, Sante Fe.
Schaafsma, Polly (1965): Southwest Indian Pictographs and Petroglyphs, pp. 6, 7, 9, 12, Sante Fe(?)
Schaafsma, Polly (1966): Early Navajo Rock Paintings and Carvings, pp. 14, 15. Museum of Navaho Ceremonial Art. Inc., Sante Fe.
Schoolcraft, Henry R. (1851): Antiquities, History, Conditions, and Prospects of the Indians of the United States, Part I, pp. 112, 338, 425, Pl. 48, Pl. 64, Pl. 65, Philadelphia.
Sims, Agnes (1950): San Cristobal Petroglyphs, pp. 5, 7, Pl. IV, Pl. V, Pl. VII, pl. VIII, Pl. XI, Pl. XIII, Pl. SIV, Pl. XVI, Santa Fe.
Smith, William Belle (1962): Personal Communication (regarding seal rock).
Smith, Watson and Louie Ewing (1952) Kiva Mural Decorations at Awatovi and Kawaika-a, Papers of the Peabody Museum of American Archaeology. Harvard University, Vol. XXXVII, no. 5, pp. 63, 97, 212—216, 299, 302, 304, Cambridge.

Spinden, Herbert Joseph (1957): Maya Art and Civilization, pp. 53—57, Pl. XLVII, Indian Hills.

Squier, E.F. (1851): The Serpent Symbolism in America. American Archaeological Researches, no. 1, pp. 110, 136, figs. 20, 24, New York.

Stevenson, Matilda Cox (1904): The Zuni Indians, Their Mythology, Esoteric Fraternities, and Ceremonies. Twenty-Third Annual Report of the Bureau of American Ethnology, p. 439, Fig. 15, Pl. XII, Washington.

Steward, Julian H. (1929): Petroglyphs of California and Adjoining States p. 227, Berkeley.

Strong, Emory (1959): Stone Age on the Columbia River, p. 120, Portland.

White, Leslie A. (1932): The Acoma Indians. Forty-Seventh Annual Report of the Bureau of American Ethnology, pp. 86, 113, Pl. 10, Pl. 11, Washington.

Wildschut, William (1960): Crow Medicine Bundles. Contribution from the Museum of the American Indian Heye Foundation, Vol. XVII, pp. 11, 12, Gluckstadt.

Wilson, Thomas (1896): The Swastika. Report of the United States National Museum for 1894, Smithsonian Institution, Pl. 13, Washington.

Die Felsbilder vom westlichen Nordamerica

VON HERBERT KÜHN

Es mag seltsam erscheinen, aber es ist doch eine Tatsache, die Felsbilder Amerikas wurden wissenschaftlich früher erforscht als die von
Europa. Nur Skandinavien macht in Europa eine Ausnahme, das
Gebiet, wo die Fülle der Bilder zur Fragestellung lockte. Das erste
Buch über die Felsbilder Skandinaviens ist das von A.E. Holmberg
von 1848, das Buch von C.G. Brunius erscheint 1868, das noch heute
wichtige Werk von Laurids Baltzer 1891—1908.

Die Felsbildforschung im übrigen Europa beginnt erst 1906, als
das erste Werk von Breuil und Cartailhac erscheint, das Buch über
Altamira.

Das erste wissenschaftliche Werk über die Felsbilder Nordamerikas
ist das von Garrick Mallery mit dem Titel: Picture-Writing of the
American Indians, Washington 1886, die Fortsetzung 1893.

Das heute noch führende Werk ist das von J.H. Steward, The Petroglyphs of California and the adjoining States, Berkeley 1929. Seitdem
ist das grosse Werk von Robert F. Heizer u. Martin Baumhoff erschienen, Prehistoric Rock Art of Nevada and Eastern California, Berkeley 1962, und die Forscher, Gebhard, Campbell Grant haben immer von neuem die Felsbilder des Westens der USA untersucht und
wissenschaftlich bearbeitet. Trotzdem ist die Fülle dieser Bilder in
Europa noch fast unbekannt. Um eine Vorstellung von der Menge
dieser Bildvorkommen zu geben, möchte ich Zahlen nennen. Steward
kennt 1929 in Kalifornien 129 Fundplätze, Campbell Grant nennt
mir im Jahre 1963 die Zahl von 300 Stationen, allein in Kalifornien.
Nevada weist etwa 100 Fundstellen auf, zusammen Tausende von
Malereien und Gravierungen.

Ich selbst habe die Bilder Amerikas zuerst 1933 in New Mexico
und in Arizona besuchen können. Ich habe darüber berichtet in dem
Buch, Wenn Steine reden, Wiesbaden 1966, 2. Aufl. 1969.

Im Jahre 1963 bot sich mir eine einzigartige Gelegenheit, die wichtigsten Felsbilder von Kalifornien und Nevada zu besichtigen. Ich
war als Gastprofessor für ein halbes Jahr an der Universität Berkeley
tätig. Ich habe dort über die Felsbilder der Welt Vorlesungen gehal-

ten. Am Ende des Semesters stellte mir die Universität einen Expeditionswagen zur Verfügung, und zwei Begleiter, die die Fundstellen der Bilder kannten, reisten mit mir, Prof. Elsasser und Allan Bascon, dazu meine Frau. Wir sind mehrere tausend Kilometer gefahren, vorbei an Felsen und Riffen, an Seen und Flüssen, und immer wieder durch die endlose, durch die quälende Wüste.

Die Bilder liegen nicht in Höhlen, sie lagern sich an freien Felswänden. Sie sind gemalt in den Farben Rot, Gelb, Schwarz, Weiss. Häufig findet man auch Gravierungen, eingeschlagen mit Steingeräten in den felsigen Untergrund. Dargestellt sind immer Tiere, Menschen und Symbole. Die Tiere noch verhältnismässig naturhaft, die Menschen stark abstrakt, naturabgewandt, oftmals in derselben Formgestaltung wie die abstrakten Menschendarstellungen in Europa. Die Symbole sind Kreise, Dreiecke, Kreuze.

Die Datierung nach den Jahreszahlen von Europa ist nicht möglich. Die Bilder können Jahrtausende alt sein, sie können aber auch vor hundert, vor fünfzig Jahren geschaffen worden sein. Im Kriege 1846–48 nahmen die Vereinigten Staaten Kalifornien. Mexico verlor mehr als die Hälfte seines Gebietes, Texas, Kalifornien, New Mexico, Arizona, Nevada, Utah und Teile von Colorado und Wyoming. Die 1848 neu in die Staaten eingefügten Länder waren so ausgedehnt, dass die Indianer noch lange Zeit als Jägervölker in ihnen leben konnten, in manchen Gegenden bis 1900, und die Pueblo-Indianer, die Ackerbauer, können in manchen Reservationen ihre alten Lebensformen bis heute erhalten. So ist die Herstellung der Bilder denkbar bis in unsere Zeit.

Deshalb sind die Bilder nur zu unterscheiden nach den wirtschaftlichen Gegebenheiten, die Bilder der Jäger, die Bilder der Ackerbauer. Ein Datum ergeben nur Bilder von Reitern, das Pferd ist erst mit den Europäern nach Amerika gelangt. Das früheste Datum solcher Bilder ist 1550, für Kalifornien 1775.

Bilder der Eiszeit, also vor 10 000 v. Chr. sind bisher nicht bekannt aus Amerika. Es ist auch der Mensch der Eiszeit selbst in einer gesicherten Bestattung, wie in Europa, in Amerika nicht zutage getreten. Soweit unsere Kenntnis bis jetzt reicht, ist der mongolische Mensch im Norden über die Beringstrasse nach dem Ende der Eiszeit gegangen, zugleich der malaische Mensch über die Inseln des Pazifik. Aus der Vermischung beider Typen entstand der heutige Indianer.

Da, wo die Tiere leben, blieb der Mensch bei der Jagd, da, wo die Tiere seltener wurden, musste er übergehen zum Ackerbau, wie in Vorderasien, wie in China, wie in Europa. Die Mehrzahl der Bilder im westlichen Nordamerika ist die von Ackerbauern. Alle Felsbilder sind Anrufungen an die Gottheit, ebenso wie in Europa, Asi-

Abb. 1. Churchill County, Nevada.

en und Afrika. Der Jäger bittet um das Tier, das Tier ist eine Wirklichkeit, daher sind seine Bilder real, wirklich, naturgegeben.

Der Ackerbauer aber bittet um die Fruchtbarkeit der Felder. Die Fruchtbarkeit aber ist unreal, ist unwirklich, ist ein Gedanke. So kann nur das Symbol der Inhalt der Bilder sein. Das Symbol weist hin auf das gedanklich Erfasste, es ist nicht eine Wirklichkeit, es ist eine Abstraktion. So ist die Mehrzahl der Bilder des westlichen Nordamerikas abstrakt, hindeutend, hinzeigend. Diese Bilder tragen einen kultischen Sinn in sich, eine Bedeutung.

So wird es die Aufgabe des heutigen Betrachters sein, den Sinn, den Inhalt der Bilder aufzufinden, und ich bin der Meinung, dass das möglich ist.

Das Zeichen Wasser. Zickzack
Sehr häufig erscheint auf den Felsbildern des Nordwestens Amerikas das Zeichen der Zickzack-Linie. Sie kann nur das Wasser bedeuten. *(Fig. 1)*. Es ist die eckige, die stilisierte Wellenlinie. Sie erscheint auf den neolithischen Tongefässen der Negade-Kultur in Ägypten unter und neben den Bildern der Schiffe. Sie erscheint ebenso unter den Schiffen auf den Tongefässen der geometrischen Periode Griechenlands als Bezeichnung des Wassers. In Nevada ist das Zeichen deutlich etwa in Churchill County, in Kalifornien in Inyo County, in Clark County (Heizer-Baumhoff, ebd.S.82 Fig.23 a).

Die Lebensquelle des Menschen ist das Wasser. Wo das Wasser nicht vorhanden ist, ist der Mensch nicht lebensfähig, ebenso nicht das Tier, und nicht die Pflanze. Das Wasser bedeutet die Grundlage der Existenz alles Lebendigen. So muss die Bitte um das Wasser an die Gottheit immer den Mittelpunkt jedes religiösen Kultes bedeuten.

Für den Ackerbauer ist das Wasser von besonderer Bedeutung, nicht nur zur Erhaltung seiner eigenen Existenz, sondern auch noch zur Erhaltung der Fruchtbarkeit seiner Felder. Auf ihr beruht sein Leben. Der Jäger kann weiter wandern, wenn das Wasser, wenn der Regen fehlt, der Ackerbauer aber, sesshaft geworden, braucht den Regen, braucht das Wasser für die Erhaltung und für den Ertrag seines Feldes. So tritt bei den Ackerbauern die Bitte um Wasser noch stärker in den Vordergrund als bei den Jägervölkern.

Ich habe bei Köln einer Prozession beiwohnen können, in einem Dorfe, genannt Gymnich, bei der der katholische Geistliche auf dem Pferde die Felder der Gemeinde im Ornat umreitet und Wasser streut auf die Felder, die Gottheit anrufend und sie bittend, den Feldern Wasser zu geben. Auch in Italien und Spanien ist die Wasserprozession üblich bis in die Gegenwart.

Im Christentum aller Konfessionen wird das Kind und der in die Religion Übertretende getauft mit dem Wasser. Beim Eintreten in die katholische Kirche weiht sich der Gläubige mit dem heiligen Wasser.

So muss auf den Felsbildern vor allem der Ackerbauvölker, in Amerika der Pueblo-Indianer, der Dorf-Indianer, das Zeichen Wasser an den Felsbildern, den heiligen Stellen der Anrufung der Gottheit, zu erwarten sein. Dieses Zeichen kommt vielfach vor.

Dass das Zickzack-Zeichen tatsächlich Wasser bedeutet, wird völlig gesichert durch unsere Schrift. (Chiera, Sie schrieben auf Ton, Zürich 1963, S. 175). Das latinische Alphabet, übernommen durch die europäischen Völker von den Römern, verwendet das Zeichen bis heute. Die Römer wieder haben es übernommen von den Griechen, und diese von Phöniziern. In dieser Schrift ist das Zeichen Zickzack das lateinische M, es heisst hebräisch mem, und das bedeutet Wasser. Einen klareren Beweis kann man nicht wünschen.

So tragen auch die Tongefässe des Neolithikums in Europa und auch in Vorderasien immer wieder das Zeichen Zickzack, das Zeichen Wasser, vor allem die Glockenbecher, die Schnurbecher, die Walternienburg-Bernburger Kultur.

Das Zeichen Wasser. Wellenlinie
Schon die Bezeichnung Wellenlinie deutet darauf hin, dass es sich um die Welle, wiederum um das Wasser handelt. Das Zeichen er-

Abb. 2. Churchill County, Nevada.

scheint vielfach in Kalifornien und Nevada, *(Fig. 2)* manchmal allein stehend, meistens aber verbunden mit anderen Symbolen.

In Europa ist die Wellenlinie das immer wiederkehrende Zeichen der sogenannten Bandkeramik, der neolithischen Kulturgruppe, die von Vorderasien sichtbar ist bis Belgien, im ganzen dem Laufe der Donau aufwärts folgend. Es ist diejenige Kulturgruppe, die über Land die Kenntnis des Ackerbaues und der Keramik verbreitet. So ist es verständlich, dass auf ihren Tongefässen immer wiederkehrend das Zeichen der Wellenlinie, des Wassers, erscheint. Die Gefässe enthalten das Wasser und sicherlich ist auch aus ihnen geopfert worden, um die Gottheit zu bitten um das Lebensnotwendigste, um das Wasser.

Wie das Ziechen Zickzack erscheint das Zeichen Wellenlinie in Europa ebenso wie in Amerika.

Die Wellenlinie findet sich ebenfalls in der Sinai-Schrift wie der Zickzack. Es verändert sich in der Schrift zum Zeichen W, in der griechischen Schrift zum Zeichen Σ, in der phönizischen und lateinischen Schrift zu S, auch sch gesprochen. In Nevada ist das Zeichen häufig, so in Clark County, Churchill County, Washoe County (Heizer-Baumhoff, ebd. S.78. Fig. 19,a).

Das Zeichen Wolke. Kammartige Figur
Ein anderes Zeichen ist schwerer zu deuten, es ist oftmals in der vorgeschichtlichen Literatur nicht verstanden worden. Das Zei-

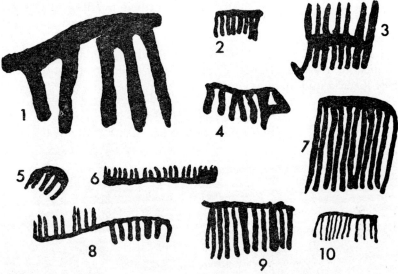

Abb. 3. Wolke-Zeichen, Nevada. 1. Churchill County, Flat Top. 2, 3,4,6,7. Clark County, Valley of Fire. 5, 10. Clark County, Mouse's Tank site. 8. Esmeralda County. 9. Washoe County, Massacre Lake.

chen erinnert an einen Kamm *(Fig.3)*, und oftmals ist es in diesem Sinne bezeichnet worden. Diese Deutung ist aber unangebracht. Ein Kamm ist kein Gegenstand religiöser Überlegungen. Es gibt in der Tat keine Religion, in der der Kamm erscheinen könnte als ein tragendes, als ein führendes Element.

Den Sinn habe ich erst in Amerika verstanden, in dem Indianerdorf Taos bei Santa Fé, New Mexico. Ich sah einer Indianerin beim Bemalen der Tongefässe. Sie trug mit Farbe das Zeichen Kamm auf, den waagerechten Strich, von dem mehrere senkrechte Striche nach unten ausgehen. Ich fragte sie, was das Zeichen bedeute, sie sagte mir auf Spanisch nubia, Wolke, so verstand ich das Zeichen. Es bedeutet die Wolke, aus der es regnet.

In der Steiermark, in Österreich, gibt es bis heute den Bauernkalender, in ihm wird der Regen noch jetzt bezeichnet mit dem gleichen Symbol, der waagerechten Linie, an die sich die senkrechten Linien nach unten anschliessen. Dieses Zeichen wird in dem Kalender aufgeführt als Regen. Das Symbol für regnerisch trägt den Halbbogen über den senkrechten Strichen.

Dieses Zeichen ist in Europa häufig im Neolithikum, etwa in der Walternienburg-Bernburger Kultur in Mitteldeutschland bei Halle, oder auf den Tontrommeln derselben Gegend. Sie wurden beim

Kult geschlagen bei der Bitte an die Gottheit um Regen. Das Zeichen Regen oder Wolke ist auf ihnen das immer wiederkehrende Symbol.

Dasselbe Zeichen erscheint in Amerika in Nevada in Churchill county, in Washoe County, Clark County (Heizer-Baumhoff, ebd. S.84 Fig.24 a und b).

Das Zeichen Fruchtbarkeit. Dreieck
Wenn die drei bis jetzt genannten Zeichen sich auf das Wasser, das

Abb. 4. Renegade Canyon, China Lake, California.

Urelement des Lebens beziehen, dann ein anderes Symbol auf den Menschen und in gleichem Sinne auf die Gottheit.

Der Ackerbauer, der Prairie-Indianer, braucht die Fruchtbarkeit des Feldes und auch die Fruchtbarkeit des Menschen, die Nachkommenschaft. In Renegade Canyon, am China Lake, California, ist ein göttliches Wesen eingraviert, viereckig wie das Feld, wenn der Pflug den Acker bearbeitet *(Fig. 4)*. Das Zeichen trägt die Andeutung eines Kopfes mit Nase und zwei Augen und rechts und links zwei Kreise. Innerhalb der viereckigen Gestalt erscheint zuoberst das Zeichen Regen, darunter immer wiederkehrend das Dreieck als das Symbol des weiblichen Geschlechtes. Unter diesen Symbolen erkennt man wieder das Regenzeichen. Wichtig ist es, dass neben dieser göttlichen Gestalt eine andere steht. Bei ihr trägt der Kopf Strahlen als Ausdruck göttlicher Kräfte, das Gesicht ist schematisch gegeben, angedeutet sind die beiden Augen. Der Körper ist wieder viereckig wie das bebaute Feld, es sind leicht angedeutete Zickzacklinien, das Wasser bedeutend, die den Körper waagerecht überziehen.

Beidemal ist die Gottheit gemeint, die dem Felde den Regen bringt. Ich meine, dass die Darstellungen lesbar, dass sie im Sinne des Denkens und Erlebens von Ackerbauvölkern verständlich sind.

Ein fast gleichartiges Steinbildwerk, eine Stele, befindet sich im Museum Kassel, stammend aus der weiteren Umgebung von Kassel, aus Hessen, aus Ellenberg. Wieder ist überraschend die Ähnlichkeit, fast die Gleichartigkeit der Symbole.

Das Zeichen Ahnenreihe. Fortlaufende Kreise

In der Nähe von Santa Barbara, nördlich von Los Angeles, California, liegen Felsbilder in den Santa Susanna Mountains *(Fig. 5)*. Die Bilder, gemalt und graviert, stellen seltsame Zeichen dar.

Eine menschenartige Figur, abstrakt im Sinne der neolithischen Menschengestalten, steht an entscheidender Stelle. Es ist offenbar die Gottheit mit zwei Füssen, die die Wolken darstellen. Es sind breite Strichlagen mit den auslaufenden Strichen, hier quer gestellt. Dass die Regenwolken gegeneinander gestellt sind, spricht nicht gegen die Deutung, Wolken können verschieden gelagert sein. Unter der Gestalt ist der Kreis gemalt, er bedeutet bei allen Völkern den Erdkreis, den Kosmos, das Ganze der Welt. So steht die Gottheit über der Welt, ihr Kopf ragt in das Ewige, ihre Füsse sind Wolken.

In ähnlicher Formgestaltung, die Gottheit über dem Weltall, wird Buddha dargestellt, Schiwa, Christus. Neben der Gottheit, und nur als solche kann die Gestaltung verstanden werden, erscheinen zwei Reihen von übereinander stehenden Kreisen, durchzogen von einer senkrechten Linie. Als ich vor dem Bilde stand, habe ich nachgeson-

Abb. 5. Santa Susanna Mountains, near Santa Barbara, California.

nen über die Bedeutung der Kreise, ich habe meine Begleiter, Campbell Grant und Gebhard, die unermüdlichen Forscher der Felsbilder dieser Gegend um ihre Meinungen befragt, auch sie wussten keine Erklärung, keine Deutung. Jedoch die Zeichen, rechts und links neben einer Gottheit stehend, müssen einen Sinn enthalten, auch wenn er unseren Denkkategorien schwer verständlich ist.

Ich meine, dass seine Bedeutung verständlich ist durch den Blick auf die tragenden Bewusstseinsformen aller Religionen. Die Grundfrage aller Religionen, aller Philosophien, ist das Problem der Herkunft des Menschen. Der Mensch erlebt sich hineingeworfen in diese Welt. Immer muss sich im Mittelpunkt seines Denkens die Frage erheben, wo komme ich her, wo kommt die Menschheit her. Die Reihe weist auf den Vater, den Grossvater, die Altvordern, die Ahnen, bis hin zum Urmenschen, zum Urstammvater, dem Adam. (Heizer-Baumhoff 1962. Pl. 14). Er muss zur Gottheit werden, zu der Gottheit, die schützend, helfend, die auch strafend und Gerechtigkeit gebend über dem Menschen steht. Die Gottheit wird der Vater des Stammes, so wie Wotan der Urvater der Germanen, Jahwe der Urvater der Hebräer, Amon der Urvater der Ägypter, Zeuss der Urvater der Griechen, so, wie wir noch heute sagen: Gottvater und Vater unser.

In der Bibel wird immer die Ahnenreihe genannt, ebenso in der Edda. Wenn die Reihen neben der Gottheit angebracht sind, können sie nur die Ahnenreihen bedeuten. Sie sind bezeichnet durch das weibliche Geschlecht, durchzogen von dem männlichen, dem Stamm, so wie wir sprechen vom Stamme Davids, vom Stamme der Habsburger, der Hohenzollern, der Romanows.

Ich meine, dass sich in diesem zentralen Sinne die Bedeutung der Reihen zu erschliessen vermag. Solche verbundenen Kreise kommen vor in Santa Susanna bei Santa Barbara, Calif., am Columbia River bei Beverly, Washington (Campbell Grant, Rock art of the American Indian, New York 1967 S. 95-. Heizer-Baumhoff, ebd. S. 76 Fig. 18 b).

Das Zeichen Stammbaum. Baum

In engem Zusammenhang mit dem Zeichen Ahnenreihe steht ein anderes Zeichen, das Gleiche bedeutend, ausgedrückt in anderen Formen. Es ist das Zeichen Stammbaum. Das Bild ist ein Baum. (Heizer-Baumhoff 1962. Fig. 95 b). Es mag sein, dass es ein wirklicher Baum ist, ein Baum mit einer geistigen Bedeutung, wie bei uns der Maibaum des Frühlings, wie der Weihnachtsbaum zur Winterzeit. Auch diese Bäume, wirkliche Bäume, tragen doch einen Sinn in sich, es ist die Fortdauer des Lebens, es ist die Erneuerung des Daseins.

Es gibt aber auch den Baum des Lebens, den Lebensbaum der Bibel und des mesopotamischen Umkreises. Auch er bedeutet die Reihe der Ahnen bis hinauf zum Urahnen, der zur Gottheit wird. In Nevada findet sich das Zeichen Baum, aber es ist gebildet wie menschliche Figuren übereinander. Ich meine, dass dieses Zeichen den Stammbaum bedeutet, ebenso wie Baumzeichen im südlichen Spanien, in Zarzalón, Batuecas (Breuil. Peint, rupestr. schém. d.l. Penins. Ibér, Paris 1933 I, Pl. XIX). Die Äste sind wie die Arme auf den Malereien der abstrakten Epoche, nach unten gerichtet, das Zeichen Wolke steht daneben. Auch in Solberg, Östfold, Norwegen (G. Gjessing, Østfolds jordbruksristninger, Oslo 1936 Pl. XX) kommt der Baum vor, er mag ein wirklicher Baum sein mit der Bedeutung der Fortdauer des Lebens, es mag aber auch der Stammbaum der Ahnen sein, zumal auch an dieser Stelle der Kreis, das Weltall, neben dem Baum erscheint. Die Art der Äste deutet auf die Arme abstrakter Menschengestalten. Mag es auch nicht immer möglich sein, den letzten Sinn deutlich zu erkennen: offensichtlich handelt es sich um kultische Gedanken, hinweisend auf die Fortdauer, auf das Ewige des menschlichen Geschlechtes.

Abb. 6. Basalt Cliff, San Bernardino, California.

Darstellungen vom Baume finden sich in Nevada in Lyon County, in Churchill County, in Kalifornien in Sierra County. (Heizer-Baumhoff, ebda. S. 158 Fig. 95 b).

Das Zeichen Radkreuz. Kreis mit Viergliederung
Ein besonders häufiges Zeichen in Amerika, in Europa und in Asien ist das Radkreuz, das Rad mit der Viergliederung, mit dem Kreuz in seinem Inneren, wie in San Bernadino, Basalt Cliff California *(Fig. 6)*. Es ist das ein Zeichen, das auch heute noch als heilig gilt, es findet sich in fast allen katholischen Kirchen, es findet sich als Mandorla hinter oder über dem Antlitz von Christus. An den Sonnenwendtagen wird es noch heute an manchen Stellen des nördlichen und mittleren Europa von dem Berge hinabgeworfen in das Tal. Die Götterbilder Skandinaviens, vor allem die von Thor-Donar,

dem Gott mit dem Hammer und mit dem Bockskopf, tragen dieses Zeichen auf der Mitte des Körpers. In der Edda wird es als Rad bezeichnet, Donar ist der Wagengott.

So ist dieses Zeichen als wirkliches Wagenrad bezeichnet worden, man hat es auch das Sonnenrad genannt, weil es bei der Sonnenwende getragen wird. Jedoch die Bezeichnung auf die Sonne ist nicht zu erklären, die Sonne ist nicht viergeteilt, sie erscheint auch nicht in vier Phasen wie der Mond. Der Sinn, verbreitet über die Welt, muss ein anderer sein, ein grösserer, ein umfassenderer.

Wenn das Viereck die Erde bezeichnet, dann muss der Kreis das Weltall bedeuten, am sichtbarsten ausgedrückt am Himmelstempel von Peking. Er steht auf viereckigem Grund, der Erde, der Tempel selber als Zeichen des Himmels, ist rund, ist der Kreis. Dieser Kreis, das Ganze, das Weltall bezeichnend, den Kosmos, dieser Kreis ist gegliedert in Vier.

In den beiden Kategorien des Denkens, wie Kant es ausdrückte, in der Zeit und im Raum, ergibt sich durch den Menschen die Gliederung in Vier. Im Raume ist es Norden, Süden, Osten, Westen, in der Zeit ist es Frühling, Sommer, Herbst und Winter. Die Vier ergibt sich durch das Bild des Menschen, er selber bedeutet ein Oben und Unten, ein Rechts und ein Links.

So ist das Zeichen Rad nicht die Sonne, es ist umfassender, es bedeutet das Ganze des Weltenalls, den Himmel und die Erde, den Menschen als Sinnbild des Kosmos. Dieses Zeichen wird das heiligste Zeichen, und so erscheint es in seinen Abwandlungen, als Kreuz im Christentum, als Hakenkreuz im Buddhismus. Christus trägt dieses Zeichen, Thor-Donar trägt dieses Zeichen in der Vorzeit. Es kann kein bedeutenderes Zeichen geben als dieses, es ist der Sinn und der tiefste Ausdruck alles dessen, was ist, es ist das All, es ist das Herrschaftssymbol der Welt als Ganzem.

Der deutsche Kaiser, als Herrscher, trägt den sogenannten Reichsapfel in der Hand bei den feierlichen Vorgängen. Er ist durch fast tausend Jahre erhalten, er befindet sich unter den Reichsinsignien in der Burg in Wien. Er ist rund und er trägt aufgeprägt die Viergliederung, das Kreuz hier in christlichem Sinne.

Das Zeichen Radkreuz bedeutet die Kraft, die Herrschaft der Gottheit über das Ganze der Welt, über den Kosmos.

In Susa, Südpersien, hat de Morgan 1889 eine bemalte Schale gefunden, jetzt im Louvre in Paris, die diese Gedanken deutlich bestätigt. In der Mitte der Schale, des Kreises, der Welt, das Radkreuz, rechts und links die Vögel, die um die Welt zu fliegen vermögen. Oben und unten die Weltmeere, bezeichnet durch die breiten Striche und oben und unten die Wolke, aus der Regen strömt.

Abb. 7. Tule River, Tulare county, California.

Das Zeichen Mensch. Abstrakte Form

Ebenso häufig wie in Europa im Neolithikum erscheint auch auf
den Felsbildern Amerikas das Zeichen Mensch in völlig abstrakter
Form *(Fig. 7)*. Der Jäger des Paläolithikums bat die Gottheit
um die Erlangung des Tieres. Das Tier ist eine Realität, ist eine Wirklichkeit. Der Ackerbauer des Neolithikums bittet die Gottheit um
die Fruchtbarkeit des Feldes. Die Fruchtbarkeit aber ist ein abstrakter Gedanke, nicht gestaltbar in der Wirklichkeit, nur darstell-
bar im Symbol, im Hinweis, im Hinzeigen auf etwas Entscheidendes.
Dieses Wesentliche ist das Wasser, ist die Fortpflanzung, ist das
Ganze des Daseins, die Welt mit den vier Jahreszeiten, ist auch der
Mensch, der um sein Leben bittet.

Auch der Mensch wird in dieser Zeit, in Amerika in der Welt
des Ackerbauers, bei den Pueblo-Indianern, ausgedrückt im Symbol.
Eine Linie wird der Körper, Linien werden Arme und Beine. Der
Kopf kann zum Kreise werden, wieder viergeteilt, denn Mensch und
Kosmos entsprechen sich im Denken dieser Epoche, in dieser Situa-
tion der auf dem Ackerbau beruhenden Weltgedanken.

So erscheint das Bild des Menschen in den Carizzo Plaints bei
Santa Barbara in Kalifornien, so in Washoe County oder in Churchill
County in Nevada (Heizer-Baumhoff, ebd.Taf.1,2;Taf.15,a,b,d).

In dieser Form erscheint das Bild des Menschen in der ältesten

Buchstabenschrift des Sinai. Sind die Arme betend erhoben, wird dieses Zeichen im Lateinischen zum E und zum H, beide den Menschen bezeichnend, noch in der Schrift unserer Tage.

Wieder sind die Ähnlichkeiten oder die Übereinstiummungen in Europa, Asien und Amerika überraschend. Ein Menschenbild mit erhobenen gewickelten Armen aus der Fundstelle Clart Hiko Springs in Nevada (Heizer-Baumhoff 1962, S.124, Abb. 61 a) zeigt genau die gleichen Formen wie Menschendarstellungen in Valcamonica, Norditalien (E. Süss, Le incisione de Valcamonica. Milano 1959. Fig. 5).

Andere abstrakte Darstellungen des Menschen finden sich in gleicher Form in Nordafrika, in der Türkei, im Kuban in Russland, in Sibirien. Die Übereinstimmungen sind derart eng, dass man nach dem Stile des Bildes allein seinen Herkunftsort nicht zu bestimmen vermag.

Das Zeichen Gottheit. Kraft und Segen

Wie kann die Gottheit dargestellt werden, das ist immer die Frage der Priester, die sich an die Gottheit wenden, die an den Felsen, meist an entlegenen Stellen allein mit der Gottheit sprechen. Sie malen und gravieren die Bilder der Gegenstände, die die Horde oder das Dorf als Wichtigstes braucht für das Leben. Moses stieg auf den Berg Sinai, die Gesetze zu empfangen von der Gottheit. So liegen die Bilder an den schwer zugänglichen Stellen, in der Tiefe der Höhlen oder auf den Höhen der Berge. Auch die Kirche unserer Zeit hat noch die Krypta, den heiligen Raum unter dem Schiff der Kirche und den Turm, der wie der Berg in die Höhe weist, in den Himmel, den Wohnsitz der Gottheiten.

Die Gottheit selbst trägt bei allen Vökern zwei Wesenheiten, einmal die Macht, die Kraft, die Stärke, zweitens das Segenspendende, das Gebende, das Helfende im Dasein.

Die Kraft und die Stärke wird bei Christus im Mittelalter dargetan durch die Mandorla, durch den Heiligenschein, durch das Radzeichen, durch die Herrschaftsgeste, die Majestas Domini. Bei Buddha wird die Macht dargestellt durch die Handhaltungen, durch seine unnahbare Überlegenheit, durch sein Zeichen, das Rad der Lehre und durch das Hakenkreuz.

Bei den germanischen Göttergestalten der Felsbilder Skandinaviens wird die Gottheit bezeichnet durch ihr Symbol, bei Thor dem Rad, bei Wotan dem Ring, der in der Edda *draupnir* genannt wird. Ihre Kraft kommt auch zum Ausdruck durch die betonte Bezeichnung des männlichen Geschlechtes, weiter durch ihre Waffen, bei Thor durch den Hammer, bei Wotan durch die Lanze. Die Herrscher des

Abb. 8. Inyo county, California.

Abb. 9. Dinwoody, Wyoming.

Abb. 10. Dinwoody, Wyoming.

Mittelalters leiten ihre Abstammung von Wotan her, und so ist es die Lanze, die bei der Übernahme der Herrschaft dem neuen Herrscher übergeben wird. Die heilige Lanze des Deutschen Kaisers, durch fast tausend Jahre verwendet, ist noch in der Schatzkammer der Wiener Burg erhalten. Bei den Merowingern und den Karolingern und den späteren Herrschaftsgeschlechtern Frankreichs ist es die Lanzenspitze, die *fleur de lis,* die das Symbol der Macht bedeutet.

Ein zweites Element ist das, was die Gottheit der Menschheit übergibt den Segen und die Güter des Daseins. Auf den Tempelbildern von Siam sitzt Buddha auf den Früchten des Feldes und des Meeres, bei Christus ist es Wein und Brot, was im Abendmahl genossen wird, bei den Göttern Mexikos das Maismehl und das Fleisch.

Bei den Bildern der Götter auf den Felsbildern Amerikas ist es das Zeichen des Wassers, das immer wiederkehrt, die Grundlage der Ernährung.

Auf den Bildern von Inyo County in Kalifornien *(Fig. 8)* ist der Körper der Götterbilder das rechteckige, das gepflügte Feld, überzogen mit dem Zeichen Wasser. Neben der Gottheit steht das Radkreuz, Symbol des Weltalls, steht auch das Kreuz mit vier Kreisen, den Weltgegenden und den Zeitepochen des Jahres.

In Dinwoody, Wyoming *(Fig. 9)* ist die Kraft der Gottheit angedeutet durch die Gestalt des Vogels, der kräftiger ist als der Mensch, weil er zu fliegen vermag. Die Flügel sind Wolken des Regens, der Körper trägt die Wasserlinien den Zickzack.

Am China Lake in Renegade Canyon, California, (Heizer-Baumhoff 1962. Pl. 18 e) ist der Körper der Gottheit wieder das Feld mit dem Wasser, der Kopf ist der Kreis des Weltalls mit den Strahlen oder mit den Hakenzeichen der Drehung. In ähnlicher Gestalt, die Hände erhoben, der Kopf als Kreis mit dem Hirschgeweih erscheint die Gottheit in Valcamonica in Norditalien oder in Russland, in Tamgaly, Kazachstan. (IPEK 21, 1964-65 Taf. 33).

In Dinwoody, Wyoming *(Fig. 10),* trägt die Gottheit den Stammbaum des Clans, der Kopf ist bezeichnet durch zwei runde Augen und über ihnen steht die göttliche Strahlung.

Ein sehr ähnliches Bild der Gottheit ist das von Peña Tú in Spanien (E. Hernandez-Pacheco Las pinturas prehist. de Peña Tu, Madrid 1914), bei Barcelona. Die Gottheit hat zwei Augen, die Nase, der rechteckige Körper ist das gepflügte Feld, bedeckt von Wolken mit Regen, und um die Gestalt herum läuft der Zickzack, das Weltenmeer. Strahlungen gehen aus von der Gottheit. Durch den doch ist sie zu datieren in die Zeit um 1800 v. Chr. stilisierte Menschen stehen zu ihren Füssen.

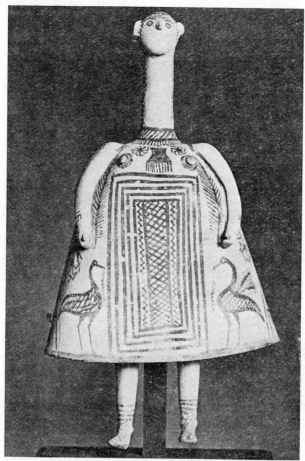

Abb. 11. Böotien, Griechenland. 8 Jh. v. Chr. Musée du Louvre.

Eine ähnliche göttliche Gestalt aus Böotien, Griechenland, in Ton
gearbeitet, mag die Betrachtung beschliessen *(Fig. 11)*. Sie befindet sich im Louvre in Paris. Der Kopf ist hoch erhoben und rund,
sowie bei vielen Göttergestalten der Felsbilder Amerikas. Der Körper
trägt die Malerei des Feldes. Um das Feld erscheint das Zeichen Zickzack, das Wasser. Vom Hals fällt die Wolke, der Regen herab. Die
Wasservögel bringen den Regen, die Arme tragen Zweige.

Bastian, der Begründer des Berliner Museums für Völkerkunde,
(1826–1905), hat von Elementargedanke oder Übertragung gesprochen. Ich meine, dass die Verwandtschaft nicht Übertragung, sondern Elementargedanke sein wird. Ich bin der Meinung, dass die

Menschheit an jeder Stelle der Erde unter den gleichen wirtschaftlichen und geistigen Gegebenheiten dieselben Gedanken zu denken und dieselben Gestaltungen zu schaffen von Natur aus gehalten ist. Immer wird das Göttliche als Hilfe, Schutz und Errettung vor ihren Augen stehen und immer wird dieses göttlich Gedachte erscheinen in den ähnlichen und in den gleichen Ausdrucksformen der Bildgestaltung.

LITERATURVERZEICHNIS

Mallery, Garrick, Petrographs of the North American Indian. 4th Annual Report of the Bureau of American Ethnology, Washington D.C. 1886.
Ders., Picture-Writing of the American Indians. 10th Annual Report etc. 1893.
Steward, J.H., Petroglyphs of California and Adjoining States. Univ. of California. Publ. in Amer. Archaeol. and Ethn. Vol. 24, 1929.
Ders., Petroglyphs of the United States. Smithsonian Inst. Annual Report for 1936, 1937. S. 405—425.
Cressman, L.S., Petroglyphs of Oregon. Univ. of Oregon Publications in Anthrop. Eugene 1937.
Jackson, A.T., Picture-Writing of Texas Indians. Austin, Univ. of Texas, 1938.
Lathrap, D., A Distinctive Pictograph from the Carrizo Plains, San Luis Obispo County, Univ. of California Archaeol. Survey Nr. 9, 1950.
Heizer, Robert F., Sacred Rain Rocks of Northern California, Univ. of Calif. Archaeol. Survey, Nr. 20, Berkeley 1953.
Baumhoff, A. Heizer, R.F. Elsasser, A.B., The Lagomarsino Petroglyph Group, Nevada. Reports of the Univ. of Calif. Archaeol. Survey Nr. 43, 1958. Nachdruck in: Heizer u. Baumhoff, Prehist. Rock Art, 1962.
Gebhard, David, Prehistoric Paintings of the Diabolo Region of Western Texas. Roswell Museum Publications Nr. 3. Roswell, New Mexico, 1960.
Ders., Rock Drawings in the Western United States. IPEK, Jahrb. f. prähist. u.ethn. Kunst, Berlin 1963 S. 46—63.
Heizer, R.F. and Baumhoff, A., Martin, A., Prehistoric Art of Nevada and Eastern California. Univ. of Calif. Press, Berkeley 1962.
Grant, Campbell, Rock Drawings in California. IPEK, Jahrb. f. prähist. u. ethn. Kunst, Berlin Bd. 21, 1964—65 S. 84—90.
Ders., Rock Art of the American Indian. New York, Thomas J. Crowell Comp. 1967.
Ders. and James W. Baird, J. Kenneth Pringle, Rock Drawings of the Coso Range, Inyo County, Calif. Maturongo Museum. China Lake, Calif. 1968.
Herbert Kühn, Santa Fe, New Mexico; Santa Barbara, Kalifornien; Nevada, in: Wenn Stein reden. Wiesbaden, F.A. Brockhaus Verlag 1966, 2. Aufl. 1969.

Method of recording and analysing rock engravings

BY EMMANUEL ANATI

Although the first recordings of rock-art are over three hundred years old and an increasing number of publications have come to light in the last one hundred years, the new methodological study of rock engravings is a relatively young field of prehistoric science. Specialists rely on experiences evolved mainly within the last generation. This subject is arousing an ever-growing interest among researchers, but they often find themselves lacking those elements which evolve with experience or with the study of recording systems; it is thus necessary to bring up to date the research situation in this field. The purpose of the methods is to obtain a documentation which should be sufficiently precise and detailed for the kind of study to be undertaken. In each project the methods must be adapted to ensure that they enable one to obtain the basic data for analysis; analysis is planned in accordance with the questions to which the projects intend to provide answers. A certain amount of flexibility must therefore be admitted in order to assure such possibility of adaptation.

The methods of recording and analysis developed in years of research in various parts of Europe and the Near East are in a state of continuous refinement. No doubt, they will evolve further as technological development is stimulated, in this case by the necessity of collecting ever more detailed documentation. Thus, previous publications are here partially modified (E. Anati, 1968, pp. 133–155); (1971, pp. 115–120); (1977, 58 pp.).

Techniques have to be adapted to the peculiarities of the material and the area which are being studied. Paintings and engravings require different techniques; where they occupy the same surface, still different problems have to be faced. In addition, the dimensions of the figures and of the decorated surfaces, their degree of preservation, the type of rock, the presence or lack of various techniques of execution and of complex stratigraphic superpositions, differences in patination and alterations of the rock surfaces, require, in each case, special approaches. We will here set forth the methods developed by the Centro Camuno of Prehistoric Studies for research in

Valcamonica: these methods are today being used in several major rock art sites in Europe and the Near East.

The collection of data starts with exploration, either carried out to obtain a discovery or with the first on-the-spot investigation, due to information previously received. It is necessary to situate the finding geographically by locating it on a map, delimit the area that it covers, provide the coordinates, describe the topographical situation and the position of the rock in relation to its surroundings: then the treatment of the rock begins.

The research is realized in four phases and 16 steps:

A. TREATMENT

1. *Cleaning the rock:* This phase includes cleaning the outcropping surfaces, excavating buried parts, and washing the rock to obtain a perfectly clean surface without remains of moss, lichen or other vegetal traces. The importance of washing is two-fold: A) it is not possible to study properly a surface that is not perfectly clean; B) since lichen and other micro-organisms are one of the major causes of the deterioration of decorated surfaces, the removal of such elements is important for preservation. In cases of rocks in a state of decomposition, it is necessary to consolidate the rock before beginning the treatment. In many instances this should be the task of a professional conservateur. Various kinds of silicones and other synthetic products are available for the purpose. Each rock treated in such way should first be carefully analysed by a specialist, in order to assure the use of a proper process. Where the possibility exists of paintings being present on the same surface as engravings, one must use special techniques to avoid altering the painting.

2. *The study of the causes of deterioration and of the degree of preservation:* Since various agents compete in causing its deterioration, an engraving has rarely been preserved in a perfect state.

For the engravings whose surfaces are exposed, the main causes of weathering are: A) mechanical factors, such as fractures due to freezing or erosion caused by water: B) chemical factors, such as the deterioration of the rock caused by corrosive processes, determined by the flow of acidic waters or by smog; C) human factors, such as trampling, recent engravings, incompetent casting or rock removal; D) biological factors, in particular lichen and other micro-organisms which damage the surface enough to weaken the signs left behind by prehistoric man.

Underground, the main causes of deterioration are: A) vegetable factors, such as roots, which often penetrate the cracks of the rock

146

and crumble it; B) chemical factors, such as the salinity or acidity of the soil; C animal factors which, however, are only of secondary importance; D) other physical factors such as frost and defrost, which combined with penetration of water in the cracks, constitute major causes of deterioration.

Five degrees of preservation have been determined: 1) excellent; 2) good; 3) mediocre; 4) bad; 5) very bad. These degrees are adaptive to the average situation of each zone. Since it is important to maintain a consistent evaluation within a single locality, fixed criteria for evaluation are established.

3. *Study of Incrustations:* Samples of possible incrustations are lifted and analyzed, various techniques are considered to assure that the

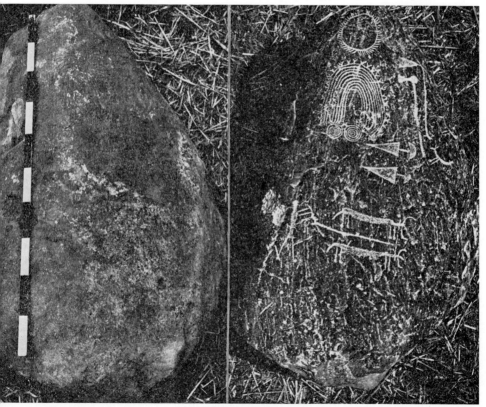

2. The stele n°2 at Bagnolo before the treatment. Incrustations prevent a clear view of the engravings.
3. The same stele (Bagnolo, n° 2) after the treatment. All the engravings are clearly visible.

best method is used to remove them where they might be covering engravings. Such incrustations are often of a calcareous nature, but there are also other types of incrustations and thus each case must be considered individually. In industrial zones, there are incrustations caused by deposits of carbon, sulphur and other materials due to smoke, which sometimes act as corrosives and must be removed from the surface.

4. *Preparation:* The surface is prepared by coloring it with very delicate colors which do not create a layer and which dilute perfectly in water. The name «neutral method» had been selected because it consists of an objective coloration which puts into relief all the engravings existing on the surface and does not permit personal interpretation. The method consists of a three-fold treatment: first, the entire rock is painted with an extremely diluted color, a tint contrasting with the rock's natural one; that is, if the surface is dark, white is generally used; if is it light, black is used. Using a paintbrush or an atomizer, all the cracks and irregularities of the rock are penetrated, homogeneously coloring the surface.

Second, when this first coloration is dry, a slightly moist sponge is passed all over the surface to remove the color which is left on the smooth surface. The coloration must be light, transparent and without thickness.

The third phase consists in the application, with a cloth or a piece of felt, of a color opposite from that used in the first coloration. The felt should be nearly dry so that it «stamps» the rock in negative, coloring only those parts which would impress the paper if the surface was used as a stamp, not penetrating into the deep parts of the engravings, into the incisions or into the natural cracks of the rock.

The preparation has three objectives: the first is to make visible to the human eye all the engravings, even the smallest, many of which are not evident without the «neutral method» coloration. With some exceptions, the treatment allows one to obtain surfaces perfectly legible in all details, clearly displaying both the various engraving techniques and the character of the border or margin of the engraving itself, to establish possible phases, and to see with clarity the instances of superimposition, of filiform engravings and of numerous other details otherwise invisible. An accurate study of historiated surfaces of the type found at Valcamonica is unthinkable, at the present stage of technology, without the proper treatment of the rock.

The second objective is protective, since the color used kills lichen and other organisms encrusted to the surface.

The third objective, of secondary interest, is to see the engravings in a way very similar to that in which prehistoric man himself saw them. In fact, from numerous cases of ochre and other coloring materials found at the base of engraved rocks (in particular, a deposit of 38 pieces of a variety of colors at the base of the Massi de Cemmo, from the presence of remains of coloration on the historiated walls of Capitello Dei Due Pini near Paspardo and from various other considerations) we know today that prehistoric man painted the engravings. Their present uncolored state seems therefore to be the result of deterioration.

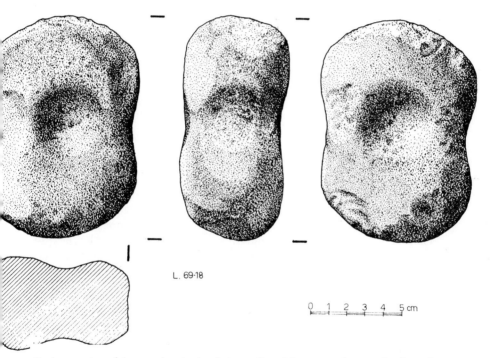

L. 69-18

0 1 2 3 4 5 cm

7. A percuter of hammering tool, of stone, found in excavation at the feet of rock n° 69 at Luine. The tool had been used on the six sides.

The engraved surfaces of Valcamonica are often of large dimensions, figures are made primarily by pecking but also linear figures and filiform incisions are present: the incisions are generally quite superficial and have a minimum difference of patina. For this type of rock art, the «neutral method» is at present the only one which allows adequate study. The result is aesthetically excellent and can be used to render legible those monuments visited by a non-professional public, such as, for example, engraved rock displayed in museums.

The color must not be the rock's own color because in such case, the accentuation achieved by coloration could easily be considered as natural. When a rock is treated with coloring, it should be clearly visible that it has been processed in such a way.

The coloration is washable with soap and water. Harmless diluents act more rapidly, but are expensive and unnecessary.

For rocks displayed in an uncovered setting, in Valcamonica's climate, the coloration fades gradually within approximately two years. If one wishes to maintain the figures easily visible, it is advisable to repeat the treatment annually, at least for the first years. For monuments located in covered areas, the treatment will last for five or six years. When repeating the coloration on rocks already treated, it is recommended first to wash off the residue from the preceding coloration.

When the treatment is completed, the rock is ready to be recorded. Here begins that collection of documentation which leads to analysis.

B. DOCUMENTATION

5. *Tracing:* Only the minute tracing of all the hammerings, engravings and incisions carried out by prehistoric man allows an in-depth study of the rock. An integral tracing of natural dimensions is necessary not only to have a good documentation in the laboratory but is, in itself, part of the study. With an integral tracing, the researcher can decide if certain signs are natural or man-made; he can observe with clarity which differences exist between one pecking and another and if certain natural forms or cracks in the surface were used and completed by man. Each rock, of the more than one thousand of which a tracing has been made in the last years in Valcamonica, has been found to be filled with innumerable details which would not have been observed without using the treatment described above and without the use of an integral tracing.

Cases of superimposition can be marked on the tracing by using ink of two or more colors, but generally when a tracing is accurate, one should be able to recognize the differences of pecking or of incisions which illustrate the succession of the superimposed figures.

Due to archive limitations, for large rocks standard format sheets of paper, 90x120 cm with a strip of 2 cm per side to overlap the adjacent leaves, are used. The scales used for the reduction are 1:5, 1:6 and 1:10. Photographic or manual reductions give, for standard leaves, the format respectively of 18x24 cm, 15x20 cm and 9x12 cm. There have been rocks whose tracing has required a mosaic of leaves. For example, the tracing of rock no. 34 of Luine, near Boario Terme, required the use of 108 leaves of standard format paper (90x120 cm). The composition of the integral tracing of this rock would require a surface of 25x34 meters. Scaled to 1:10, it can instead be exposed on any wall 3.40 meters long and 2.50 meters high.

4. Checking of the tracings upon rock n° 34 at Luine. Several leafs of polyetylene with the tracings are awaiting to be controlled.

6. *Photographing:* As regards the methods of study here elaborated, three different types of photographs are used, each for a different reason: I-General views to locate the rock in its surrounding and to have an image of its entity; II-A mosaic of the engraved zones, especially necessary for laboratory and archive work; III-Photographs of details such as the techniques of pecking of incision. The latter is preferably carried out with micro-lenses allowing enlargements of the negatives of 5 to 10 times the natural size and obtaining, in a manageable format, details enlarged up to 100 times. A group of hammerings of 5 millimeters can thus be studied when enlarged up to half a meter. This is useful not only to distinguish among differences of hammerings, but also to determine the type of tool used and its material (such as stone, ivory or metal). It should be noted that, because of documentation needs, it is advisable to pho-

151

tograph each rock, first at the moment of discovery, and then at every phase of the washing and treatment. Stereo-photos may be helpful in some cases to illustrate topographical relationships between surface and figure.

7. *Casting:* A cast can be interesting for display in a museum or for decorative purposes: if well done, it is attractive, from an aesthetic point of view and as such, undoubtedly, has its value. Rarely, however, does it have uses in the type of scientific reserarch here described, when the original rock is of easy access. No cast can at present be a complete substitute for the original in a meticulous analysis. Casts may, however, be used to study details of superimpositions or to compare and define different kinds of peckings or of incisions.

Casts are made for preservation of data when necessary: when the original rock risks destruction or is in the process of deteriorating, or when the rock is too porous to be effectively colored itself.

There are three principal types of cast: A-*Casts with liquid materials*. Negative casts are made by spreading a liquid which solidifies on contact, such as silicone, synthetic rubbers, polyester, plaster, plastiline. B-*Casts on contact:* There are negative casts made by adhesion to the engraved surface, of a solid plane which, when wet, molds itself to it and then, loosening itself, retains the negative impression. There are cardboards which are excellent for this purpose; they are delicately shaped when wet: they are allowed to dry, removed, solidified and utilized for the printing of positives. Sheets of silver or thin copper leafs may be used in the same way. They do not need wetting and may be solidified by spray or by a backshield of plaster. C-*Positive casts:* these casts are made by a paper, nylon, or film which, by a process of coloration by pressure, obtain the positive figure of the historiated surface. The kind of rubbing or «frottage» which is used by schoolchildren to reproduce coins, is the simplest of positive casts.

With any of these methods, near-perfect results can be obtained today. All three have size limitations and may be executed only for modest portions of rocks. They also have limitations of form, especially type C., for which good results are obtained mainly on flat or almost flat surfaces.

8. *Numbering:* The systematic numbering of all the historiated figures on the same surface serves to facilitate the work of analysis. In fact, a reference to a number is more precise and briefer than a reference to a figure which must be newly described each time it is mentioned.

The number is marked on the tracing or reduced tracing of the rock. The reductions are duplicated in various copies, then cut out; one serves for the typological analyses of the figure, another for the analysis of groups and scenes. The reference to the numbers of the original tracing greatly simplifies the work.

9. *Cataloguing the figures:* The purpose of the catalogue is to give a consistent typological definition which establishes the identity of each figure. It is the basis for all subsequent elaborations; it follows the order of the numeration and contains the definition of essential data such as typology, style and context. The catalogue is constructed on the basis of a typological list, used for all rocks (see the appendix).

The catalogue also serves as an index for the rock, since it generally starts with the point of access to the engraved surface and follows a constant direction to the most remote figure. The information is so organized as to be easily fed into a computer system, for eventual calculation of the comparative data. For each rock group, the catalogue is based on a reasonable and logical typological table.

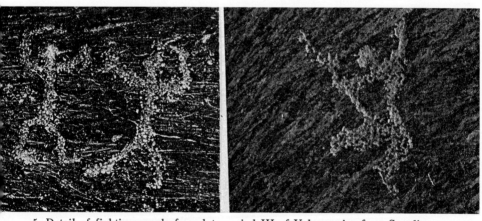

5. Detail of fighting couple from late period III of Valcamonica from Seradina II, rock n° 9. The peckings made by the prehistoric artists are visible very clearly after the treatment.
6. Human figure from period IV of Valcamonica. Seradina III, rock n° 13. Compare the difference in the texture of peckings between this and the previous example.

10. *Differentiation of groups, scenes and style:* The differentiation of techniques and the associations of figures determine groups made

1. A case of numerous superpositions concentrated on one restricted surface. Seradina III, rock 9-B. Engravings from two phases of period III and three phases of period IV are found upon this surface.

by the same tool, or by the same hand, or in a certain style; it is a necessary step for subdividing a historiated rock into chronologically and ethnologically significant sections.

As already mentioned, a numbered copy of the tracing is cut up by groups and scenes. The «cards» which result are catalogued by subject matter. According to each case, it is possible to group together, for example, scenes having a defined mythological character, scenes showing some ritual, hunting scenes, artigianal scenes, agricultural scenes, battle scenes, scenes associated with repeated symbols, as well as compositions associated with particular subjects and compositions of a more abstract nature.

11. *The study of superimposition, of the degree of preservation and of the patina:* This item is particularly important for the deter-

154

mination of the relative local chronology of each rock. The cases of superimposition are analysed in their order of distribution on the rock; groups of engravings are classified according to their degree of preservation; possible differences of patina existing among engraved figures on the same surface are differentiated. The data obtained from these three analyses are compared and the succession of the phases of depiction or engraving existing on the same rock can thus be determined. Any stylistic difference among the recognized phases must be noted for possible clues in determining their chronological significance. Furthermore the stylistic successions of numerous rocks must be examined and those characteristics which are consistent and repeated in the stylistic evolution of the entire group must be defined.

12. *Study of the techniques of execution:* This study is preferably carried out on greatly-enlarged photographs. The type of pecking or hammering, of engraving, of incision or of polishing, is classified according to evaluations of A — Regularity, B — Degree of concentration of the peckings, C — Dimensions.

A — Regularity: The pecking can be all alike, varied or quite differentiated. As far as we can tell, the regularity depends on the material of the incisory tool: stone, metal, horn, bone, etc., have all been used as raw materials for the working tools; and on the method of hammering used, either direct pecking, done only with the incisory instrument, or indirect, done with the aid of a mallet or striker. At the foot of the historiated rocks of Valcamonica, of Monte Bego and elsewhere, instruments used for the engravings have been found; contemporary primitive people have been observed while making stone engravings with the same methods (Anati, 1966, pp. 7—11: Id., 1973, pp. 5—51). Recent comparative experiments executed on rocks of the same hardness and with similar instruments enabled us to reach quite firm conclusions regarding the identification of the kind of tools used by prehistoric men, their raw material and the pecking-technique which was used in each specifič case.

B — Degree of concentration: The average number of blows per square centimeter is counted; thus a reference is provided, respective to other engravings, of engravings from other rocks or other periods.

C — Dimensions: The average depth and average maximum width of each type of hammering found is calculated. For filiform engravings, linear and polished, the depth, the maximum width and the cross-sections of the engravings are calculated.

This may be done using negative micro-casts made with plasticine or latex, or directly on the rock itself with the help of a comb-micromater. The data obtained from the study of the techniques of execution will undoubtedly increase, allowing a more precise classification of engravings than that which has been done up to the present.

13. *Rocks File:* The file on a rock is a formulary which includes the principal elements of each engraved rock and which is identical, as a formulary, for all rocks analysed, allowing for comparisions. This file, a copy of which is presented in the following pages, is constructed so that all the data collected can be reported on perforated cards or on magnetic tape, for future computer analysis.

C. ANALYSIS

14. *Analysis of components:* The components are analysed on the basis of three criteria: A — Stylistic analysis; B — Chronological analysis; C — Ethnological analysis.

A — In stylistic analysis, a concise description of the typological characteristics and of the style of each group found on the rock is given. When parallels exist with complexes whose identity is already firmly established, it is useful to utilize them to contribute to the development of a view, as clear as possible, of the stylistic-typological psysiognomy of each rock group. The basis of an effective stylistic analysis is to pin down the significant variables, thus eliminating those details which are shown not to be particulary relevant.

B — The chronological analysis results in a summary of the considerations which help to determine, first, the relative and then the absolute chronology of the various phases; notice must be taken of indications of possible chronologically valuable elements found in each group, such as figures of weapons or of tools of particular interest for comparison with excavation findings, descriptions of occupations and of rites which may have a chronological value, types of dress, the presence of symbols of a known age, techniques of engravings which are known to be recurrent in a certain period and other details suitable for contributing to the dating of the phase.

C — The ethnological analysis should result in a summary of those data which permit the reconstruction of the daily life, the activity, the socio-political structure, the economy, the beliefs and the external contacts of prehistoric man for each phase represented.

15. *Discussion:* The results of the three types of analysis must be compared and discussed so as to present a coherent view on the chronological evolution of styles and subjects.

16. *Synthesis of the collected data:* Finally, the conclusions drawn

from the elements collected in the preceding steps, are synthesized to form a general view of the rock, of its figures, of what they reveal about their significance and the life and beliefs of their artists. One can also make comparisons with other similar rocks or other findings, as long as such considerations are comprehensive and systematic. On the other hand, it is advisable to avoid casual, approximative, vague and sporadic comparisons, as they would carry the risk of being misleading.

The analysis of the rock concludes the technical study and forms the start of the actual research, the fitting of the rock into a wider archeological and cultural framework, the study of the historical and artistic significance represented by the rock figures collected.

The increasing number of rock art sites discovered in recent years, the variety of their figures and of their chronological context, as well as profound studies concerning their meaning, are making rock-art into a paramount source of information for some stages of human culture. In order that it may become an objective source, the archaeologist must present reliable and comparable data. In other words, research in prehistoric art must leave its stage of infancy and reach adulthood. The purpose of the present paper is to contribute to an evolution of this discipline in such direction.

A. TREATMENT:
B. DOCUMENTATION:
C. ANALYSIS:
D. SYNTHESIS:
 1. Cleaning;
 2. Study of the degree of preservation and
    of deterioration;
 3. Study of possible incrustations;
 4. Preparation;
 5. Tracing;
 6. Photographing;
 7. Casting;
 8. Numbering;
 9. Cataloguing the figures;
10. Distinguishing groups, scenes and styles;
11. Study of superimpositions, degree of
    preservation, and of the patina;
12. Study of techniques of execution;
13. Rock file;
14. Analysis of the components;
15. Discussion;
16. Synthesis of the collected data.

REFERENCES

Anati, E:

1966 — Utensili litici per eseguire le incisioni rupestri e il loro metodo d'impiego. *SIBRIUM,* Vol. 8 (1964—66), pp. 7—11.

1968 — I metodi di analisi e di archivio dell'arte rupestre, *B.C.S.P.,* vol. 2 (1966) pp. 133—155.

1971 — Methods of Analysing and Recording Rock-Art, *B.C.S.P.* vol. 6 (1971), pp. 115—120.

1973 — Luine (Darfo) — Campagne di ricerca 1968—1970, *Notizie degli scavi,* (1972), pp. 5—51.

1977 — *Methods of Recording and Analysing Rock Engravings,* Capo di Ponte Edizioni del Centro, 58 pp.

* Maps and diagram by Lars Tangedal, Historical museum, Bergen.

A. LOCATION:
    1 - coordinates ....   2 - region ....
    3 - locality ....   4 - rock number...............
B. REALIZATION:
    1 - date of tracing: ......   2 - date of index:... 3 - date of analysis:.....
C. ROCK COMPOSITION:
    I - type of rock:
        1 - sandstone;   2 - calcareous;   3 - schist;
        4 - granite;   5 - conglomerate;   6 - other   ....
    II - type of surface:
        1 - smooth;   2 - smooth with fractures or local breaks;
        3 - slightly rough;   4 - very rough;   5 - irregular;   6 - very irregular.
    III - color:
        1 - surface color............... 2 - rock's internal color ....
    IV - geological age
D. ROCK DEFINITION:
    I - position of rock in the valley:
        1 - east side;   2 - west side;   3 - outside valley.
    II - inclination of engraved side:
        1 - vertical or almost; 2 - very tilted; 3 - horizontal or almost;
        4 - not in situated.
    III - direction faced by engraved side:
        1 - north;   2 - east;   3 - south;   4 - west;
    IV - general dimensions of rock:
        1 - maximum length;   2 - maximum width;
    V - total size of decorated surfaces in sq.m.
E. GENERAL INFORMATION CONCERNING THE FIGURES:
    I - total no figures:
    II - styles represented:
    III - cases of superimposition (indicate the number of all the superimposed
        figures):
        1. ...... on ......   5. ...... on ......   9. ...... on........
        2. ...... on ......   6. ...... on ......   10. ...... on........
        3. ...... on ......   7. ...... on ......   11. ...... on........
        4. ...... on ......   8. ...... on ......   12. ...... on........
    IV - degree of figure preservation:
        1 - excellent; 2 - good; 3 - mediocre; 4 - difficult to decipher;
        5 - indecipherable;

F. QUANTITATIVE DEFINITION OF TECHNIQUE (MARK
QUANTITY OF FIGURES PER TYPE)

    I - types of techniques
        1-painted........ 2-pecked engravings...... 3-incisions ....
        4-polished engravings........ 5-high and low reliefs.........
        6/8-other techniques ....
        9-prevailing technique of depiction on the rock....... = ...%

    II - type of contour
        1-very regular   2-regular   3-irregular
        4-very irregular   5-non-existing

    III - type of peck-marks
        1-direct peckings..... 2-indirect peckings..... 3-other type ......

    IV - density of the peck-marks
        1-deep peck-marks
        2-superficial peckings covering the entire surface
        3-superficial pecking leave spaces between pecks
        4-sparse peckings covering over 50% of the surface
        5-peckings covering between 50% and 20% of the surface
        6-peckings covering less than 20% of the surface

    V - average size of the peck-marks
        1- 1 to 3 mm.   2- 3 to 6 mm.   3- above 6 mm.

    VI - relation between linear figures and figures with fully engraved spaces
        1-linear figures, n. ....=.................%
        2-figures represented with contour, n. ....=.................%
        3-figure with fully engraved spaces, n. ......=.................%
        4-other types (define) ....=.................%

    VII - depth of engraving in mm.
        1-maximum .... 2-average .... 3-minimum..........

G. ENCLOSURES

    I - Presence of encrustations: type: ....
        Join to appendix eventual results of analyses. Ref.
    II - Rock plan: attach general plan of rock, marking the outline, north
        indicator, the points of maximum length and width, and the location
        of the concentration of the figures
    III - Sections of rock: provide the sections in the same scale as the plan
    IV - This rock has been mentioned already in the following
        publications:
    V - Further remarks

Name.............................   Date ....

2. CLASSIFICATION OF FIGURES

TYPOLOGICAL LIST	Prehistoric styles				La-ter figu-res	Un-cer tain	Total
	I	II	III	IV			
A. HUMAN FIGURES:							
I. Simple human figures:							
1. with raised arms («praying»)							
2. with open arms							
3. with lowered arms							
4. in profile							
5. other							
II -Human figures with clothes and ornaments:							
1. with feathered headdress							
2. with simple helmet							
3. with feathered helmet							
4. with other ornament or hat on head							
5. with skirt or other type of dress ...							
6. with armor....................							
7. with feather decorations on body							
8. with more elaborate dress or orna-ments							
9. with masks							
10. other							
III -Human figures with weapons and tools in hand:							
1. with stick							
2. with hoe or other small agricultural instrument							
3. with hammer							
4. with scythe...................							
5. with axe							
6. with dagger or sword							
7. with halberd							
8. with lance							
9. with shield							
10. with shield and offensive weapons (dagger, sword, lance, etc.)							

2. CLASSIFICATION OF FIGURES

TYPOLOGICAL LIST	Prehistoric styles				La-ter figu-res	Un-cer tain	Total
	I	II	III	IV			
11. with bow and arrow							
12. with plough							
13. with wagon							
14. with other weapons or tools in hand							
15. with undefined weapon or tool ..							
16. with other objects							
IV - Mythological antropomorphic figures:							
1. with horns and «Cernunnos»							
2. hybrid (anthropo-zoomorphic) ..							
3. with large hands							
4. without arms							
5. without legs («praying bust») ...							
6. without arms and legs							
7. without head							
8. «phi» and other schematized figures							
9. other							
V - Persons on animal-back:							
1. simple person on horseback							
2. armed persons on horseback							
3. person standing on horseback ...							
4. persons riding other animals							
5. others							
VI - Other anthropomorphic figures:							
1. anthropomorphic figures with two or more heads							
2. ———————————————							
3.							
TOTAL A)							

2. CLASSIFICATION OF FIGURES

TYPOLOGICAL LIST	Prehistoric styles				La-ter figu-res	Un-cer tain	Total
	I	II	III	IV			
B. ANIMAL FIGURES:							
I - Wild quadrupeds:							
1. cervidae with branched horns ...							
2. capridae and cervidae with un-branched horns							
3. wolves, jackals, foxes, etc.							
4. squirrels, hares, mice and other rodents							
5. quadrupeds of uncertain identity							
6. other wild quadrupeds							
II - Domestic quadrupeds:							
1. dogs							
2. cattle.........................							
3. horses							
4. goats							
5. sheep.........................							
6. pigs							
7. other domestic quadrupeds							
III - Flying animals:							
1. ducks, geese							
2. hens, chickens							
3. small wild birds...............							
4. large wild birds							
5. other flying animals							
IV - Other animals:							
1. fish							
2. serpents							
3. other animals..................							
TOTAL B)							

2. CLASSIFICATION OF FIGURES

TYPOLOGICAL LIST	Prehistoric styles				La-ter figu-res	Un-cer tain	Total
	I	II	III	IV			
C. FIGURES OF BUILDINGS-VEHICLES AND HEAVY IMPLEMENTS:							
I - Buildings:							
1. buildings on a platform							
2. buildings with a ladder							
3. buildings with solar disks							
4. buildings with human figures							
5. buildings of complex nature							
6. other buildings							
II - Vehicles:							
1. four wheeled wagons							
2. two wheeled carts							
3. sleds and other vehicles for land use...........................							
4. boats							
III - Heavy implements:							
1. ploughs							
2. looms							
3. anvils							
4. ladders							
5. traps							
6. other heavy implements							
TOTAL C)							
D. WEAPONS AND IMPLEMENTS NOT HELD BY HUMAN FIGURES:							
I - Weapons:							
1. triangular-bladed dagger with crescent-shaped pommel							
2. other triangular-bladed daggers .							
3. sub-triangular bladed daggers....							
4. other daggers							
5. swords......................							
6. halberds							

2. CLASSIFICATION OF FIGURES

TYPOLOGICAL LIST	Prehistoric styles				La-ter figu-res	Un-cer tain	Total
	I	II	III	IV			
7. battle axes							
8. lances							
9. bow and arrow							
10. shields							
11. other weapons							
II - Implements:							
1. axes							
2. hoe							
3. hammer							
4. scythe							
5. sickle							
6. others							
III - Other objects:							
1. «palette»							
2. pins and fibulae							
3. bracelets and necklaces							
4. horns, trumpets and other musical instruments							
5. pots and other vessels							
6. other							
E. SYMBOLIC, SCHEMATIC, and ABSTRACT FIGURES:							
I - Symbolic figures:							
1. oculi-shaped...................							
2. idol-shaped							
3. horn-shaped (bucrania)							
4. spirit signs							
5. hand prints							
6. foot prints							
7. others							
II - Conventional signs:							
1. crosses and derivative figures							
2. triangles and derivative figures ..							

2. CLASSIFICATION OF FIGURES

TYPOLOGICAL LIST	Prehistoric styles				La-ter figu-res	Un-cer tain	Total
	I	II	III	IV			
3. squares, rectangles, and derivatives							
4. stars							
5. «celtic roses»							
6. «author marks»							
7. signs of numerical value							
8. repetitive ideograms							
9. raetho — etruscan inscriptions							
10. latin inscriptions							
11. other inscriptions							
12. other conventional signs							
13. others							
III - Cup-marks, disks, and spirals:							
1. single cup-marks							
2. group of cup-marks							
3. group of cup-marks arranged geometrically							
4. cup-marks and small grooves							
5. cup-marks linked by a groove							
6. cup-mark and radial arrangement (like a rayed star)							
7. simple disk.							
8. cup-mark and disk							
9. concentric disks with central cup-mark							
10. concentric disks with series of cup-marks							
11. disk with internal rays (like a wheel)							
12. disk with external rays (like a rayed sun)							
13. disk with rays only on one side (Paspardo type)							
14. disk with a tail (like a comet)							
15. spiral and double spiral							
16. spectacle spiral pendant							

2. CLASSIFICATION OF FIGURES

TYPOLOGICAL LIST	Prehistoric styles				La- ter figu- res	Un- cer tain	Total
	I	II	III	IV			
17. labyrinth and semi-labyrinth							
18. meanders and other figures based on a circle form................							
19. others							
IV - Topographical figures, lattice-work, point and lined, symmetrical and asymmetrical zones:							
1. points and groups of points							
2. lines and groups of lines........							
3. «grill-shaped» figures							
4. «lattice work» figures							
5. simple «topographical» figures ..							
6. complex «topographical» figs							
7. other internally hammered surfaces							
8. others							
V - Other symbolic, schematic, and abstract figures:							
1.							
2.							
TOTAL E)							
F. OTHER FIGURES:							
I -							
II -							
TOTAL OF FIGURES ON THE ROCK							

2. CLASSIFICATION OF FIGURES

TYPOLOGICAL LIST	Prehistoric styles				Later figures	Uncertain	Total
	I	II	III	IV			
APPENDIX - A Qualifications and activities) I -Human figures - sex: 1. masculine .... 2. feminine .... 3. undeterminable							
TOTAL							
II -Human figures - occupations: 1. hunting.................... 2. animal breeding .... 4. fishing .... 5. war .... 6. religion .... 7. other occupations .... 8. no occupation recorded							
TOTAL							
III -Wild quadrupeds: 1. wounded by weapons .... 2. trapped................... 3. other figures in hunting scene ... 4. others in a herd............ 5. others isolated .... 6. other figures...............							
TOTAL							
IV - Figures of dogs: 1. connected with hunting scenes ... 2. not connected with hunting scenes 3. uncertain							
TOTAL							

TYPOLOGICAL LIST	Prehistoric styles				La- ter figu- res	Un- cer tain	Total
	I	II	III	IV			
V - Other figures of domestic quad- rupeds: 1. connected with human figures ... 2. not connected with human figures 3. uncertain							
TOTAL							
VI - Flying animals: 1. connected with human figures ... 2. not connected with human figs. ... 3. uncertain							
TOTAL							

APPENDICE — B

List of the catalogued figures, which apply to more than one section. (For example: a human figure whose head is decorated by feathers is counted in section A-II-1. If it holds an axe, it should appear in this appendix, marked in the second column by the number A-III-5. If the same figure has other relevant attributes, these should be indicated in the third and fourth column).

Number of the fig.	Class in which it was counted	Second classification	Third classification	Fourth classification
1.	....	....	....	....
2.	....	....	....	....
3.	....	....	....	....
4.	....	....	....	....
5.	....	....	....	....
6.	....	....	....	....
7.	....	....	....	....
8.	....	....	....	....
9.	....	....	....	....
10.	....	....	....	....

N.B.: In the «figure classification» each figure must appear only once.

Is the location of rock pictures an interpretative element?

BY GRO MANDT

1. *Presentation of the problem*

The subject of this article is the interpretation of rock pictures. The question to be considered is the extent to which the location of the pictures contributes to their interpretation. I shall try to throw light upon the problem by means of analyses of the geographical and topographical locations of rock pictures in Western Norway. The analysis is based primarily on the group of rock pictures traditionally termed «agrarian», which are usually dated to the Bronze Age. Problems connected with dating will not be taken up in this particular study.

2. *Social and ecological background*

2.1 The rock pictures as part of a society

As an introduction I want to point out the importance of seeing the rock pictures in a social perspective. Whatever interpretation the pictures are given, they must be considered a product of their own time, made by and for a certain society. It seems therefore unsatisfactory to study the rock pictures as an isolated artistic or religious phenomenon. If they are not seen as part of a greater social entity, an essential dimension of the interpretation will be lost.

2.2 The influence of the environment on social and economic structure

Within the framework of this paper, it is not possible to outline a picture of the Bronze Age society of Scandinavia. It seems relevant to point out, however, that Scandinavia in the Bronze Age was hardly one homogeneous culture area. The ecological conditions are very varied in the different parts of Scandinavia, and this must have effected the development of society. In particular the economic conditions — and the connected social organisations — must have been diverse. The open, fertile fields of Southern Scandinavia must have offered much better opportunities for the farming economy than, for instance, the hilly and often meagre terrain of Western

Norway. Sheltered and productive hillsides may be found along the coast and fjords of Western Norway, but they are few when compared with the unproductive areas. Thus only 4 to 5% of the area is farmland today *(Ahlmann* 1962: 168). It therefore seems reasonable to believe that people in these regions continued to exploit the resources of the sea, the woods and the mountains in the Bronze and Iron Ages.

In this connection I find it less interesting to ask whether farming or hunting was the main occupation in Scandinavia in the Bronze Age. It is essential, however, to realise that different forms of adaptation to the environment probably occurred. Determined by the ecological conditions, the different farming activities were of varying importance in relation to «old» occupations such as hunting and fishing. The economic and social differences were reflected in different customs, which again influenced the material remains. The rock pictures are part of these material manifestations. In my opinion this is an essential reason for studying them in a general social connection — also including religion — instead of stressing the interpretation of single motifs isolated from their context.

3. *Fertility-cult and farming*

The rock pictures have for a long time been accepted as a religious phenomenon. Many interpretations have been put forward, but I shall concentrate on one which has proved of great importance in understanding Scandinavian rock pictures. In the 1920's Oscar Almgren, in a pioneer work, formulated his hypotheses on the interpretation of the pictures *(Almgren* 1927). He sees the rock pictures from the Bronze Age as a reflection of cult actions to promote fertility in a peasant community, a cult rooted in the prehistoric religions of the Near East. A great many of the later interpretations are extentions of and adjustments to Almgren's hypotheses.

After it had been generally accepted that many of the elements of the Bronze Age rock pictures seem conprehensible only in relation to a fertility religion, agriculture became a timely word. In accordance with this Gutorm Gjessing in 1936 introduced the term «agrarian» rock carvings, and since then this word has been commonly used, at least in Norway *(Gjessing* 1936: 1). In Gjessing's opinion it is more relevant to use a term referring to the presumed occupation of the makers of the rock pictures, than to use the traditional terms for distribution and age: «South-Scandinavian» and «Bronze Age» carvings. In Gjessing's opinion these terms are not fully adequate, because «agrarian» rock pictures are not found only in Southern Scandinavia (strictly Denmark and Scania), and it is not definitely proved that all of them were made in the Bronze Age.

Gjessing's arguments for putting aside the distributional and chronological terms deserve full agreement. Though his alternative is also interpretative — a principle which ought to be avoided — it will nevertheless be used here, for lack of a more suitable term.

The basis of Almgren's fertility-centered interpretation was the motifs of the rock carvings, and they were also decisive for Gjessing's occupational term. But another element of the agrarian carvings has gradually come into use in order further to emphasize the connection with an agrarian fertility cult and -magic; that element is the location. It has been said of the agrarian carvings that they are mainly situated in areas of old and productive farmland, and that they are usually found close to cultivated fields and pastures (*Hagen* 1962: 108, *Marstrander* 1963: 1). The counterpart has been considered as being the hunters' carvings, picturing game and usually located in the woods and by the sea, that is in hunting terrain (f.i. *Hagen* 1962: 50). These observations, probably correct in many cases, have through the years become something of an axiom. The connection of the agrarian carvings with farmland and the hunters' carvings with hunting areas has been considered the rule, other forms of location as exceptions.

4. Contrasting views regarding the hypothesis of agrarian connection

In archaeological research it is necessary to arrange and classify the material. In order to elucidate the social processes which have resulted in the material remains, one must place the material into different «boxes». However the «boxes» must not be looked upon as being constant and once and for all defined in relation to each other.

As pointed out, it is the motifs and the location that have been used to place the agrarian carvings into the box «fertility-cult in connection with agriculture», and the same elements have defined these rock pictures as being different from hunters' carvings. If the use and basis of these «boxes» are accepted in advance in an interpretation, many of the elements of the rock pictures will escape the analysis. Since the main subject of this contribution is whether location is an interpretative element, the motifs will not be considered here. Instead I shall draw attention to some general «irregularities» as far as location is concerned.

In Norway large groups of agrarian carvings are found in the productive agricultural areas of Østfold, Rogaland and Trøndelag (fig. 1).* A great many of these localities, however, are situated by

* Maps and diagrams by Lars Tangedal, Historical Museum, Bergen.

172

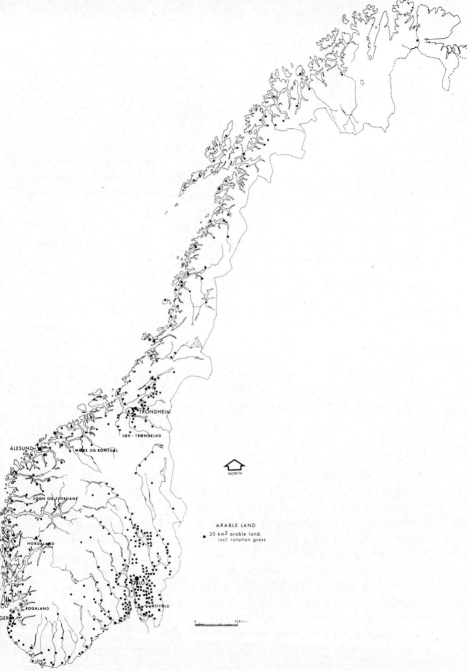

Fig. 1.The distribution of arable land in Norway. (Reproduced from Sømme 1961, map 12). In Østfold, Rogaland and Trøndelag the distribution of agrarian carvings coincides with the arable land, but this is not the case in the inland districts of Eastern Norway, north of Oslo.

173

heavy clay fields, cultivated in late historic times (*Hagen* 1967: 152). On the other hand there are very few examples of agrarian carvings in the inland districts of Eastern Norway (*Marstrander* 1963, fig. 1). This is an area with easily cultivated moraine soils, districts having an agrarian economy as far back as the beginning of the Late Stone Age (*Hinsch* 1955: 55). As just mentioned, Trøndelag has large and characteristic localities of agrarian carvings (*Marstrander* 1963: 6 f.). In the very same districts there are many large and as characteristic localities of hunters' carvings (*Gjessing* 1936). Examples of the two groups may also be found on the same farm, the different motifs can even be represented on the same rock, for instance at Bardal (*Gjessing* 1936: 30, pl. LV). This mixing of motifs is also found both in Eastern and Western Norway (*Engelstad* 1934: 69 f., *Mandt Larsen 1972: 34 f.*).

5. *Analysis of the location*
5.1 Hypothesis

On the basis of the above mentioned relations, I shall put forward the hypothesis that location in productive farmland is not an integrated element of agrarian carvings. This hypothesis will be tested on the material from a limited area. As mentioned in the introduction, the analysis is based on the rock pictures in Western Norway, in the three counties Hordaland, Sogn og Fjordane and Sunnmøre.

5.2 Definitions

In the following «image-localities» are separated from «cup-mark-localities». *Cup-mark-localities* have cup-marks as their only motif — appearing from 1 up to 100 — and they are often arranged intentionally, for instance in circles or rows. *Image-localities* may also have cup-marks, even in numerical predominance, but in addition one or more images are represented among the motifs: boats, human figures, foot prints or different kinds of geometrical figures. This distinction is made for two reasons. On the one hand it is the location of the image-localities which is in focus when the presumed connection to farmland is concerned. On the other hand cup-marks are almost undatable when found as a single motif.

Distinction is further made between two kinds of location: Macro-location and micro-location. *Macro-location* is the geographical distribution of the localities in the three counties. *Microlocation* is their topographical situation, that is in what kind of terrain they are located.

174

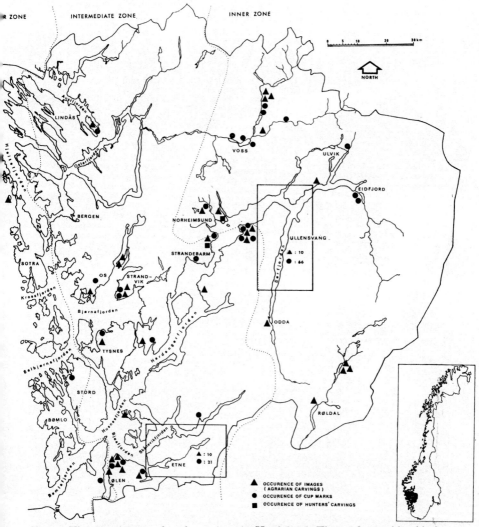

Fig. 2. The distribution of rock carvings in Hordaland. There are considerable
concentrations in the two areas marked off with squares, Etne and Ullensvang
(numbers given).

The analysis is only concerned with what is called *fixed sites,* that
is rock pictures on mountainsides, solid rock and earthbound boul-
ders. Unattached stones may have been moved from their original
position. The few examples of decorated grave-stones from Western
Norway are not included in the analysis, since they are considered
an element of the burial customs, and as such have no relevance to

175

Fig. 3. The distribution of rock carvings in Sogn og Fjordane and Sunnmøre. In Luster, the area marked off with a square, there is a considerable concentration of cup-mark-localities.

the question of a possible connection between the agrarian carvings and farmland.

5.3 The macro-location

In the county of *Hordaland* the majority of the localities of rock pictures occurs along the fjords in the southern and central parts, with some in the inland districts (fig. 2). There are areas with remarkable concentrations of agrarian carvings in the south, for instance in Etne and Ullensvang (especially along Sørfjorden). The Sørfjord-district is dominated by cup-mark-localities, more than 50 having been found. In the coastal districts there are only 3 localities, and in the northern part of the county also only 3.

In the county of *Sogn og Fjordane* there is a concentration of localities, mainly with cup-marks, in the inner districts of Sogn, especially in Luster (fig. 3). The majority of the image-localities occurs in the coastal areas of Sunnfjord and Nordfjord, many being situated on comparatively big islands. Apart from these, some localities are found in the central parts of Nordfjord.

The four fixed sites of *Sunnmøre* occur in the coastal district.

5.4 The distribution in relation to the ecological conditions

As previously mentioned, Western Norway is a marginal area where agriculture is concerned. Owing to climate and soils, the conditions are bad for the cultivation of cereals and root-crops. The main agricultural occupation is the growing of grass and cattle-breeding. (*Ahlmann* 1962: 168).

The environment and the living conditions are, however, not the same on the windblown islands of the coastal districts, in the sheltered fjords and inlets farther inland and in the easternmost mountain areas. The following survey of the living conditions is only concerned with such «natural» occupations as agriculture, fishing and hunting (*Sund* 1963: 119). The survey is based upon the present ecological pattern, because the climatic conditions in Western Norway of today presumably do not differ essentially from those of the sub-Boreal period (*Frenzell* 1966).

In the *outer zone*, consisting of the islands and the outer seashore, fishing is the main occupation, while agriculture is very poor (*Ahlmann* 1962: 168). The *intermediate zone*, consisting of the regions around the central parts of the fjords, have comparatively large agricultural areas (*Norge* 1963: 175 f.). To a certain degree fishing takes place in the fjords, but this occupation was more common in earlier times. These districts also have relatively large woods, with woodland animals such as deer. The *inner zone* consists of the inner parts of the fjords, with steep hillsides and mountain areas. The cultivated areas are small because of the topographical conditions but, on the other hand, the more continental climate is favourable to cultivation (*Ahlmann* 1962: 168—169). The breeding of goats and sheeps is typical for these districts (*Norge* 1963: 213). Apart from this, people have exploited the ample resources of the fjords and the mountains.

This short survey shows that the intermediate, and to some degree the inner zone, offer the most diverse ecological resources. As previously shown the majority of *Hordaland's* agrarian carvings occur in these districts, that is in the districts also most favourable to agriculture, at least in the form of stock-breeding. In this connection it is, however, worth noting that in Hordaland the only two (small) examples of hunters' carvings occur in the very same area: one in the intermediate zone and one in the inner zone (*Mandt Larsen* 1972: 142). The majority of agrarian carvings in *Sogn og Fjordane* occurs in the outer zone, as do the two large examples of hunters' carvings of Ausevik and Vingen (*Bøe* 1932, *Hagen* 1969).

With regard to the macro-location no exclusive preference seems to have been made for locating the West-Norwegian agrarian carvings in cultivable areas. Further there seems to be no distinct division between the distribution of the agrarian carvings and the hunters' carvings; on the countrary, their occurrence seems to coincide.

5.5. The micro-location

The hypothesis that farmland-location is not an integrated element of the agrarian carvings will also be tested in relation to the topographical location.

In the analysis I have tried to define location-categories for the sites based on their topographical conditions. The classification is based on the relation of the sites partly to the present settlement, partly to situations in the terrain. Relation to the present settlement — especially farmsteads — is used in the analysis because the built-up area of a parish is determined by local climate and soils, and these are the relations relevant for the classification. Further elements of classification are exact altitudes, distance from the sea, and the nature of the terrain — whether it is flat or hilly.

5.5.1 Location-categories

On the basis of these criteria four main location-categories have been distinguished for the rock pictures of Western Norway (fig. 4):

	COASTAL ZONE						FARM ZONE						MOUNTAINSIDE ZONE					
	SHORE LINE		FLAT TERRAIN		HILLY TERRAIN		FLAT TERRAIN		HILLY TERRAIN		OVERHANG-ING ROCK		FLAT TERRAIN		HILLY TERRAIN		OVERHANG-ING ROCK	
	I	CM	I	CM	I	CM	I	CM	I	CM	I	CM	I	CM	I	CM	I	CM
HORDALAND	3		3		12	4	8	16	9	17	1		7	47	1	6	2	3
SOGN OG FJORDANE	1		5		6		3	5		8			1	102	1	21		
SUNNMØRE					1		1		2									

I   ▪ occurrence of images

CM ▪ occurrence of cup marks

Fig. 4. The topographical locations of the fixed sites of agrarian carvings in Western Norway, in relation to the location-categories.

I)   *The coastal zone* is characterized by close vicinity to the sea — maximum 300 m from the shore — and by low altitude — up to about 40 m above sea-level.

II) *The farm zone* includes the built up area in a parish («bygd»), up to a maximum of 250—300 m above sea-level.

III) *The mountainside zone* includes the mountain summer farms and the surrounding areas having about the same altitudes, from about 300 m to about 900 m above sea-level.

IV) *The high mountain zone* includes areas over 900 m above sea-level, that is the areas above the mountainside zone. In this zone there is one single site, having only cup-marks, and this will be no further considered in the following.

In the first three main location-categories further distinction is made between flat and hilly terrain. Other subdivisions are: for the coastal zone the actual shoreline, and for the farm zone as well as the mountainside zone, overhanging rock («heller»).

I am fully aware that this classification system to some degree is based on personal judgment. The topographical location of the West-Norwegian rock pictures is as varied as the landscape, and the transition between the categories is as flexible as the transition between the different kinds of terrain. Nevertheless, I believe that the classification reveals a certain tendency as far as location is concerned.

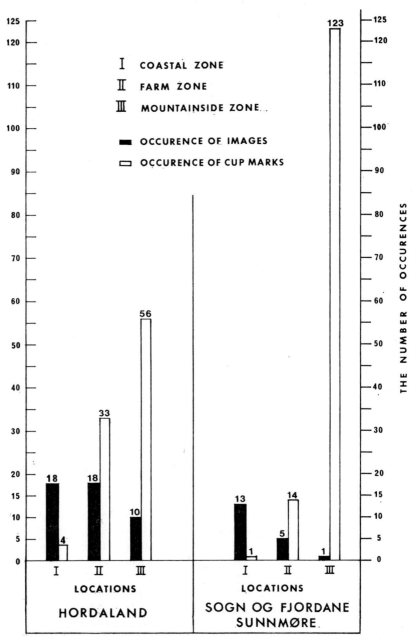

Fig. 5. The distribution of image- and cup-mark-localities in Hordaland and Sogn og Fjordane/Sunnmøre respectively, expressed in actual numbers.

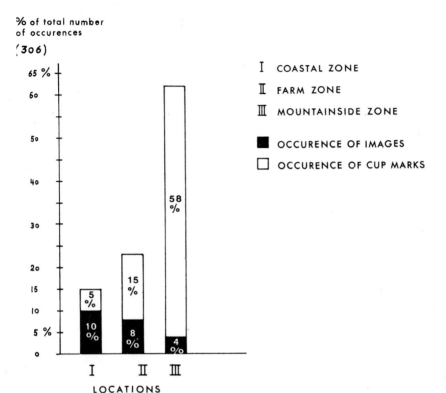

Fig. 6. The distribution of image- and cup-mark-localities in relation to the location-categories, expressed in percentages of total number (306).

5.5.2 Evaluation of the topographical location

According to the traditional hypothesis of farmland-connection, the «ideal» location of agrarian carvings would be the cultivated fields and the close vicinities of the farmsteads. Translated into my classification system this location is identical with the *flat terrain of the farm zone*. The table fig. 4 shows that only a minority of the image-localities of the West-Norwegian agrarian carvings occur in this zone: in Hordaland 8, in Sogn og Fjordane 3 and in Sunnmøre none.

Connection with the sea is a characteristic feature of the location of the West-Norwegian image-localities. The diagram fig. 5 shows that Hordaland has the same number of image-localities in the coastal zone as in the farmzone. On the other hand the number of image-localities is small in the mountainside zone. The topographical distribution of the cup-mark-localities reveals an opposite tendency in

Hordaland. In Sogn og Fjordane this pattern of distribution is further emphasized. In this county nearly three times as many image-localities occur in the coastal zone as in the farm zone, and only one in the mountainside zone. The distribution pattern of cup-mark-localities is the same as in Hordaland, that is the majority of the sites is found in the mountainside zone. The diagram fig. 6, showing the three counties as a whole and the numbers expressed as percentages, clearly reveals the strong connection of the image-localities with the coastal zone, and the marked predominance of the cup-mark-localities in the mountainside zone.

With regard to the topographical location of the hunters' carvings in Western Norway, we note that it is not distinguishable from the location of the agrarian carvings. The hunters' carvings are located in the same topographical zones as the majority of the image-localities of agrarian carvings in Hordaland and Sogn og Fjordane respectively. In one case motifs from hunters' carvings and agrarian carvings occur on the same knoll (*Mandt Lasen* 1972: 34—35).

A summary of the micro-location is as follows:

I) The majority of the image-localities of the West-Norwegian agrarian carvings occurs in topographical location-categories different from the presumed «ideal» location of agrarian carvings. As a whole, location in the coastal zone predominates.

II) The majority of the cup-mark-localities occurs in the mountainside zone, while few are located in the coastal zone.

III) The topographical location of the hunter's carvings is not distinguishable from that of the image-localities of the agrarian carvings in Western Norway.

6. *The importance of the location for the interpretation of rock pictures*

In my opinion the above analysis confirms the hypothesis that connection with farmland is not an integral element of the agrarian carvings. Neither the geographical nor the topographical distribution shows a primary and intimate relation between the agrarian carvings and cultivated areas. The problem of the cupmark-localities of the mountainside zone will not be considered in this connection. They have been dealt with by Johannes Bøe, who saw them as manifestations of summer pasturing in the mountains in the Bronze Age (*Bøe* 1944). In my opinion, however, both the dating of the cup-mark-localities and the age and character of early summer pasturing are yet too uncertain for judging this hypothesis.

On the basis of the lack of connection between the agrarian carvings and cultivated areas in Western Norway, one is inclined to ask if this implies a different interpretation than that of a fertility-cult concerned with the subsistance of the farmer. In my opinion, however, this interpretation includes two elements which ought to be separated. Fertility-cult is one element, agricultural rites to secure fertility is another. The cult concerned with securing the farmer's livelihood is just one field of application in a fertility-centered mythology. Still further, myths and rites concerned with fertility are only one part of the religious system probably known to the makers of the rock pictures.

The evaluation of the different motifs of the agrarian carvings is not a subject for this contribution. In my opinion, however, a great number of the motifs should most likely be explained in relation to conceptions of fertility. But that does not imply that I will in advance accept that the agrarian carvings as a whole and wherever they occur are connected with agriculture.

7. «Primitive» religion
7.1 Vegetation-rites

In almost every religion there are vegetation-rites and -symbols, which may appear almost identical to the rites and symbols of cultivation (*Eliade* 1958: 265). In vegetation-symbolism a new world is made while the old one dies, just like the vegetation fades away and new plants grow. Conceptions of the eternally regenerating life, of immortality and the salvation of the soul form part of the vegetation-symbolism — a symbolism very common to hunters and cattle-breeders (*Eliade* 1958: 267).

In the agricultural rites the conceptions of the sacredness and re-birth of vegetation are accentuated, and more dramatically expressed. All organic life is seen as a unity, and women and sexuality are considered analogous with the cultivated fields and the sowing. From these conceptions grew more abstract ideas about the rythm or life, and death as rebirth (*Eliade* 1958: 361).

Whether the universal vegetation-rites or the specified agricultural rites may be reflected in the rock pictures is difficult to ascertain. Nevertheless it is important to be aware of the possibility of connecting the agrarian carvings with a sphere of ideas other than the agrarian fertility-cult.

Against this background, I put forward the hypothesis that neither the location nor, in my opinion, the motifs of the rock pictures primarily reflect the economy of the society in question. A brief survey of the religious life in a «primitive» society may serve to elucidate this statement.

7.2 The complexity of religious life

The religion of a society consists of a diversity of rites, myths, symbols and divine conceptions, of manifestations of the divine and the sacred, and of religious experiences and theories, for instance about the creation of man and the world (*Eliade* 1958: 24 f.). Religion is an integrated part of all the activities of the community, necessary and decisive in both social, political and economic relationships (*Goode* 1968: 89 f.). «Primitive», pre-modern man is a genuinely religious being, to whom every aspect of life can become sacred, in contrast to the profane. Actions that to modern, irreligious man appear exclusively physiological, like for instance nourishment and sexuality, become sacraments to the religious individual, actions bringing him in touch with the sacred. Man learns about the sacred because it manifests itself through objects, myths and symbols, that is through hierophanies (*Eliade* 1969: 6 f.).

In the complex religious system of a prehistoric community, the rock pictures constitute a part, a concrete expression of the abstract metaphysical superstructure. In my opinion it may be considered a hierophany, a manifestation of the sacred. Though a detail only, it reflects parts of the whole system, not only a fragment of it.

8. *Conclusion*

My conclusion is that the above survey has confirmed the hypothesis that the rock pictures do not primarily reflect the economy of the society in question, and the cult and magic connected with subsistance. Rites securing the livelihood of a society constitute elements of the religious system, but they are only fragments in a greater complex. Religion is concerned with so many other aspects of human and social life in addition. Diverse considerations may have played a part for the choice both of the motifs and the location of the rock pictures, considerations which modern man may never be able to realize, and not necessarily of a practical magic kind. Therefore I consider the location of the rock pictures to be of no value where interpretation is concerned, at least when it is evaluated as an isolated element.

The only conclusion with regard to prehistoric economy to be drawn from the analysis of the location of the rock pictures in Western Norway, is in my opinion that people settled and carved their pictures in areas presenting an abundance of desired resources, whether these were fish and game, fields for cultivation and pasture, or a combination of these, or even a resource or value to us unknown.

Some problems concerning the relation between rock art, religion and society

BY JARL NORDBLADH

Traditional research on petroglyphs, in my own opinion, been characterized by the uncritical approach of conventional history of religions also in the Nordic countries. As a result, we have today a number of explanations which do not add very much to our understanding. The petroglyphs are presented as a more or less isolated phenomenon without an explicit place in a hypothetical society of their time.

I should like to try a different approach, one giving more consideration to the scientific demand for an integrated presentation of knowledge. In this way the petroglyphs might in the future be given a more significant role in a socio-economic context.

1. *Current difficulties of general archaeology*
   — relation theory — method
   — formulation of problems; description and analysis
   — concept of theory
2. *How petroglyph research usually has been carried out*
   — production of data
   — manipulation of data
   — dating
   — interpretation
3. *What the petroglyph researchers generally agree on*
   — data
   — dating
   — organization of entities
   — interpretation
4. *What the petroglyph researchers agree less on*
   — data
   — dating
   — interpretation
5. *The concept of paradigm*
6. *Criticism of the hypothetical paradigm of petroglyph research*
   — lack of basic theory

1. *Current difficulties of general archaeology*

The archaeological science of the Nordic countries is — in my opinion — being side-tracked into a dead end which is perhaps not easily seen. The greatest concentration of the work carried out today is, generally speaking, an enormous collecting of data. On a more strict level of research the efforts are mainly directed towards problems of methods in relation to the working up of data. These efforts are made in opposition to traditional research, which is often understood to be impressionistic, meaning — among other things — that it is difficult to check.

The construction and testing of valid methods handling the archaeological material is, of course, important as well as laborious. Perhaps that is why the fatal mistake has been made of limiting the opposition towards traditional research to strictly methodological questions. There seems to be a lack of awareness of the fact that the older methods to a great extent were supported by generally accepted theories and values of reality, as well as by archaeological reality. Consequently, the same criticism ought to be directed towards the theories supporting traditional research. Many of these are no longer adequate.

The cul-de-sac of the main part of present archaeological science which in certain respects is shared by other sciences, is:

    there is a limitation in constructing methods relating only to the research material

and

    there is an omission in working with an explicit theory relating to the problems and explanations.

This blindness is well manifested in the concept of artefact-research.

186

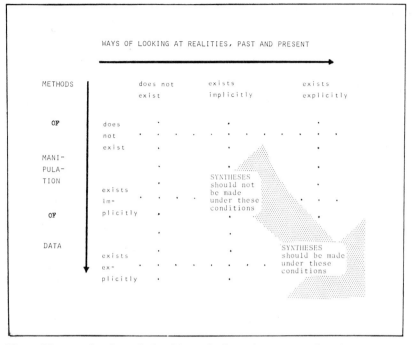

Fig. 1. Diagram showing relationship method- — theory — explanation.

Without a formulated theory, it must be very difficult to perform processes such as the testing of hypotheses.

The diagram in fig. 1 shows the consequences of this hostitlity to theory on the explanatory level.

What effect may this have on scientific work and its anticipated results? Let me first briefly discuss one possible view of the beginning of the research process. How do the problems come to exist and how can they be formulated?

Discription of the problem
From a general diagram of the research process (fig. 2) it is possible to discuss the problems of this matter. There are, in short, two main groups of problems, but not a real dichotomy. They are rather directions with different main points:

Problems of knowledge with the starting point in the dissatisfaction with the lack of knowledge of certain conditions

Problems of existence with the starting point in the dissatisfaction with a certain social reality

187

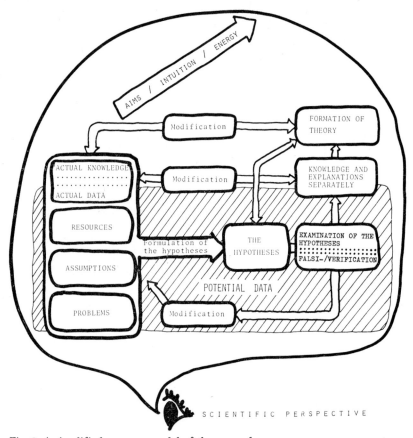

Fig. 2. A simplified common model of the research-process.

The scientific problem has nothing to do with artefacts which must be examined, properties that can be observed, described and measured or scientific techniques. The problem must be determined and described in other terms than methodological ones. The description of the problem must clearly incorporate:
— who has the problem
— what is the problem
— in what situation does the problem appear
— existence and character of earlier descriptions, analyses and solutions

The description of the problem must be provided with a statement, explicitly saying what the solving of this problem implies and what such a solution could possibly entail.

Analysis of the problem

After a presentation of the problem an analysis ought to follow, which must deal with the factual problem. This has still nothing to do with methods. Discussions of method should only come after the analysis of the factual problem.

To accomplish a good analysis of a problem is essentially more difficult than to practise methods, no matter how exclusive, on new combinations of measureable variables. It is important to stick to the problem and not to be tempted by questions of measuring and data-collecting.

The original description of the problem often contains vague and unclear terms. These must be made more precise. The meaning of the concepts and terms in question is the important matter, not their measurability. That something can be described and measured does not in itself clarify anything.

Unambiguousness of terms and concepts must not, however, be an end in itself. Terms used in the social sciences cannot always be given a hundred per cent agreement in meaning. We are often forced to accept a certain vagueness. This vagueness must be supplemented with necessary comments.

We must consider whether new data are required. If so, we must make them precise and examine how the data collected could form part of the problem-solving. It is of course important to find out — before the data research is carried out — what has been done before. If it is necessary to continue collecting new data, the analysis of the problem is of fundamental significance. It is one of the tasks of this very analysis to determine whether new data are needed or not.

A poor analysis of the problem can endanger a whole research project, no matter how well is is carried out later. From the economic point of view this is the origin of the most serious mistakes. The description and the analysis of the problem demand a large share of the total research. Often they are too superficial and too generally expressed, on a few pages, in many cases written afterwards.

Often too little attention is paid to the very beginnings of the research. If you start with assumptions accepted without reflection, the path towards the question of data manipulation has been entered upon — a long and weary path. As a result a multitude of data constellations is obtained and then transmitted more or less directly to terms of reality.

I have already suggested that most often archaeological problems are not very precise. If the problem is not clear, for instance because of the research situation, it should be stated that one of the goals is to map and determine the problem closely, to increase the knowledge of the structures and the qualities of the problem.

Concept of theory
Determination of the problem requires that it can be fixed in relation to reality, with the aid of concepts sufficiently clearly defined. Unfortunately this rarely happens. Many of the basic concepts with which archaeological science is working, no longer satisfy the demands which form a concept. Either some of the terms are not real concepts, only words belonging to our ordinary language. They can be used only as long as nobody questions them. Or these words can also be real concepts, constructed in an unsuitable way, for instance delimiting only too restricted a part of reality, leaving the rest without qualities. They then become isolated units and are not part of a greater context — in any defined way.

A concept can of course be denoted by several different terms. What I refer to here is not these terms but the concepts they represent, and it is therefore quite useless to provide the terms with definitions. The proper way is to work vice versa. A semantic analysis of the term is not at all the same as a definition of the concept. Sometimes, however, it is a possible way of understanding what concept is hidden in a text.

The main thing to watch then is not to use terms which belong to ordinary language too much. A term must work like a signal within the sentences, not like one of many other words. When the terms are used too often and too vaguely they will soon become part of our ordinary language, and we shall have semantic difficulties in our discussions (e.g. the terms ecology, milieu, culture). This is one of the main reasons why terms must be exchangeable.

As regards concepts the exchange situation is quite different. Here changes are often made because of new knowledge of reality, or because the created concept is too difficult to use in such a situation. What, then, is a real concept? This is a hard question to which there is more than one answer. But a concept must have certain qualities in order to be used successfully. It must be given certain criteria, such as kind and degree of interaction with other concepts, the degree of appliciability and prolongability and so on. We can illustrate this with the connotation (the content) and the denotation (the extent) of the concept.

It is of vital importance whether the concept is to be used as a goal or as an instrument for the investigation; whether we are going to end with a real part of reality or start with an assumption not to be questioned.

190

The concept is established by a definition, which should be explicit, but *the* definition does not exist. Depending on the circumstances, different kinds of definitions should be chosen.

There are for instance:
descriptive, real, normative and operational descriptions; and definitions by enumeration, dictionary definitions, survey definitions, all representing different kinds of dimensions.

If the concept behind the term is explicitly supplied with a definition, it is possible for the reader to discuss the usefulness and significance of the concept, and finally to check if it has been correctly used by the writer in question.

The sets of concepts are the very body of scientific work, with static or dynamic functions. Therefore it is indefensible not to use these valuable tools as much as possible. If they are used within an investigation, the tolerance of unclearness, unnecessary complexity, etc. is more a matter for the research society. On the other hand, if the concepts are obscure in the explanatory part of the investigation, the matter concerns the whole of society, which is a far more serious concern. Misuse in the latter context is far too common in scientific work, including archaeology.

2. *How petroglyph research has usually been carried out*
Having stated these two considerable difficulties in archaeological research, I should like to come to the particular field of research connected with the petroglyphs. I will exclusively keep to the area commonly considered as belonging to the Nordic Bronze Age.

This research consists of combinations of the following units:

Production of data
Aims to obtain reliable and sufficiently comprehensive material for research.

The determination of the material
— nature of rock
— structure of the rock surface, fissures and glacial striations included
— damages by weathering and other forces
— direction of the gradient of the rock surface
— carving techniques
— depth of the carvings
— delimitation of the image area

The description
— choice of the method of description
— formation of the descriptive concepts

The reproduction
— determination of the documentation contents
— determination of the documantation forms (tracing, casting, design, scale, photo, photogrammetry, etc.)

The topographical determination
— arrow indicating North
— height above sea level
— natural environment on micro- and macro-level
— cultural environment, e.g. nearness to roads, bridges, cultivated land

Manipulation
— data regarding size, techniques, etc.
— geographical diffusion of certain figures and motifs
— mutual nearness of the petroglyph sites
— appearence of certain figures on the single image area
— determination of compositions according to content, style and position

Dating
   Internal dating
   — study of juxtapositions
   — study of style
   — study of formal seriation
   — study of curving lines

   Dating in relation to other chronologies
— stratigraphy, for instance in connection with other ancient monuments, such as graves
   — datable finds made in connection with the petroglyph sites
   — situation in relation to earlier sea or lake level (possible only in certain areas)
— analogies of images on other kinds of archaeological objects (e.g. «razors», the Wismar horn)
   — analogies of real objects, depicted by the petroglyphs (e.g. datable weapons of bronze)

Interpretation
   In relation to the contemporary cultural background
   — questions of technology (e.g. what kind of ship, plough, carriage is depicted?)
— questions of economy (e.g. what kind of economy is depicted?)

- questions of society (e.g. relations to the contemporary society, regarding social stratification, occupational groups, the sexes)
- questions of religion (e.g. the relation to our ideas of the religion of the Bronze Age culture, known from other sources)
- questions of cultural topography (e.g. the nearness of the petroglyphs or certain motifs to other phenomena such as old highways, waterways, sites, graves, places for sacrifice, place names)

In relation to the general history of religions and psychology
- analogies in written sources, for instance Tacitus (partly the same as the next two items)
- analogies in other religions, past and present
- analogies in surviving myths ad folklore
- phenomenology
- assumptions about «primitive» man and about «levels» of societies and religions

In relation to contemporary natural background
- questions of climate
- questions of natural topography (e.g. the structure of the landscape, the distribution of land, sea, fresh water, mountains, plains, woods)

3. *What the petroglyph researchers generally agree on*
   Data
   It is of great importance that new data are published and recorded in a reliable and usable way. The uneven quality of such documents has constantly caused research difficulties.
   It is of vital importance of course, how the image area appeared originally, something that has not yet been possible to determine.

Dating
The petroglyphs are commonly considered to belong to the Nordic Bronze Age. Some categories (e.g. the cup marks) may be older; some may be younger, from the beginning of the Iron Age.
   One of the signs most important to the research is the «ship», mainly because it is very common, both chorologically and chronologically. On this particular image, studies of style and formal seriation have been based. Chronology has been stated in relation to a chronology based on mental artefacts.

Organization of entites
I stated above that I would like to confine myself to the Southern

Scandinavian Bronze Age area, but here I make a small exception, caused partly by the traditional way of delimiting the material. The Scandinavian petroglyphs have been devided into two main categories, one connected with a more northerly area and a hunting and fishing society, the other with a more southerly area and a society based on stock-breeding and agriculture. There are contacts between these categories (for instance at Nämforsen and Evenhus), but the chronological and cultural circumstances of these contact areas are uncertain. The differences are said to be more on the economic than on the mere geographical level. As regards the category of stock-breeders and farmers, attempts have been made to look at the material as a whole, consisting of limited local areas. Today this kind of approach seems to be difficult to employ. Instead studies have been directed towards more regional approaches.

Interpretation
There is general agreement that the petroglyphs are connected with a religion. This religion is expressed by images from an economic system — as well as from other cultural sub-systems — mainly based on stock-breeding and agriculture, but also hunting and fishing. Among the images of human beings males are most common. Images of females are extremely rare.

The «image-language» of the petroglyphs is considered to show changes of religion. The images are said to develop from single signs towards more complicated representations with, among other things, objects and human beings. This has been interpreted as reflections of a change of religion, from non-personal superpowers to personalized gods.

Many of the images have been interpreted as referring to the obtaining of success in agriculture and stock-breeding, as connected with sacrifice and cult ceremonies in honour of the superhuman. Truly profane scenes may occur, but they are very rare and without importance to the petroglyps as a whole.

The gradual vanishing of the petroglyphs towards the end of the Bronze Age is said to be a consequence of the introduction of a new religion from abroad. This new religion is characterized by a goddess, who appears naked, wearing two double necklaces as her only attributes. Discoveries of sacrifices of, for instance, double necklaces and small bronze figurines form important evidence for this interpretation.

4. *What the petroglyph researchers agree less on*
Data
The documentation and identification of single images or details

sometimes give different results. These results often lead the interpretations in different directions.

Dating

Differences in the dating of single petroglyphs or petroglyph sites
may appear (for instance the tomb at Kivik).

This is also the case with som metal objects said to be important to the chronological determination of the petroglyphs (for
instance the Wismar horn). No system of dating is fully accepted
yet, not even the method of curving lines analysis.

Interpretation

There seems to be agreement that the petroglyphs are part of a
religion, but there are many different ideas of what this religion
meant. Sun cult, rain cult, death cult and worship of gods are among
the explanations suggested. They are all, it is said, forms of fertility
cult.

Furthermore there is discussion about whether the signs represent
powers or gods, or if the religion in non-iconic, with a god who must
not be depicted.

For the work of interpretation, literary sources from different
epochs, geographical and cultural areas have been used. There are
divergent opinions about whether these sources support the hypotheses or not.

Another interpretation of the images is that it is the very making
of them that is most important, not how they are arranged. Partly
influenced by this view are questions such as the following: it is the
place of the image-making or the point and length of time that is
important. There is no general agreement on these questions or
whether the images on one site are the work of one person or of
several persons at the same time or at different times.

The origin of the petroglyphs has been explained in several ways,
one of which is that they began already during the Neolithic period
and that their great frequency during the Bronze Age is connected
with the definite break through of agriculture, *or* that the petroglyphs are only a part of a common European world of images, which
in our areas have been preserved because of the resistant material.

During the last few years some of the descriptive terms have been
much criticized. Based on studies on the West coast of Norway, where
the topographical conditions of agriculture are very limited, it has
been suggested that the images were used, not only by mainly agricultural societies, but also by societies with a more mixed ecconomy.
This permits a suggestion of a possible change of meaning of certain

195

images. Morphological similarities do not necessarily mean seamantic similarities. Inside the large area of the Northern Bronze Age there could have been regional differences due to environmental and economic situations. Thus differences in style, iconography, uses of symbols and ritual patterns can very well have existed. This view has not yet been fully discussed or proved, but is really threatening the general picture of the Bronze Age and the petroglyphs.

5. *The concept of paradigm*

By this quick look at petroglyph research and at examples of what is more or less agreed on, I have wanted to outline the framework of this research and the theories, problems and methods governing it.

The American historian of science Thomas S. Kuhn has created a concept in a way resembling such a framework, which he calls a paradigm.

A paradigm is mainly characterized by two qualities:

1. it has the power to attract several researches around a basic scientific problem

and

2. it has been able to show, by successful trails, that it has discovered a fruitful way to solve the problem.

Very often, however, the basic problem is so extensive that it requires the solution of many part-problems all the time. The researchers gathered around the paradigm are then sharing a common — though often vaguely formulated — aim and have agreed on how this aim should be accomplished.

The paradigm gives its members motivations, concepts, definitions and theories which are gradually taken for granted and are no longer criticized, unless this element of criticism is part of the common and established aim. By not questioning the basis and certain areas of the research, many and interesting results can soon be attained.

Another quality is that the paradigm contains explanations considered to be very successful, but at the same time there are no demands for explanations of all problems immidiately.

As guides of the research some central publications, for instance text books to which we return again and again, can function. Lectures, congresses and circulating, unpublished articles can serve this function too, of course.

By providing the very basis of the research approach and this not being questioned, quick results will thus be obtained. These, however, soon tend to exist on subtle levels, where often differences of

196

degree are discussed and where the results are of interest only to an inner circle of researchers. Very often they cannot arouse any common interest because of their abstract and highly specialized level.

However, care has to be taken that this lack of common interest does not give a negative bias to research production within the paradigm.

Paradigms are often rigid: that is, their aim is not to produce revolutionary new knowledge of explanations and concepts. Thus the results are often to a certain extent known in advance. They can never produce unexpected news — which could threaten the paradigm. This is, among other things, a consequence of the problems chosen.

Other problems, with different backgrounds, in conflict with the paradigm, are rejected as unscientific or metaphysic, as belonging to another discipline or as something so problematic that it has no solution.

Because of this the paradigm, if strong, may among other things protect certain parts of society from problems and knowledge not wanted there.

This free interpretation of Kuhn's concept of the paradigm seems to agree quite well with the framework of Nordic research on petroglyphs. I find it worth considering, as it could predict how the research will proceed in the future, if a shift of paradigm does not occur. I am not going to point out the consequences of this comparison here; that would require much more thorough studies.

It would, however, be extremely interesting to hear how the scientists working within this field look at the future, what possibilities their researches will give, their limitations, needs and ultimate goals.

6. *Criticism on the hypothetical paradigm of petroglyph research*
Nordic petroglyph research is about a hundred years old. Has the basic attitude to the material changed during this time? Have really competing explanations been produced, resulting in any different views of the Bronze Age society? I can only discern one major event, taking place at the turn of the century, when it was suggested that the petroglyphs were remnants of a religion. Since then no change in the direction of this research has occured.

This situation need not, of course, be negative. To change a basic attitude or produce comperting explanations is not in itself a virtue. But it seems surprising that during the last fifty years or so no change has occurred.

New data, new methods and new ways of asking questions have

only produced knowledge, which was already there in embryo in certain main themes. However, there have been other results, in an area which not everybody would call an area of knowledge, although it certainly is: they have stressed and deepened the knowledge of the complexity of the problems. For some scientists this process has resulted in doubts about the old basis of the research.

Here it would be appropriate to have a discussion on some of the bases of petroglyph research and how this was once consolidated. In this connection I should like to make the statement that isolated results of older research cannot be criticized, only their logical structure. They once functioned in and belonged to the researcher's own society. Criticism of older results or opinions built on criteria other than logical ones is in fact, criticism of a certain society or parts of it. To isolate scientific questions and results and to see changes in them as a straight and undisturbed research process is a false abstraction. Such a procedure can only show later researchers thoughts as possible influences and inspirations.

Before I enter on the study of religion and the petroglyphs, I should like to comment on some peculiarities from which presentday research suffers. Almost every new publication on the subject has, as an introductory chapter, a history of this research, which is frequently repeated with minor adjustments. But this the researcher demonstrates first of all that he is dependent on earlier research. We never see an explicit, scientific perspective as a starting point or an explicit way of looking at history or an attempt to give an explicit view of man.

This lack of basic theory has a negative effect on the ultimate results. These are not being supplied with a more precise frame of reference. The result of the research, freed from its implicit paradigm, is atomistic, without a conscious or explicit structure.

After this statement about the lack of theory in archaeological science, I want to stress one of the central concepts of method, used with especially great unclarity and contradiction in petroglyph research, the *interpretation*. Interpretation is used indiscriminately in petroglyph research, from the very recognition of certain lines and surfaces on the rock as a depiction of, for instance, a bull, to statements of this animal as a part of a fertillity cult.

The first step after the perception and registration that something exists is the discernment that lines and surfaces together form an entity, for instance a bull, or that it is a shape we are unable to translate. For this step I would like to recommend the use of the concept *identification*.

We can probably agree that, by identifying an image on the rock as a picture of a bull, we have not interpreted it. We have discerned it and possibly described it and thus been able to identify it. But reality does not appear without mediation. A description is not an explanation, so let us continue.

Does interpretation come next? Unfortunately the issue is not that simple. Interpretation is nothing independent; it is totally dependent on something, and that is the process of asking and explaining. Is interpretation the same as explanation then? No, it is not that easy.

Interpretation is dependent on what kind of explanation we are aiming at and on what level it is given.

Let us continue with the image in our example, which we have identified as a picture of a bull. Let us see what this picture represents, what it means.

Item: Let us consider why this meaning is chosen for just this image, why the image has just this form, with these special accentuations.

Item: Let us consider why there has been a need for just this meaning.

Item: Let us consider of what wider context the image of the bull is a part — that is, what part of reality has been transmitted into a picture.

Item: Let us consider from what part of reality the meanings of the pictures come.

Item: Studies of style, choice of motifs, close meanings of images, dimensions, etc., are only studies of superficial phenomena. Let us look for the real function of this «reconstructed», postulated religion within the society. What does it mean to the social and economic structure of this society, its stability, its dynamics, etc.?

Item: Let us consider this postulated religion in relation to the religions of other societies. Religion serves different concrete functions in different societies. Its main function can be within the society or between societies. Here there are possibilities of classification of the function and structures of cultures. It is possible to look at religion from the point of view of the society, as well as to look at the society from the point of view of religion. However, only by combining these two perspectives we will get a full picture.

Item: Let us look at the society as a whole. Even if, for example, the religions of two societies should be different in performance and structure, the wholeness, the deep structure of the societies can be the same. A difference in religion is not itself an essential criterion for dividing cultures into different categories.

If we desire to go further or in another direction, all these levels of the synthesis can claim to be levels of interpretation. An isolated «interpreting of the petroglyphs», does not mean anything in a scientific context if the frame of reference is not stated.

With this in mind, it is important that the scientist states the level of the interpretation of his investigation. On this level it is important to say if the result is expected or unexpected, and it is possible to fit in the unexpected result with the established theory or not.

For the general reader of the reports the different interpretations are often very difficult to survey. It can be difficult to see if an interpretation is on the same level as another, if they conflict or not.

A possible way of looking at such a conventional situation, more or less simulated in fig. 3, can illustrate the dilemma. By the interpreter's taxonomy it is easy to see that the dilemma of the reports is very difficult to solve.

However, I have not yet managed to obtain a clear picture of petroglyph research. That depends partly on the difficulties connected with the reconstruction of thoughts and procedures hidden behind the individual research results hinted at above and partly on my lack of basic knowledge of the theory of science necessary to transfer the paradigm concept to this specific archeological field of work.

The paradigm concept is far from clearly delimited. Furthermore, it has been created in order to be used for analysis of dynamic

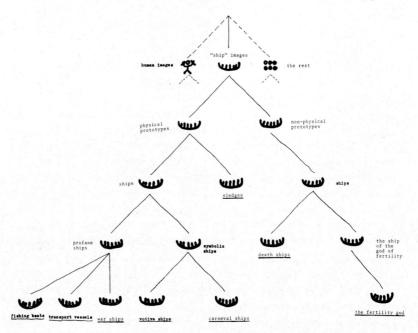

Fig. 3. A taxonomic possibility to arrange interpretations of ship images.

conditions such as the growth of knowledge and the changes of scientific ideals within the research society. Also non-logical factors like social and economic conditions have to be taken into account. The English linguist Margaret Masterman has analysed Kuhn's paradigm concept, and among other things reached the conclusion that it consists of three main factors, the metaphysical, the sociological and the constructional — corresponding roughly to world view, scientific habits (intellectual, verbal, behavioural, mechanical, technological) and the puzzle-solving activities. The paradigm concept is thus difficult to use because of the context (comparisons of different sciences — comparisons within one science — comparisons within a certain field of research of one science), but at the same time it is a very attractive concept. It has been used within many sciences where it has successfully replaced older views such as research tradition, schools of research, conventional history of research, etc.

7. Criticism of the history of religions
The research into the history of religions was very active from the middle of the nineteenth century. Theology had expanded and the comparative study of religions had started, in collaboration with Christian mission, philosophy and psychology. In Sweden scientists like Nathan Söderblom in Uppsala and Martin P:son in Lund were for decades the leaders of this new research.

Theories of the history of religions were worked out, mainly influenced by idealism and evolutionism, with the relation between man and superman as the primary object. The existence of supernatural and superhuman powers was never questioned and because of that the main work resulted in different ideas about these superpowers. The supernatural and the superhuman in themselves were meant to be inaccessible to knowledge.

This is where the ordinary history of religions still stands, despite developed methods and theories.

By an evolutionary way of thinking *one* starting point was the capacity for thinking of the so-called primitive man. *The other* was that the superior from of religion, Christianity, and only slightly inferior forms such as Islam, Judaism and Buddhism, contained remnants of older religions, even magic. This chain was seen as a development of the experience of the superhuman, from a naive belief that the superpowers could be influenced and directed by man towards a trusting belief that the superpower were one and only one power and that it was selfcontrolling and cared about man.

By studying different primitive cultures knowledge was gained about different ways of being connected with the superhuman. Several concepts were constructed. Soon it was impossible to relate these to other concepts, constructed from experiences of other societies. From this store of religious concepts the archaeologists often borrowed. Even today the archaeologists use these concepts, both synonymously and contrastingly, mostly making them meaningless.

What, then are, the relation between cult-ceremony-rite-sacrifice-magic etc? There is, I believe, only one relation — chaos. This is because the archaeologists have not transformed these concepts into a model, useful for prehistoric situations. They have only used the concepts in a passive way, as references for their work. But these concepts have no scientific-historical definite signification and usage; they are highly controversial, with different meanings in different authors of the historiy of religions.

Another sign that these concepts have served their time is that most explanations which have been made with the aid of these concepts have ended up as mixtures of competing categories. These mixtures seldom have a character; they are rather diffuse masses between two extremes.

How then is the situation on the level of theory? It is not much better. We can even find statements about the advanced religion of the Bronze Age which is said to have left primitivity. The question is on what theory of science this statement is built, which sees the change from impersonal powers to personal gods as a progress.

Analogies from primitive or advanced religions are often used to support discussions of the history of religions in archaeology. This use can only serve the construction of hypotheses, not verify or reject them. The construction of hypotheses is of major importance and thus the analogies have a great mission.

But often a very serious mistake is made in this process, a mistake quite difficult to discover, hidden on a theoretic level. If analogies from studies of the history of religions are mixed with examinations of oral or written reports from members of a certain society, two different systems are mixed: a system or a model with which the researcher is working in order to understand or explain the religion of a certain society and the system or the model according to which the members of the society in question understand their religion. The consequences of getting these mixed are then hidden in the archaeological hypotheses.

The great difficulties archaeologists have in penetrating the jungle of the history of religions have frightened many researchers away from comprehensive interpretation. Some want to leave this kind of interpretation to the historians of religions, some would like to collaborate.

We might sometimes wonder why archaeologists are not suprised that all their hypotheses about the petroglyphs can get support from the history of religions. Hence we cannot depend on this as reliable support.

It is time once again, I think, to consider whether the petroglyphs reflect a religion, and this argument must be put forth with the aid of a reformed science of religions. With the existing view of religion as an independent system in an evolutionist orbit, research on the petroglyphs can only come to conclusions about conceptions of the qualities of the superhuman. To quote a modern textbook in the science of religions could be very instructive here; the science of religions, if it wants to be a science, is reduced to description. It cannot in a real sense explain the religious phenomena.

8. A structuralistic way of looking at religions

I started by talking about man's need for a total view of reality and that such a total view is also a demand on science. The French structuratist Claude Lévi-Strauss has researched the classifications of primitive man and thereby discovered that earlier theories that man lived to a great extent in chaos are wrong. On the contrary, in a primitive society man has just as strong a need for coherence as we have, and his ways of thinking do not differ from ours. His classifications have the same purpose as ours, even if his way of classifying and his categories are different.

Influenced by Lévi-Strauss, his colleague Maurice Godelier has etablished a general theory about the structure and function of myth. He has made it theoretically possible to apply this theory to all primitive societies. I think it would be possible to take the concept of religion from this source and use it later in archaeological research.

Lévi-Strauss has found that the structure of myth corresponds to the structure of society; that is, the words used to describe the myth are more than just superficial loans from the society.

These corresponding structures have been explained by the meaning of myth in society. It is extremely dependent on society. Godelier considers that mythical thinking is a way of describing and understanding reality by analogies.

Man's relation to society and to nature can be divided into two categories. One, he can control directly, the other he cannot. The contents of these two parts depend on the very nature of the society. To place a certain item in the not-directly-controllable part — the superhuman and the supernatural — is not analogical thinking in itself. We must take a further step.

Analogy has the power to move thinking out of one part of reality into another. Thereby we win understanding and a total view of the wholeness of nature and society. For instance, the superhuman and the supernatural are described in terms of culture.

By the process the supernatural and superhuman realities are described in terms and with a structure we find in the controllable part of reality. This gives a comprehensive view of the totality.

Mythical thinking starts from a wish to know reality, but the results of the analogical process will be an illusory explanation of a series of causes and effects on which existence is thought to be based. Growing from mythical thinking there is mythical acting or magic. This makes it possible to influence the superhuman and the supernatural, because these categories have been connected to a system of causes and effects which is the same as in the directly controllable world. In this way mythical thinking is divided into two parts, one of theory and one of practice, *one religious,* with description and explanation of the supernatural and the superman, and *one magical,* with man's ability to influence the supernatural and the superhuman.

That is then that how mythical thinking has a directing effect on society, not only through circumstances concerning magic, but also because of the analogical process which gives the cause and effect used in religion a way back to the society with greater power. Explanations are raised to a higher dignity, a more absolute level.

Magic, acting with its rules of restriction and obligation, can of course be seen as acting upon itself, an activity with a special purpose, but which at the same time reflects ideas about how cause and effect can be influenced in ruling actual phenomena.

Mythical thinking as presented here has many advantages, useful for further development in an archaelogical context for instance. Religion and magic are no longer independent systems, but systems which together with the knowledge of the controllable world form a whole, an explanation of reality.

A consequence of this is that isolated research into the archaelogical history of religions would be impossible without religion to the rest of reality.

If we say that religion is a way of explaining the not-controllable world, then our object of examination will be that part into which a society places the not-directly-controllable reality.

If on the other hand by religion we mean that part of reality which *is* superhuman, this part would be the object of examination.

In some societies we do not find this object in the not-controllable world, but in the controllable. The results of such an investigation are not of real archaeological interest. It is not science — it is theology.

I have earlier talked about how petroglyph research could work and what aims it could have according to a pradigm. A view on religion is evolving, to some extent outside this paradigm, as part of a better defined society. This approach I see as a very promising one with many possibilities.

Unfortunately, our present knowledge of the Bronze Age society (if there was only one society) is very limited and at the same time highly controversial, making more comprehensive explanations of a social or religious kind very difficult.

By directing our studies towards social problems I think we shall attain better opportunities of judging the importance of religion. There are social anthropologists, such as Radcliffe-Brown, who feel that religion has a fundamental function as a regulator of norms of value, social organization, etc. This is a statement which is, perhaps, not altogether true. On the contrary, it must be one of our aims to find out whether religion and magic in a given society were of much importance or not. From the existence of belief in superhuman powers it does not absolutely follow that these powers are given much attention or are of any great importance in the community.

9. Petroglyphs as visual messages

Finally, I should like to go back to our material, the petroglyphs themselves. In spite of the fact that they form the basis of our research, the images have very rarely been considered as part of a living Bronze Age society. Too often they are regarded only as links between man and superman. However, these images, must also have been part of the common environment and this point is of some importance. If we see them as pictorial messages with a religious function, they also had the power of affecting those of the members of the society who were in contact with the milieu where the images were depicted. The petroglyphs must have had a function there, perhaps a most important one. What I have in mind here is not some form of magic or workship. I mean that the images must have had a historical significance also, after they had come into existence.

Every society has channels for transmitting and receiving messages. The same channel (music, speech, pictures, etc.) can have different functions and different channels can have the same function. Therefore comparative studies are needed, including the channels of communication in other societies.

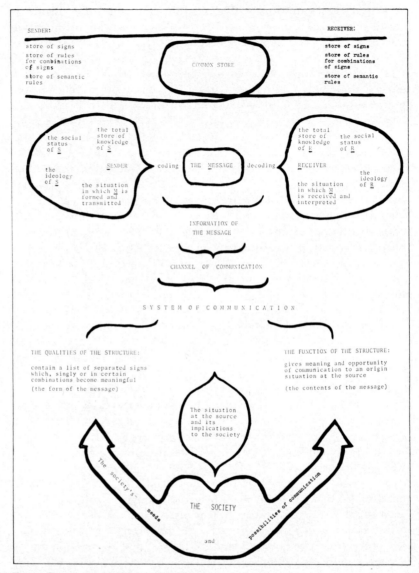

Fig. 4. Communication as a semiotic system.

Elements of visual communication have for a long time been of great interest to the science of archaeology. By their construction, in which we believe we find abstract parts of reality, the images form a special kind of research material, which to some

206

extent must be handled quite differently from the usual archaeological material. They can be seen as products of analogous thinking and seeing, as symbols, and are therefore looked upon as advanced products of civilization. From here the step to assigning them to a religious world has been tempting, partly because of the great number of images impossible to identify and explain. Very often, therefore they have been taken for magical images.

The petroglyphs are almost always regarded as picture frames only. I believe, however, that it is very difficult to determine directly from the picture as such, i.e. as a physical artefact, what part of a system it belongs to religious or profane. I am more inclined to think that the meaning of a picture is more likely to be found in relation to the situation of its application.

But our knowledge of the circumstances in which the pictures were used is still very limited. No comprehensive studies or field-work have been carried out to determine if the physical pictures really were important parts of the type of ancient monument we call petroglyphs. That today we find them very impressive, is quite a different matter.

How can we get hold of the function or funtions the petroglyphs may have had? There are different possibilities. Some have been explored for a long time, others have not yet been tried.

One possible way would be to begin, so to speak, at the other end of the problem, not with a possible religion but with the petroglyphs themselves, seen as messages, transmitted along a channel of communication from somebody to somebody else, containing information affecting mainly a certain part of the society (fig. 4).

By this way of looking at the data the image will be seen from three different angles:
— the picture as such
— the picture in relation to its object
— the picture in relation to its users

Recently this view has been expressed by influences from linguistics. Applied to petroglyph research, the structure shown in fig. 5 appears.

Such an approach would, among other things, provide a better opportunity for examining the relationship between religion and the systems and channels of communication, formed by the images of the society.

Of course none of the material treated here is pure communication. It must have been guided by desires and decisions of different kinds and it is our task to see the petroglyphs not only as instruments of

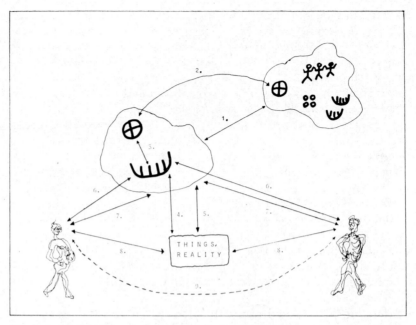

Fig. 5. A simplified linguistic model applied to petroglyphs:

1—3 *Syntactic* studies:
   1) between picture frames
   2) between signs of different picture frames
   3) between signs inside a single picture frame

4—5 *Semantic* studies:
   4) between sign and thing
   5) between message-contents and reality

6—8 *Pragmatic* studies:
   6) between user and image
   7) between user and message
   8) between user and reality

If 1—8, communication, 9, is possible.

communication but as instruments of acting upon reality with transforming and/or preserving purposes.

I have here tried to indicate som new, possible ways for petroglyph research partly on the theoretical-methodological level, partly on the explanatory level.

There is no reason why petroglyph research should work with a worse scientific apparatus than other archaeological fields. On the contrary, this image research has interesting interpretative problems — of a kind not existing in general archaeology — and real hard work is demanded to build up a suitable research frame. This

208

framework, if properly made, would give knowledge not only of the special kind of archaeological material which the petroglyphs are, but also of aspects of the society, extremely difficult to obtain through other materials.

My research has been a study of petroglyph research rather than a study of petroglyphs. That is why my comments for the moment have a preliminary, abstract form, where I have chosen assertion in preference to argumentation. That I myself have broken many of the rules of thumb I have proposed in this paper is not of great interest. On the contrary, I think, that my experience in this respect is rather typical of a student who wants to understand a certain branch of archaeology. The situation could be made easier if the researchers occasionally took the time to look back — and also forward — at their strategy and results, seen in a larger context.

ACKNOWLEDGEMENTS

This manuscript was finished five years ago. No reawakend, I hope it still has some life. I would like to acknowledge with thanks my friends and colleagues at the Department of Archaeology, University of Gothenburg for their interest and help at my preparatory seminars on this subject. I am also particularly grateful to Helga Ohlsson for her invaluable assistance with the English translation.

REFERENCES

L'Analyse des images. Communications. Ecole Pratique des Hautes Études. Centre d'Études des Communications de Masse. No 15. 1970 (Bibliography).

Anthropological Approaches to the Study of Religion. Ed. by Michael Banton. A.A.A., Monographs. 3. London 1969.

Berner Öste, Mia: Om termer, begrepp och definitioner, Uppsala 1968.

Communication and Culture. Readings in the Codes of Human Interaction. E. by Alfred G. Smith, New York 1966.

Eco, Umberto: Den frånvarande strukturen. Introduktion till den semiotiska forskningen. Lund 1971. (Original ed. La Struttura assente, Milano 1968).

Ehnmark, Erland: Att studera religionshistoria, Stockholm 1963.

Eriksson, Einar: Kring forskningsprocessen. Föreläsningar vid doktorandkurs vid Lunds tekniska högskola (arkitektursektionen). (Blueprint) Lund 1970.

Feuerbach, Ludwig: Vorlesungen über das Wesen der Religion. Stuttgart-Bad Cannstatt 1960.

Godelier, Maurice: The Origins of Mythical Thought (Myth and History). New Left Review. September — October 1971, No 69.

Guiraud, Pierre: La Sémiologie. (Que Sais-je? No. 1421), Paris 1971.

Jorn, Asger: Helleristningerne. Kunst eller religion. Information. 6 August 1969.

Kuhn, Thomas S.: The Structure of Scientific Revolutions. (Foundations of the Unity of Science. Vol. II. No. 2.) Chicago, 2nd ed. enl. 1970.

Leroi-Gourhan, André: Les religions de la préhistoire. (Mythes et Religions). Paris 1971.

Lévi-Strauss, Claude: Det vilda tänkandet, Stockholm 1971. (Original ed. La pensée sauvage, Paris 1962).
Liungman, Carl J.: Semiotik. Strukturalism. Semiologi, Lund 1971.
Masterman, Margaret: The Nature of a Paradigm. Criticism and the Growth of Knowledge. Ed. by Imre Lakatos & Alan Musgrave, Cambridge 1970.
On Method in the History of Religions. Ed. by James S. Helfer. History and Theory, Studies in the Philosophy of History. Beheft 8. Middletown, Conn. 1968.
Törngren, Anna: Opium för folket. Till kritiken av religionshistorien, Stockholm 1969.
For general bibliographies of petroglyph-research in Southern Scandinavia, see:
Fredsjö, Å, Janson, S. & Moberg, C.-A.: Hällristningar i Sverige, Oskarshamn 1969.
Glob, P.V.: Helleristninger i Danmark (Rock-carvings in Denmark). Jysk Arkeologisk Selskabs Skrifter. Bind VII. Copenhagen 1969.
Kontaktstencil. Organ för Nordiska Arkeologistudenter. No. 4. (Blueprint), Copenhagen 1972).
Most recent discussion:
Norwegian Archaeological Review. Vol. 3, 1970 & Vol. 4, 1971.

An attempt at a framwork for visual analysis of rock art

BY JAN ROSVALL

The art concept*

It is a surprising fact that the central concept in the field of research in question is the *art*[2] concept. This is surprising for, at least, two reasons.

Firstly, that a term from a neighbouring discipline, sometimes misused, has been made into a guiding light in the rock-art branch of *archaeology*. Furthermore, if the use of the concept art can be easily accepted in this context also, for several reasons this means that the concept must be carefully defined, in a way which is in accordance with the method by which material is treated, and then eventually used in the way accepted.

We must be aware of some misleading interpretations of the term art. Of course art, like any other vaguely defined term, can be used in many unspecified ways, just like the term «normal»[3], which conveniently can be used with any meaning suitable for the moment. This lack of precision must of course be avoided.

Thus, the first interpretation of art which is inappropriate in this context, is the one[4] which has its starting point in ourselves and our conventions in aesthetics, politics, religion etc. It is a scientific mistake[5] to use this kind of value concept in historical disciplines; the results are anachronistic.

Secondly, there is the concept of art which is based on the view that it is permissable,[6] on the whole, to remove any picture from its original environment and spiritual context, in order to treat it as a work of so-called pure art, on subjective and aesthetic grounds alone. The misunderstanding underlying this treatment of a picture is a result of the positivist and romantic outlook in science which arose during the nineteenth century.

Because of the proposed limitations, one is tempted to look for a concept of art which is pertinently constructed. It is not possible for me to present any such here, but there are ideas waiting to be developed. But, in any case, it is perhaps not a bad thing to exclude inadequate components and concepts. I will therefore leave the field of definition open for now.

However, there is one other aspect of the art concept that could serve as a point of departure in our search for guidance. I refer to the use of the term «art» in the disciplines of art history and the science of art.

Rock pictures and science/history of art

My remarks are partly based on the possibilities existing in the science and history of art which are of importance for the description, analysis and interpretation of rock-pictures. Of course many different schools of thought and methods exist in these disciplines[7]. Until now, however, no research in this field has emerged containing anything of great consequence for the discussion of rock-art.

On the contrary, practically all standard works on general art history begin with a section or chapter on pre-historic or proto-historic art forms — as a mere prelude, or rather, in many cases, as the beginnings of art — brought about by an evolutionistic point of view. I will not deny the value of presentations of early art, either included in larger works or by themselves, but they should treat their material in accordance with its nature, function and origin, and not as an apology for historicism, or any other likely reason.

As the needs arise out of the situation, it is not yet easy to show what methods would be applicable for our needs. Research methods are formed or fitted according to the description of the problem and the aims of the investigation, as well as to the character and body of the material that it is intended to deal with. Furthermore, it is a well-known fact[8] that methods are not universally applicable, even with some modifications. However, I would like to mention the research plan[9] of the late professor Erwin Panofsky, well established for several decades.

I am here referring to the iconological approach, which has proved very useful in certain important contexts of Western art history,[10] ranging from the ancient world to late classical periods. It has mainly been applied to painting and sculture, but also architecture is included on the list. The main features of this plan are shown below.

The plan is presented as a tripartite scheme, with the Panofsky's three levels listed on the left and with brief explanations in the middle column. On the right an attempt at indicating which components and procedures in the research on rock-art would correspond to the proposed plan is shown.

212

The iconological approach, after Panofsky

LEVELS:	CHARACTERISTICS:	SPECIALLY FOR ROCK-ART:
PRE-ICONO-GRAPHICAL DESCRIPTION	Establishing a catalogue, guided by e.g. the historical-critical theories and their derivations in the history of art.	Technical analysis, identification of elements, topographical situation.
ICONOLOGICAL ANALYSIS	Elementary discussion of the material collected. Comparative studies, compositional and other forms of analysis with regard to the visual structure of pictures handled.	Discussion of picture-composition analysing the images not merely as (visual) artefacts, but as visualising means. Quantitative correlations, e.g. with matrices.
ICONOGRAPHICAL INTERPRETATION	General discussion of the material investigated and its role in a proper context. This involves intricate analysis of the history of ideas, religion, politics etc, and in what way the pictures treated form part of the situation.	Synthetical analysis of the role of the rock pictures in their (archaeological) context, explained as components in the interaction of socio-economic-religious and other forces or directions.

N.B.
The scheme does not explicitly include the unquestioned introductive and terminal components of investigations[11] which in an executive situation must be added.

Personally I am no proselyte of the Panofsky school, and of course it has received a considerable amount of criticism.[12] However, the framework presented could be useful for investigating rock-art.

On the other hand, it is easy to see that research work on rock-art archaeology is actually being carried out at all levels for the framework mentioned. But this activity very often does not give a total view nor include a comprehensive hypothesis of its subject, nor upon rock pictures as a type of formation in the visual medium.

About style

A discussion of the concept rock-art necessitates a comment on the term style.[13] There are not many serious art historians, with generally accepted aims, who any longer use this term much.[14] But of course, «style» is a convenient term for indicating a certain period or class or art.[15] It is evident that complete and «homogeneous» works of art as a rule are characterized among other things by a consistent treatment of the particular elements of the pictures, and they are dependent on a principal formation. In general it is the «homogeneity» suggested above, which is intended when the term style is used. This implies that the concept of style has a descriptive function and that it is not of an explanatory nature.

The concepts of style can often be derived from the *original use*[16] by the performing artist himself, or at least as a descriptive term established some time after the introduction of the phenomenon in question.

This kind of term, with a documentational value of its own, is closely related to that which is sometimes used by art historians for *characterizing*[17] works of art.

«Baroque» was for example originally used in this way, meaning something which was looked upon negatively,[18] by people living with it or some time afterwards.

On the other hand, «Baroque» can be used to describe a painting or a building which has *certain defined qualities.*[19] Even if this term is a-chronological, it is agreed by most art historians that this specific term cannot very well be used except for the «Baroque» period.

Thirdly, «Baroque» is a term which defines a *certain period*[20] of Western art history, as mentioned in the second example.

Beside these kinds of emotional, expressively descriptive concepts of style, we can also recognize at least one more of importance.

I refer to the comprehensive concept «style»[21] which takes into account and also *integrates motifs, compositions, social and other functions as well as visual action* of groups of pictures, buildings or theories of town planning.

As a result, specialized concepts of style for certain purposes have developed, and some of these concepts seem to have a fair chance of working out well in the restricted fields for which they have been constructed.[22] Of interest here is of course Bertil Almgren's study on curving lines,[23] which in some respects corresponds to the concept of style referred to. Unfortunately this study has not, as far as I know, been published yet. The style-concepts are not means of dating, at least not directly, they are descriptive more than anything else. In certain cases it is not the chronological aspect of the style-conceps which are of value, but rather the possibilities to establish certain groupings. In many situations, however, they will form excellent criteria for relative chronology.

In general, however, style has proved a not very useful term and should be avoided both as a descriptive and as a chronological concept.[24] This is a consequence of the broad outlook of the research field, and also the diversified purpose of the modern discipline which interprets visual phenomena. An outline of this situation must of necessity be avoided here, even if it could be of value for the correct understanding of latent possibilities, which it is my task to indicate.

As a concluding remark I would like to say that we must never forget that pictures and monuments — in their proper environment — are means of visualizing, on their own terms, the whole ideology of man in the society that produced them,[25] not just means of «depicting», for example, an agricultural or religious system.

This means that the pictures cannot be made use of just by selecting details which seem interesting for some particular reason. A picture is an entity[26] which cannot be arbitrarily fragmented without at the same time losing the content, inner or superficial, and the function, visual or practical, of the picture.

These demands quite obviously involve both an analysis and a good knowledge of the environment of the sites[27] from which certain views of interest were originally defined, and which were also clearly accessible to man as long as they were actually valuable to him.

Visual analysis of rock pictures

What I am looking for is a way of regarding, an analysis and interpretation of rock-art as consisting of pictures. Not primarily in the sense of physical artefacts — optically recognizable — but rather as *visual structures*[28] which obviously follow distinct rules but are all the same very different from mere archaeological objects.

It is not adequate, nor sufficient, to bring together fragmented descriptions of isolated geometric characteristics, sculptural forms, notes on identifiable colour tones etc. A pictorial analysis[29] should rather incorporate an elaborate treatment of the composition *as a whole,* as well as modes of constructing perspective, the scale and abbreviations used — both optical and abstract — and also the way the physical matter is treated, just to mention some central aspects.

It is perhaps most important that all these attributes should be synthesized into a relevant total visual analysis of every picture in question, as well as of whole assemblies of rock-picture areas.

This kind of description and analysis should also include a comprehensive testing[30] of those possible places where one might visually grasp the whole or part of the pictures, either *en ensemble* or in separate parts. In line with this it would be appropriate to try the total views[31] of Max Raphael, and also those of Leroi-Gourhan and Laming-Emperaire.

All this means that we must take into consideration the *spatial character*[32] of the physical-topographical environment and the iconological possibilities which this would allow, when interpreting the pictures. Naturally the analysis of the spatial concept needs to be closely connected with a study of the *time elements*[33] incorporated.

Instruction and visual analysis

Before continuing, it is necessary to make a brief statement about the general background of rock-art research. It must be pointed out that our common Western education is either *verbal-descriptive* or *mathematical-analytical* or a combination of both, depending on how the situation is viewed.[34]

This educational dualism is obviously the cause of many futile and unnecessary misunderstandings — which is the case also in rock-art archaeology. But there is one thing that is of far greater importance in this context. What I mean is that both of the above-mentioned bases of our educational system almost totally exclude the training of *active* visual comprehension of the environment and its components. In consequence this also guides the situation in rock-art investigation, generally speaking.

It is in most cases quite futile to look at rock-pictures separated from their proper context and physical background,[35] in the way that has been more and more common since movable pictures evolved during the Renaissance,[36] and this for obvious reasons.

Documentary value of reproductions

In this connection we also have the problem of correctly evaluating different kinds of documents reproduced from the originals, as for example by tracing, graphic design, frottage, casting with plaster and siloprene, photography — also orthogonally rectified. Furthermore, we must consider the scale of the reproduction, take account of three-dimensional form and tactility, depth of carved lines, colour fragments etc., before transforming the original information. One must never forget that every kind of reproduction is an abstract translation into a model, conventionally legible.[37]

Rock pictures are not comparable to archaeological artefacts in general, they are *intentionally visualized messages*. The different character of archaeological documents will for obvious reasons cause correspondingly different pictorial perceptive situations for the observer — be it the investigator himself or any other person. There-

216

fore the decision to choose a method of documentation[38] is not only of importance for the convenience of fieldwork, or merely being fitting for the character of the rockpictures themselves. In any case it is no question of «taste».

One must certainly consider the effects caused by the final reproductions,[39] whatever these might be, and also the intermediate stage of the documents before they at last meet the hand, or rather eye, in the shape of a printed book or perhaps a photocopy.

I do *not* mean that a generally accepted system[40] of depicting rock-art should be recommended. On the contrary, the specific character of different pictures ought to be taken into account. What is needed is that every corpus of rock-pictures should be accompanied by an explanation[41] of the system used. Preferably this should include not only a description, but also the reasons for the choice of reproductive means, as well as a discussion with regard to the visual character of the pictures in question.

A framework for visual analysis of rock-pictures

The introduction above aims at presenting the situation of rock-art research, briefly considered from a visual point of view. Subsequently some problems and consequences of the situation had to be shown, in order to reach a generally acceptable level of discussion. Bearing this basis in mind, we shall now proceed to look upon a plan for a framework for rock-art interpretation, with a visual approach.

The proposal is preliminary and intended for discussion. It has not yet been adopted and this implies that certain components and terms need be modified. Depending of the comprehensive and theoretic character of the frame, there are components which will perhaps not be very easy to uncover directly, e.g. «allegory».

The frame proposed is not thought of as a scheme with levels in a ranking order, but rather built up of fairly interrelated aspects on rock-pictures. The necessary basic analysis in practical applications, including description of morphological elements, is presumed to be integrated with — or preceding — the interpretation according to the frame.

By these remarks I do not consider that I have given a framework for description, analysis and interpretation of rock-pictures which is immediately functional. My contribution is rather intended to be a comment on one central aspect of the rock-art complex, that is whether the rock-pictures should be regarded as visual art.

217

An attempt at
A FRAMEWORK FOR VISUAL ANALYSIS OF ROCK PICTURES

Categories:	*Description:*
Material (physical matter) *and* artistic techniques	**ARTISTIC MEANS OF EXECUTION** *eg: «expressive», «impressionistic» . . .* rather restricted possibilities ⟷ a choice within the framework of cultural conventions
Coding language possibilities	**«ABSTRACTION»**[47] All rock-pictures, if treated as works of art, are in some way to be regarded as abstractions (of reality) according to definitions of the concept «art». The range of morphological modus is known as styles. The graph below shows some exponents and their relation. «abstract»[48] ⟷ «stylized» «naturalistic» «realistic» «veristic» ⇕ *«scale» of figurative character*
Rules of perspective: «levels of (un)reality»[46]	**«ABBREVIATION»** In the visual, and conceived, surface of pictures there is an intermingling of the different possible visual components, which makes possible the enrichment of the total message, if desired. The forms of «abbreviation» can be visual, expressive, intellectual.
Elementary components, *and their* visual function	**«CONTENTS»** types[43] of visual entities: <table><tr><td>SIGN</td><td>SYMBOL</td><td>ALLEGORY</td><td>NARRATIVE</td></tr><tr><td>*definitional* basic visual element</td><td>*conventional & definitional* consisting of signs and/or depictive</td><td>*conventional* artifically structured character; can also consist of signs and/or symbols</td><td>*illustrative*[44] depictive with elements of signs, symbols, perhaps also alluding to allegories</td></tr></table>
Physic context[45]	**«SITUATION»** The components of visual entities are as a rule elaborated upon, and have connecting elements, e.g. architectonic environment, verbal information such as inscriptions, human performances such as liturgy, all of iconological significance. Without these connecting elements the visual art components cannot be meaningful with regard to their intended function.
Signification	**«MEANING»** Conventional and expressive entities — Socially meaningful context[42] when used — Total decoding

NOTES

*   This paper contains some remarks that have emerged both from my experience in fields not directly related to rock-art research and from work
which I for some years have been involved in together with Jarl Nordbladh — that of publishing the corpus[1] of rock-carvings from Kville, prepared by Åke Fredsjö. Having said this I should like, in this context, to
stress the importance of dealing with rock-pictures as visual entities, but
nevertheless as a firmly integrated part of the socio-economic-religious
aspects of the societies that produced them for certain needs.

1. Hällristningar ... Rock-carvings. Kville härad (hundred), Svenneby parish
   (county of Bohuslän). Documentation: Åke *Fredsjø*, editors: *Jarl Nordbladh & Jan Rosvall*. Studies in North European Archaeology. 7, Göteborg 1971.
2. e.g. the key-word *art* of this symposium: «International Symposium on
   Rock-Art at Hankø ...»
   See *Jarl Nordbladh* and *Jan Rosvall*, A symposium on petroglyphic
   art at Hankø, August 6th to 12 th 1972. Fornvännen 68 (1973), pp. 52—56.
   Concerning «art», see for example:
   Hermann Bauer, Kunstgeschichte. Eine kritische Einführung in das Stu-
   dium der Kunstgeschichte. München 1977. (p. 14; passim)
   «Art», in: Encyclopedia of world art, vol. 1. New York — Toronto — London 1959.
3. According to The Random House Dictionary of the English Language.
   New York, College edition 1969.
4. *Meyer Schapiro*, Style. Anthropology Today. An Encyclopedic Inventory. Prepared under the chairmanship of *A.L. Kroeber*, Chicago, Ill.,
   2nd imp. 1954, pp. 287—312. «The analysis and characterization of the
   styles of primitive and early historical cultures have been strongly influenced by the standards of recent Western art.» (p. 290)
5. *Schapiro* 1954 op. cit., «The critic like the artist, tends to conceive of
   style as a value term; ... 'style' in this normative sense ... seems to be
   outside the scope of historical ... studies of art ...» (pp. 287-8)
6. This situation is understood (p. 210), even if not explicitly described, in
   Arnold Hauser, The Philosophy of Art History, London 1959. Original
   edition: Philosophie der Kunstgeschichte. München 1958 (Methoden mo-
   derner Kunstbetrachtung, München 1970.).
   The series «Art in context» is devoted to this problem, e.g. *Marilyn
   Aronberg Lavin*, Piero della Francesca: The Flagellation, London
   1972.
   This view is also stressed by *André Chastel*, in: The studios and styles
   of the Renaissance, Italy 1460—1500, 1966. (e.g. pp. 228 ff.)
7. See for example:
   Bauer 1977 op. cit.
   Hauser 1958/59 op. cit.
   Hans Jantzen, Über den kunstgeschichtlichen Raumbegriff. Sitzungs-
   berichte der Bayerischen Akademie der Wissenschaften. Philosophisch-
   historische Abteilung. Jahrgang 1938, Heft 5. (Aslo Darmstadt 1962, separately printed.)
   Heinrich Lützeler, Kunsterfahrung und Kunstwissenschaft. Systematische
   und entwicklungsgeschichtliche Darstellung und Dokumentation des Um-
   gangs mit der Bildenden Kunst. I—III. Freiburg/Br. 1975.

8. The problems of transferring methods into new fields of application, particularly archaeology, are discussed by:
   Don Brothwell Stones, pots and people: a plea for statistical caution. Science in Archaeology. Edited by *D. Brothwell & C. Higgs,* London, 2nd ed 1969, pp. 674 ff.
   Carl-Alex Moberg, Remarques pragmatiques sur quelques problèmes théoriques dans l'archéologie de la Scandinavie occidentale aux environs de 1300 avant J.C. Archéologie et calculateurs. Colloques internationaux du Centre de la Recherche Scientifique. Sciences humaines, Paris 1970, pp. 31 ff.
   Carl-Axel Moberg, Comment to paper by Sibson. Journal of the Royal Statistical Society, B. vol. 34, no. 3, 1972, pp. 311—349; p. 348.
9. Summarized in *Erwin Panofsky,* Studies in Iconology. Humanistic Themes In the Art of the Renaissance, Oxford 1939, Paperback edition New York 1962. (pp. 3—17)
10. As a representative example could be mentioned *Erwin Panofsky,* Renaissance and Renascences in Western Art. 2 vols, Uppsala 1960.
    Another important publication, exponent of an analogous direction, is *Günther Bandmann,* Mittelalterliche Architektur als Bedeutungsträger, Berlin 1951.
11. The research procedure is described in a multitude of publications, not the least in behavioural sciences. A short discussion with an example is given in *Jan Rosvall,* Quantitative Methods and Art History. Art Research In Scandinavia (ARIS) 1 (1969), pp. 40—50. (pp. 41-2)
12. Lately, especially with regards to analysis of concepts, by *Göran Hermeren,*
    — Ikonografi och ikonologi. Bildanalyser och bildtolkningar i konstforskningen: typer, metoder och argument. (*Mimeo, not dated*)Konstvetenskapliga institutionen, Lunds universitet.
    — Representation and Meaning in the Visual Arts. A Study in the Methodology of Iconography and Iconology, Lund 1969.
    — Om komparativa metoder i konstvetenskap. Konstvetenskaplig Bulletin nr. 5 (February 1971), pp. 32—34.
13. «... the conception of style came to be soonest and most systematically developed in connection with the visual arts ...» according to *Hauser* 1959 op. cit. (p. 207). The terms is briefly described, for example by *Schapiro* 1954 op. cit.: «By style is meant the constant form ... in the art of an individual or a group.» (p. 287), and «... in general the description of a style refers to three aspects of art: form elements or motives, form relationships, and qualities (including an all-over quality which we may call the 'expression').» (p. 289)
    Bauer 1977 op. cit. (pp. 9 ff, 74 ff, 87 ff)
    «Stil», Kindlers Malerei Lexikon, Band 14, München 1976.
    Erwin Panofsky, Das Problem des Stils in den bildenden Kunst.
    In: Aufsätze zu Grundfragen der Kunstwissenschaft, Berlin 1964.
    Gregor Paulsson, Konsthistoriens föremål. Uppsala universitets årsskrift 1943:5. (passim)
14. For instance, concerning the early Renaissance in relation with mediaeval art and thought, in a recent representative book it is stated that «If we explain the Early Renaissance as merely the culmination of mediaeval trends of thoughts and the later or High Renaissance merely as a foretaste of the Baroque — then it has virtually ceased to have any positive validity

of its own. Of course, this sort of a trick may be played on any historical period ...» *Michael Levey*, Early Renaissance. Harmondsworth 1967. (p. 13).
Frederick Antal, Remarks on the method of art history. The Burlington Magazine 1949:2 pp. 49—52; 1949:3, pp. 73—75.
The situation seems to be the same in the field of literature and linguistics: « ... there is no accepted definition on style ...» *Peter Cassirer*, On the place of stylistics. Style and text, Skriptor, Trelleborg 1975. (p. 1)

15. «Skall man fatta de arkitekturhistoriska sammanhangen måste man också se byggnaderna och deras formspråk som utslag av allmänna tendenser i sin tid och sitt land. Dessa gemensamma tendensers utslag i formspråket kallas stilar.» but «Stilstudiet i och för sig leder inte till full förståelse av helheten eftersom det mest gäller formspråkets visuella motiv. Det tjäner emellertid igenkännandet och karaktäristiken på ett förträffligt sätt och är därigenom nära nog oundgängligt som hjälpmedel särskilt när det gäller att skilja epoker, byggnadsskolor, arkitektpersonligheter och andra faktorer från varandra.» This explanation is cited from *Elias Cornell*, Arkitekturhistoria, Stockholm — Uppsala 1968. (Textdel, pp. 24-5) Also: *Elias Cornell*, Humanistic inquiries into architecture, Göteborg 1959. (Swedish edition: Om rummet och arkitekturens väsen, Göteborg 1966.)

16. Exemplified by:
    Levey 1967 op. cit. (p. 14), and
    Anthony Blunt, Artistic Theory in Italy 1450—1600. Oxford 1940. Paperback edition, Oxford 1962. (p. 1)

17. «Utöver stilstudiet — som ofta kallas stillkritik — behöver man emellertid ett mera allsidigt sätt att karakterisera arkitekturen i olika epoker, regioner, kulturstadier och vad det kan gälla. Helhetens sammansättning blir då vad man främst skall inrikta sig på.» *Cornell* 1968 op. cit. (Textdel, p. 25). *Cornell* 1959, 1966 op. cit.

18. *Bo Lindwall*, Barockens epok. Stockholm 1968. «... i måleriet en bild eller en figur i barockstil, i vilken proportionsreglerna inte iakttagits ...» (p. 178)

19. « ... Barock ist ... eine ganzheitliche Ordnung aus Architektur und Dekor.» *André Chastel*, Die Kunst Italiens, Darmstadt — München — Passau 1962. (II, p. 183)

20. «That the same names, 'baroque' ... should be applied both to a unique historical style and to a recurrent type or phase is confusing.» *Schapiro* 1954 op. cit. (p. 296)

21. « ... it is clear that the history of styles cannot be seen simply as a slow approximation to one particular solution. Different styles concentrate on different compensatory moves, largely determined by the function the image is expected to perform in a given civilization.» *E.H. Gombrich*, Action and Expression in Western Art. Non-Verbal Communication. Edited by *R.A. Hinde*, Cambridge 1972, pp. 373-93. (pp. 373-4)
    In this connection *Cornell* emphasizes (1968 op. cit.) that «Varje kultur, region, tidsepok utvecklar sin uppfattning, sitt sätt att artikulera helheten och dess förhållanden. Den bildar sin egen *integrationstyp*, sin helhetstyp ...» and «Sättet att sammanfoga och indela helheten är betecknande från det minsta till det största.» Textdel, p. 25); *Cornell* 1959, 1966 op. cit.

22. «Painting and experience in fifteenth century Italy. A primer in the social history of pictorial style» by *Michael Baxandall,* Oxford 1972.
    «Studies in roman imperial art» by *Per Gustaf Hamberg,* Uppsala 1945.
    «Art Nouveau» in *Nikolaus Pevsner,* Pioneers of modern design, Harmondsworth 1970. (pp. 90 ff)
    «The meaning and diffusion of the Empire Style» by *Mario Praz,* in: The age of Neo-classicism, The arts council of Great Britain, London 1972 (pp. lxxxix ff)
    «Mannerism» by John *Shearman,* Harmondsworth 1967.
23. Bertil *Almgren,* Die Datierung der bronzezeitlichen Felszeichnungen in Schweden. Actes du VII Congrès international des sciences préhistoriques et protohistoriques, Praghe 21—27 aout 1966. Rédigé par Jan Filip, Praha 1970, p. 674.
    The method is described in
    Bertil Almgren, Bronsnucklar och djurornamentik. I—II, Uppsala 1955.
24. «Upptäckten att den kulturperiod som man räknat med inte entydigt låter sig fångas in under en term har lett til kritik mot själva epokbegreppet [the Renaissance].» As referred by *Sven Sandström,* Renässansskedet, Stockholm 1965. (p. 13) Cf note 14 above.
    Gregor Paulsson, Konstvetenskap och konstkultur. In: Kritik och program, Uppsala 1949. (p. 139)
25. *André Leroi-Gourhan,* Les hommes préhistoriques et la religion. La recherche, numéro 26 (septembre 1972) pp. 723-32.
    André Leroi-Gourhan, Interpretation esthétique et religieuse des figures et symboles dans la préhistoire. Archives de sciences-sociales des religions, no 42, 1976, pp. 5—15.
    André Leroi-Gourhan, Sur les aspects socio-économiques de l'art paléolithique. In: L'autre et l'ailleurs, hommage à Roger Bastide. Présenté par J. Poirier et F. Raveau, Paris, Berger-Levrault, 1976, p. 164—168.
    Morton H. Levine, Prehistoric art and ideology. American anthropologist vol. 59 (1957), pp. 949—964.
    Jarl Nordbladh, Images as messages in society. Prolegomena to the study of Scandinavian petroglyphs and semiotics. In: New directions in scandinavian archaeology. Ed. by Kristian Kristiansen & Carsten Palludan-Müller. (The National Museum of Denmark.) Studies in scandinavian prehistory and early history, Vol. 1, Copenhagen 1978.
26. *E.H. Gombrich,* The Visual Image. Scientific American, vol. 227, number 3 (September 1972), pp. 82—96. «The chance of a correct reading of the image is governed by three variables: the code, the caption, and the context.» Further: «... how much we take for granted when we look at a picture for its message. It always depends on our prior knowledge of possibilities.» (p. 86)
    Rudolf Arnheim, Art and visual perception. A psychology of the creative eye. The new version. Berkeley and Los Angeles 1974. «... at no time could a work of art have been made or understood by a mind unable to conceive the integrated structure of a whole ...» (p. 5)
27. *Dale Ritter,* Medicine men and spirit animals. (Paper delivered at International Symposium ... 1972 op. cit.)
    Cf also *Cornell* 1968 op. cit.: «Om blickpunkter och vistelsezoner i regel ger sig utan vidare är förloppet av upplevelsen inte lika självklart ...» (p. 13); *Cornell* 1959, 1966 op. cit.
28. In this respect, the thorough research of *Gregor Paulsson* is of great

importance. The principal publication is «Konstverkets byggnad», Stockholm 1942. The following passages are taken from «Tanke och form i konsten. Studier för en betydelseslära», I. Stockholm 1933. «Vi måste utgå från helheten. Denna är en betydelse, som är bildad av former, om vilka vi endast vet att vi med vår nuvarande kunskap inte kunna isolera dem på rent formal väg.» (pp. 7—8), «Bildstrukturen dominerar över detaljerna och förändrar deras kvalitet.» but «Vad menas då med bildstruktur? I första hand givetvis byggnaden av bildzoner, förgrund, mellangrund, deras förhållande till varandra, deras dominerande funktion i bilden. Alla dessa bestämningar äro emellertid formala. Vad är det som gör skillnaden i min upplevelse av dem?» (pp. 19—20) — «Det är den enhet, som bildas av uttrycket, ej som sådant men i dess förhållande till ett föremål, som ger ett konstverk dess betydelse.» (p. 21)

29. A lay-out of a comprehensive pictorial analysis is demonstrated in *Rosvall* 1969 op. cit. (pp. 45-7)

30. Cf. *Gro Mandt Larsen,* Bergbilder i Hordalend. En undersøkelse av bildenes sammensetning, deres naturmiljø og kulturmiljø. (Rock-pictures in Hordaland. An analysis of the composition of the pictures and of their ecological and cultural background.) Acta Universitatis Bergensis. Series Humaniorum Litterarum, 1970 No. 2, Bergen — Oslo 1972. (especially pp. 81—93, 147-8)

31. *Max Raphael,* Prehistoric cave paintings. The Bollingen Series, IV, Washington D.C. 1945.
   André Leroi-Gourhan, Préhistoire de l'art occidental, Paris 1965. English edition: Treasures of Prehistoric Art, New York 1967.
   André Leroi-Gourhan, The Evolution of Paleolithic Art. Scientific American, February 1968, pp. 59—71.
   Annette Laming-Emperaire, La signification de l'art rupestre paléolitique, Paris 1962.
   Annette Laming-Emperaire, Système de pensée et organisation sociale dans l'art rupestre paléolithique. L'homme de Cro-Magnon. 1868—1968. Anthropologie et archéologie. Avant propos de Gabriel *Camps* et Georges Olivier. Centre de recherches anthropoligiques, préhistoriques et ethnographiques. Conseil de la recherche scientifique en Algerie, Paris.
   For a critical recapitulation, see
   Peter J. Ucko & Andrée Rosenfeld, Palaeolithic Cave Art. London 1967.

32. Cf. *Leroi-Gourhan* 1965 op. cit., and *Cornell* 1968 op. cit. (pp 11-13).

33. «En byggnad med sin odelbara helhet av exteriör och rum får sin fulla mening genom den handling som vi kallar ett besittningstagande.» *Cornell* 1968 op. cit. (p. 12)

34. This dichotomy has been stated principally by *C.P. Snow,* in «The Two Cultures — a Second Look.» Swedish edition, Malmö 1965.

35. Stated by, for instance, *Leroi-Gourhan* 1965 op. cit., and *Mandt Larsen,* 1972 op. cit.

36. Suggested by *Raymonde Moulin,* Lemarché de la peinture en France, Paris 1967. (p. 21)

37. An interesting example is *R.A. Weale,* Die Tragödie des Pointillismus. Palette (Basel) 40, 1972, pp. 16—24. (also versions i French, English, Italian and Spanish).
   Jarl Nordbladh and *Jan Roswall,* Documentation as a part of the research

process. Some considerations actualized by the application of photo-grammetric measuring techniques in history of culture. Norwegian archaeological review vol. 8 (1975): no. 1, pp. 54—62.

38. *Asger Jorn*, Om gengivelse, tydning og datering af broncealderens helleristninger. (in the danish paper Demokraten Århus, not dated).
Jan Rosvall, Quantitative methods and art history. Art research in Scandinavia (ARIS) vol. 1 (1969) pp. 40—50. (especially pp. 44 ff)

39. *Harold Curwen*, Processes of Graphic Reproduction in Printing, London, rev. ed. 1967.
S.K. Matthews, Photography in Archaeology and Art, London 1968.
Alf Arnamo, Tryckteknik idag och i morgon. Grafiskt forum 1972: 11, pp. 3—8.
Ole Brinch, Kontorskopieringsmetoder i vardagstrycket. Grafiskt forum 1972: 11, pp. 9—15.
Nordbladh & Rosvall, 1975 op. cit.

40. Cf. *Jorn* op. cit. « ... om nordiske arkaeologer i fremtiden kunne blive enige om alle at holde sig til et bestemt skema for tegnede gengivelser af helleristninger.»

41. An attempt is shown in Hällristningar ... Svenneby ... 1971 op. cit. («The Editors' Comments» pp. 1—5)

42. According to the discussion on «Symbolmilieu» in *Gregor Paulsson*, Die soziale Dimension der Kunst, Bern 1955. Also: *Gregor Paulsson*, Kunst, Gesellschaft, Symbolmilieu. Stil und Überlieferung. III. Berlin 1967.

43. Concerning the concepts *sign, symbol, allegory, narrative*, consult the mentioned monograph for a thoroughly analysed art historic complex: Per *Gustaf Hamberg*, Studies in Roman Imperial Art, Uppsala 1945.

44. A complication of importance which needs special consideration, is that « ... there must be a great difference between a painting that illustrates a known story and another that whishes to *tell* a story.» *Gombrich* 1972 op. cit. (p. 391)

45. In accordance with, for instance, *Günther Bandmann*, Ikonogolie der Architektur. Jahrbuch für Ästhetik und allgemeine Kunstwissenschaft, 1 (1951), pp. 67. Cf. note above, id.

46. Exemplified by *Sven Sandström*, Levels of Unreality. Studies in Structure and Constructions in Italian Mural Painting during the Renaissance, Uppsala 1963.

47. «If art is thus seen as ... an exercise in reduction (conventionally referred to as 'abstraction') ...» *Gombrich* 172 op. cit. (p. 373)

48. This term, or concept, is part of a complex not easy to comprehend. A short but enlightening discussion is given in *George Mills*, Art: An Introduction to Qualitative Anthropology. Anthropology and Art. Readings in Cross-Cultural Esthetics. Edited by *Charlotte M. Otten*, Garden City, New York 1971, pp. 66—92. (p. 72): «Commonly a distinction is made between naturalistic and abstract art. This is misleading ...»

Die Felsbilder Sibiriens

VON HERBERT KÜHN

Ganz neu ist in unser Wissen um die Felsbilder der Welt ein Gebiet eingetreten, das uns bisher nicht bekannt war, es ist das Sibirien. Felsbilder sind durch die Arbeit der russischen Gelehrten aufgefunden worden, die oft gleich, in manchem aber auch völlig andersartig sind gegenüber dem, was uns an anderen Fundstellen bekannt war. (Abb.1)

Der Entdecker selbst, Professor *Aleksej Pawlowitsch Okladnikow* von der Universität Nowosibirsk in Sibirien, ist zu diesem Symposion geladen worden, er konnte, wie so oft Gelehrte der UdSSR nicht zu uns kommen, und so sei es mir erlaubt, über seine neuesten Entdeckungen an dieser Stelle zu berichten.

Dabei möchte ich bemerken, dass ich die persönliche Bekanntschaft von Okladnikow 1969 in Linz machen konnte. Wir haben mehrere Tage sprechen können über die Probleme, die Aufgaben, die Ergebnisse. Es war mir möglich, eines seiner spannenden Bücher in deutscher Übersetzung im Verlag Brockhaus, Wiesbaden, unterzubringen, es trägt den Titel: Der Hirsch mit dem goldenen Geweih, Wiesbaden 1972.

Aus dem westlichen Russland waren im Jahre 1936 die Felsbilder von Karelien, am Onega-See von *W. J. Raudonikas* veröffentlicht worden. *A. A. Formozov* hat 1961 und 63 berichtet über die Felsbilder im Kaukasus und *Danilenko* und *Gladilin* über Felsbilder der Ukraine. Auch Felsbilder in Kasachstan sind bekannt gemacht worden.

Jedoch die Bilder in Sibirien waren dem Europäer unbekannt. Wohl gab es kurze Berichte von Reisenden über Felsbilder an der Angara und an der Lena, aber Genaueres war nicht bekannt.

Die Arbeiten von *Okladnikow* an der Angara begannen 1934 durch eine wissenschaftliche Expedition, ausgesandt von dem Museum der Stadt Irkutsk. Die Ergebnisse waren so bedeutend, dass die Akademie der Wissenschaften in den Jahren 1951-59 immer wieder Forscher zur Bearbeitung der Felsbilder berief. Ein grosser Staudamm wurde errichtet an der Angara, viele Felsbilder mussten dem Plane geopfert werden, und so wurde die wissenschaftliche Bearbeitung dringend erforderlich. Viele der gefährdeten Bilder wurden abgenommen von den Felsen und in das Museum von Irkutsk gebracht. Auch an dieser Arbeit war Okladnikow beteiligt. Die wichtigsten Bilder liegen südlich von dem Orte Bratsk und nordwestlich von Irkutsk, im Bette der Angara auf den sogenannten Steinernen Inseln. Bis 1962 konnte die Arbeit fortgesetzt werden. An 14 verschiedenen Stellen im Tale der Angara wurden Felsbilder entdeckt, vermessen, gezeichnet und aufgenommen oder nach Irkutsk verbracht. Es wurden die gemalten Bilder von Zauberern gefunden, und dann auf der zweiten Steinernen Insel die naturhaften Gravierungen von Elchen, (Fig. 2) darunter Bilder von hoher künstlerischer Qualität, eingeschlagen mit Steinwerkzeugen in den anstehenden Fels. Die Datierung ergibt sich durch neolithische Skulpturen von Elchen aus Ausgrabungen in Sibirien. Die Bilder sind geschaffen worden im Mesolithikum und im Neolithikum. Sie sind in das 8. bis 5. Jahrtausend zu datieren.

Wie in Europa verlieren die Bilder allmählich an Perspektive, an Tiefenerstreckung. Immer mehr verlagert sich der Schwerpunkt auf die Umreissung, auf die Umrisslinie, immer mehr tritt die Fläche in den Vordergrund und immer mehr führt die Gestaltung zu auf das Abstrakte. Die Darstellungen des mittleren Neolithikums sind völlig abstrakt, genau wie in Europa, Afrika, Amerika, Australien. (Fig. 3).

Auch an der Lena fanden sich Felsbilder, vor allem bei Schischkino, dann östlich vom Baikal-See, bei Chobdo-Somon. Weiter ergaben sich Bilder an der Selenga bei Ich-Alyk, fast alle abstrakt.

Aber die grösste Überraschung boten die Bilder am Flusse Amur, nahe der Grenze Chinas, bei Komsomolsk mit dem Fundplatz Sakatschi-Aljan und bei Chaborowsk mit dem Fundplatz Scheremetjewo. Es fanden sich Bilder von Masken mit tief eingeschlagenen Linien, seltsame Bildungen von eigenartigem Charakter. Sie stellen Geister dar, Dämonen, den Urvater, ein Wesen, das mehr ist als der Mensch. Fast immer sind nur die Gesichter gegeben, fast nie der Körper. (Fig. 4) Okladnikow erinnert an Menhire in Sibirien mit ähnlichen Masken und mit ganzen Menschengestalten, aus der Gegend des Jenissej. (Fig. 9) Aber die Maskendarstellungen am Amur sind doch noch anders. Am nächsten stehen ihnen Masken auf Tongefässen der neolithischen Kultur von Jomon in Japan. Es gibt auch ähnliche Tonfiguren der gleichen Zeit aus Japan. So spricht Okladnikow von einem pazifischen Charakter dieser Gravierungen der Masken in seinem Buch, Der Hirsch mit dem goldenen Geweih, 1972 S. 105. Aber eine solche Fülle von gravierten Masken im Gestein gibt es wieder nicht in Japan, und so sind diese Masken-

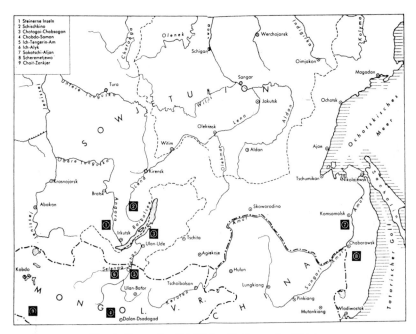

Fig. 1. Karte der Felsbilder-Stationen in Sibirien.

Fig. 2. Gravierungen von Elchen im Tale der Angara.

Fig. 3. Chotogoi-Chabsagan am Baikalsee.
Stilisierte Menschenbilder.

Fig. 4. Sakatschi-Aljan. Maske.

228

Fig. 5. Sakatschi-Aljan. Hirsch.

Fig. 6. Sakatschi-Aljan. Masken mit Strahlenkranz.

bilder eine besondere Eigenart der Gegend um den Amur. Sie gehören offenbar dem Neolithikum an. Dieser Epoche muss auch
der Hirsch mit dem goldenen Geweih zugerechnet werden, (Fig. 5),
ein eigenwilliges Bild eines Tieres aus derselben Gegend, aus Sakatschi-Aljan am Amur. Das Geweih ist nicht golden, aber Okladnikow
hat Märchen von seiner Grossmutter gehört, die von dem Hirsch
mit dem goldenen Geweih erzählen, und so hat er dieses Bild mit den
Spiralen im Körper aus Sakatschi-Aljan als den Hirsch mit dem goldenen Geweih benannt.

Die Maskenbilder am Amur und am Ussuri sind schon von
Reisenden in diesen Gegenden beobachtet worden. Im Auftrage der
Russischen Geographischen Gesellschaft erforschte die Gebiete des
Fernen Ostens von Russland ein Deutsch-Russe Richard Maak. Im
Jahre 1860 erschien seine Arbeit, gewidmet den Gebieten des Amur
und des Ussuri. In dieser Arbeit werden Felsbilder genannt, Maak
spricht von menschlichen Gesichtern, von denen Strahlen ausgehen,
von Tieren, vor allem Vögeln und Schlangen. Er findet keine Deutung, keine Erklärung der Bilder, auch die dort eingeborene Bevölkerung vermochte keine Auskunft zu geben. Dann folgen Berichte von
Reisenden in den Jahren 1873. 1899 berichtete Berthold Laufer, der
bekannte Chinaforscher, geboren 1874 in Köln, später Kurator am
Field Museum in Chicago, über die Bilder in der Zeitschrift American Anthropologist. Im Jahre 1908 besuchten F.F. Busse und Fürst
Krapotkin die Bilder.

Es war im Jahre 1935, als Okladnikow auf Veranlassung der
Akademie der Wissenschaften in Moskau mit Teilnehmern seine Arbeiten am Amur und am Ussuri begann. Er setzte sie fort bis 1970.
Dabei wurden viele neue, bis dahin unbekannte Bilder gefunden
und sorgfältig bearbeitet. In einem Artikel im Speh Bd. 23, 1970-73.
S. 95 f. berichtet er über diese neuen Funde. (Abb. 6) Mit seiner Er-
laubnis lege ich hier die neuesten Bilder vor.

Er hält sie für neolithisch, in diesen Gegenden zeitlich später als in
Europa. Es gibt Tongefässe aus dem Orte Wosnesjenowka nahe der
Mündung des Flusses Chungara am dem unteren Amur. Einige der
Gefässe dieses Fundplatzes tragen in Malereien die gleichen Masken,
sie besitzen auch die Spiralen und auch die Schlangen, wie sie
ebenso bei den Felsbildern erscheinen. Die Radiokarbondatierung
für diesen Fundplatz ergab 2500 Jahre vor unserer Zeitrechnung,
also ein Neolithikum, das dem Beginn der Latènezeit in unseren
Gebreiten entspricht.

Die zeitlich jüngsten Bilder Ostsibiriens sind die der Reiter mit
Standarten von der Westseite des Baikalsees, von der Lena und der
Angara. Es sind Bilder der Kirgisen und andere Turvölker

dieser Gegend aus dem 7. und 8. Jh. nachchristlicher Zeit. Chinsesische Quellen der T'ang-Zeit berichten über sie. Als ihr Wohngebiet wird der Fluss Angkola, das ist Angara, genannt. Die Stämme werden als Kurikanen bezeichnet. Die Grabmäler türkischer Herrscher berichten von feierlichen Besuchen dieser Stämme, das Datum bestimmt sich auf 552 n. Chr. Das ist das erste genau bezeugte historische Datum in der Geschichte der Kurikanen.

Die Arbeiten von Okladnikow, sein russisch geschriebenes Buch über die Felsbilder an der Angara und sein anderes russisches Werk über die Bilder jenseits der Lena bringen neue Erkenntnisse. Am wichtigsten aber erscheinen mir die Entdeckungen der Maskenbilder am Amur, sie zeigen eine neue, eine eigenartige Darstellungskraft, sie bringen eine neue Dimension der Bilder an den Felsen, sie erweitern unser Wissen um die Felsbilder der Welt.

Zur kulturellen Stellung der nordwestdeutschen "Sonnensteine"

VON WOLFGANG DIETRICH ASMUS

Neben dem bekannten Stein mit figürlichen Darstellungen von Anderlingen Kreis Bremervörde mit seinen Beziehungen zu Skandinavien besitzen wir aus Nordwestdeutschland 3 grosse, untereinander merkwürdig ähnliche Bildsteine, deren fast gesamte Bildfläche von einer beherrschenden Darstellung eines konzentrischen Ringmusters (sogenannten Sonnenmusters) bedeckt ist. (Abb. 1) Sie haben im skandinavischen Norden keine direkte Parallelen, sind aber bisher mit den *hellristningar* in Verbindung gebracht worden.

Die betreffenden Bildsteine stammen alle aus einem relativ eng begrenzten Raum im Küstenbereich der Nordsee. Das ist bekanntlich ein Gebiet, welches vor allem in der Bronzezeit nahe Verbindung zum nordischen Kreis der Bronzezeit hatte, aber auch im Bereich des frühen Metallhandels entlang der Nordseeküste nach Westeuropa lag.

Es handelt sich um die Bildsteine von

Beckstedt, Kreis Grafschaft Hoya (Bezirk Bremen)[1]

Harpstedt, Kreis Grafschaft Hoya (Bezirk Bremen)

Horsten, Kreis Wittmund (Ostfriesland).

Im Gegensatz zu den beiden erstgenannten Objekten mit eingemeisselten konzentrischen Kreisen und einer Grube im Zentrum auf der flachen Seite des Steinblocks weist der 1,10 m-hohe Bildstein von Horsten mit 17 ineinander-gestellten Kreisen im Zentrum ein 3,4 cm-weites durch den Felsblock führendes Loch auf.[2]

Alle genannten Funde wurden leider nicht in ihrem prähistorischen Verband geborgen. Im Hinblick auf die zentrale Durchlochung des Steines von Horsten («Seelenloch»?) hat man bei diesem die Frage nach einer evtl. Zugehörigkeit zu einem westeuropäischen Steinkistengrab gestellt, einer Form, die in Ostfriesland mehrfach belegt ist.[3] Die Verwendung von Bildsteinen im Bereich von Grabkammern in Norddeutschland ist für die ältere nordische Bronzezeit mit dem Götterstein von Anderlingen, Kreis Bremervörde (Mont. II) belegt.[4]

Sonnenbilder der genannten Art sind in Westeuropa im Äneolithikum bzw. der älteren Bronzezeit nicht selten. Aus Schottland wurde

232

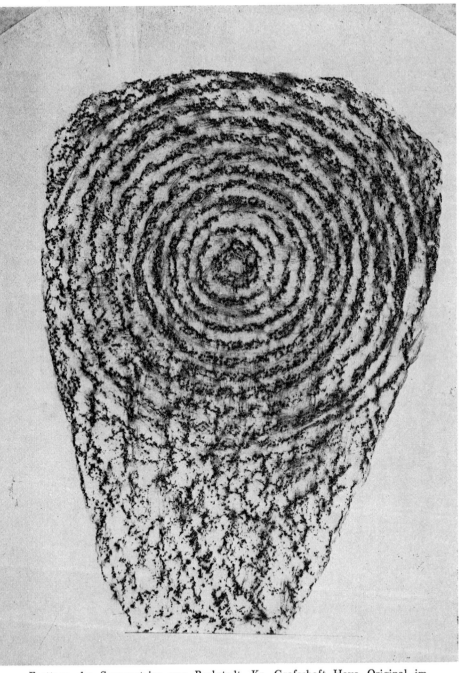

Frottage des Sonnensteins von Beckstedt, Kr. Grafschaft Hoya Original im Väterkundemuseum Bremen.

zum Beispiel ein Sonnenstein aus einer Grabkammer bekannt, der in seiner Gestalt und vor allem durch die Einmeisselung von konzentrischen Kreisen, die um eine kleine Grube angeordnet sind, den Bildsteinen von Beckstedt und von Harpstedt in hohem Masse entspricht. Der schottische Stein stand nahe an der Wandung der Grabkammer einer neolithischen Anlage. Vor ihm befand sich eine Nachbestattung der mittleren Bronzezeit. Ein Zusammenhang dieses Steines mit der genannten Nachbestattung wird von den Ausgräbern vermutet.[5]

Eingemeisselte, konzentrische Kreisdarstellungen der beschriebenen Art kennen wir in grösserer Anzahl von äneolithischen Grabbauten Westauropas, sowie auch von einzeln liegenden Felsen Irlands, zum Beispiel aus der Grafschaft Kerry (Gortboy).[6] Auch in der Bretagne lassen sich entsprechende Beispiele finden. In der Grabkammer des Tumulus von Gavr'inis gibt es Beispiele.[7] Ähnliche Darstellungen sind auch in der irischen Boyne-Kultur[8] vorhanden, die denen der norddeutschen Funde gegenüberzustellen sind. In der Rückwand der Seitenkammer des bekannten Tumulus von New Grange[9] befindet sich zum Beispiel über einem flachen, muldenförmigen Steinbassin eine entsprechende Bilddarstellung. Sie besteht aus drei nebeneinander liegenden verschieden grossen Wiedergaben von konzentrischen Kreisen. (Abb. 2). Auch das Innere der megalithischen Grabanlage von Dowth im Boyne-Tal weist eine besonders eindrucksvolle Bilddarstellung der genannten Art auf.

Auf Grund von Vergleichsfunden und diesbezüglichen Beobachtungen wird die Frage nach der kulturellen Einordnung der nordwestdeutschen «Sonnensteine» und ihrer bisherigen Einordnung in die grosse Gruppe der «Bauernzeichnungen» in Skandinavien neu gestellt.

Dabei darf die Verbindung der südskandinavischen Felsbilder zu westeuropäischen Einflüssen (zum Beispiel schiffsdarstellungen auch in der Bretagne)[10] nicht übersehen werden. Die nordwestdeutschen Fundobjekte bilden möglicherweise eine Brücke zwischen West- und Nordeuropa.

FUSSNOTEN

1. *H. Asmus:* Abklatsche von Bildsteinen, «Die Kunde» N.F. 17, 1966, S. 126, ff.
2. *K.H. Marschalleck:* Bodendenkmalpflege im Niedersächsischen Verwaltungsbezirk Oldenburg, Nachrichten aus Niedersachsens Urgeschichte, Heft 34, 1965, S. 128 ff.
3. *Marschalleck* a.a.O.

Abb. 2. Bildstein in der Seitenkammer des Grabes von New Grange (Irland).

4. *K.H. Jacob-Friesen:* Einführung in Niedersachsens Urgeschichte, Hildesheim 1963, S. 286, — *Brønstedt:* Nordische Vorzeit, Neumünster 1962, S. 90.
5. *St. Piggot und T.G.E. Powell:* The Excavation of three neolithic chambered Tombs in Galloway. 1949. Proceedings of the Society of Antiquaries of Scotland, Bd. 83, 1948/49, S. 103 ff. — *W. Nowothnig:* Zur Deutung der kreisverzierten Steine von Beckstedt und Harpstedt, Kreis Grafschaft Hoya, «Die Kunde» NF. 7, 1956, S. 91 ff.
6. *Seán P.O. Riordáin:* Antiquities of the Irisch Countryside, London 1953. (Abb. 66, 1 und 2).
7. *Péquart und Le Rouzic:* Corpus des Signes Gravés des Monuments Mégalithiques Du Morbihan, Paris 1927, S. 57 ff. und Tf. 103, 120, 121, 123, 124.
8. *T.G.E. Powell:* The Passage Graves of Irland PPS. 4/1938.
9. *G. Coffey:* New Grange... and other Incised Tumuli in Irland, Dublin 1912.
10. *Péguart und Le Rouzic:* aa.O. S. 61 und Tf. 44—46.

The Movement of styles of the rock-pictures in Europe[1]

VON HERBERT KÜHN

In the art of the rock pictures throughout thirty millennia, one recognizes two primary leading means of expressions: the naturalistic and the abstract style. These leading expressions signify more than styles, they represent basic ideas. I consider these formations to be sensoric and imaginative.

The art of the Palaeolithic period seems to be naturalistic; the following period, Mesolithic art, is stylizing, both are sensoric. The art of the Neolithic period (about 4000-1600) is abstract. This form can be called imaginative. In both of these periods, Palaeolithic and Neolithic, there are no exceptions to these characteristic formations.

Some signs in Palaeolithic art have been considered as being abstract symbols; however, they represent traps, fences, ditches and paths. In effect, they carry realistic meaning.

From the Neolithic period, no naturalistic representions has been found. This is due to by the particular way of life, the economic structure. On the one hand we have a hunter, and on the other a cultivator of land and a breeder of cattle. The hunter is a consumer, the cultivator a producer.

The hunter aims at a direct realistic object, the animal. It constitues his maintenance, nourishes and clothes him, in effect, it provides him with the foundations of his life.

The world of Neolithic man, the farmer and cattle-breeder, is directed by the idea of fertility. Fertility, however, demands imagination, abstract speculation. And this can only be expressed by symbols.

It is the new foundation of town, writing and trade which demands the emergence of a new form of realistic life. This appears at the period of the Bronze and Iron Ages. As a result, three different styles can be distinguished.

Within the naturalistic style of the Palaeolithic period there are three groups: the linear form of the Aurignacien period, the pain-

[1] The main points of view in the lecture have been treated in detail in the author's richly illustrated book: Die Felsbilder Europas, Stuttgart 1971.

236

ting form of the Middle-Magdalenian, and the expressive-swinging form of the Late-Magdalenian.

The next period is characterized by the stylizing art of Eastern Spain. There are three stages. The first period shows a naturalistic, but plain form like Calapatá, Albarracín, Charco del Agua Amarga. The second period demonstrates the form of the stylized human figures like Valltorta, Gasulla. The third stage shows the transition toward the beginning of the abstract style, the geometric form. The static element eliminates the dynamic. The expression of art is now bounded, firm, fixed, unmoved. It is the symbol which rules this world, with the meaning of the supernatural and the metaphysical.

These pictures appear especially in Southern Spain, in France, in the oldest engravings of Valcamonica in North Italy.

The next form, the third style of the prehistoric period, leads to more reality, to more movement, I may call it the realizing style. This kind of expression is to be seen in the pictures of ships and gods in Scandinavia, in the majority of the pictures of Valcamonica and also in the newly found engravings of Austria and Switzerland.

These three horizons of the rock pictures signify not only in Europe but all over the world that the idea of life underwent several changes in the period before written history.

Never before our time was it possible for man to look so deeply into the growth, the evolution, the development of spirit, form and expression of the inner life of the man. The investigation into the meaning of the rock pictures means the conquest of a new dimension of mankind. This is the special mission of the symposium.

Zur Zeitstellung der österreichischen Felsbilder

VON ERNST BURGSTALLER

Seit 1958 im Toten Gebirge in Oberösterreich die ersten Felsgravierungen in den Alpen bekannt geworden sind, konnten wir rund 30 weitere Stationen inventarisieren, sodass sich derzeit eine lange Kette von Belegstellen durch die österreichischen Alpen von Niederösterreich bis Tirol hinzieht, an die sich nunmehr auch die 1968 entdeckte schweizerische Fundstelle in Carschenna anschliesst.[1]

Mit wenigen Ausnahmen liegen fast alle diese Fundstellen in schwer zugänglichen Bereichen meist in düsteren Schluchten und Felspassagen und oft in der Nähe dürftiger Wasserstellen in Höhen bis zu 1700 im bewaldeten Hochgebirge.

In der Regel bestehen die Fundstellen nur aus 1-4 Bildfelsen, doch gibt es auch einige Grossfundstellen, die sich mit 15-20 Bildfelsen bis zu 1 km lang durch das Gelände erstrecken. In diesem Fall setzen die Bilder meist mit einem besonders eindrucksvollen Felsblock ein und enden auch mit einer bemerkenswerten Felsformation, wie z.B. im Fundgebiet «Höll» am Warscheneck im Toten Gebirge mit einem Durchkriechstein, bzw. einer Versturzhöhle, unter deren Boden ein unterirdischer Fluss mit unheimlichem Tosen talab stürzt. (Abb.1)

Für mehrere dieser Fundstellen sind im Volksmund merkwürdige Namen im Umlauf, die auf Elemente des Volksglaubens Bezug haben, wie «Höll», «Hexenwand», «Frauenwand» (bekannt nach den Berggeistern der «Saligen Frauen»), «Notgasse», «Kienkirche» usw., vergleichbar einigen Geländenamen wie Val d'Inferno, Valée des Merveilles, Gorge du diable, Salles des Fées usw. an einzelnen französischen und oberitalienischen Fundstellen.

Die österreichischen Fundbereiche befinden sich ausnahmslos im Kalkgebirge. Sogar die einzige Belegstelle in den Zentralalpen, die mitten in das Urgestein eingelagerte Fundstelle der «Frauenwand» am Faschauner-Törl, liegt in einem tektonischen Fenster aus Kalkgestein. Die eigenartigen Verwitterungsprozesse dieses Gesteins gestatten eine genauere Beobachtung der unterschiedlichen Abwitterungsgrade der nebeneinander liegenden Gravierungen, als dies anderwärts der Fall sein dürfte, haben aber den Nachteil, dass sie so nach-

Abb. 1. Fundstelle «Höll» am Warscheneck im Toten Gebirge in Oberösterreich, Bildfelsen XII. Rechte Seite der Hauptbildwand mit Darstellungen von
Pferden und Reitern, darunter die eines Pferdes mit näpfchenförmigen Hufen,
weiteres eines Hirschen vor einem stilisierten Baum, eines Fadenkreuzes und
einer Mühle. Phot. Ernst Burgstaller.

haltig einwirken, dass die Umrisslinien der offensichtlich ältesten
Bilder, wie die der naturalistischen Tierhäupter, sich manchmal nur
mehr schattenhaft von der Felswand abheben und unrettbar zerstört
werden, wenn man versucht, die Gesteinsoberfläche etwa mit einer
Bürste von der Kleinstflora zu reinigen.

   Ausser den unterschiedlichen Abwitterungsgraden bietet auch die
Beobachtung der Placierung der Bilder untereinander manches
Kriterium zur Erstellung einer relativen Chronologie, insbesondere,
wenn die Bilder knapp über dem heutigen Niveau liegen oder bis zu
mehreren Dezimetern unter dieses hinabreichen, sodass mit einer be-
trächtlichen Erhöhung des Geländes am Fusspunkt der Felsen seit der
Entstehungszeit der Bilder gerechnet werden muss.

Deutliche Unterschiede weisen die österreichischen Felsbilder untereinander auch hinsichtlich der Gravierungstechnik auf. Bilder, die durch einfache Strichritzung enstanden sind, liegen neben solchen, die aus den Felsen gehöhlt oder durch Aneinanderreihung von Punzen hergestellt wurden. Nicht unvermerkt sei, dass die oben erwähnten naturalistischen Tierbilder in unerhört gekonnter Erfassung der charakteristischen Merkmale der jeweiligen Tiergattung wie mit einer nirgends unterbrochenen Linie gezeichnet sind.

Bereits durch diese Feststellungen dürfte ersichtlich geworden sein, dass es sich bei den österreichischen Felsbildern nicht um die Produktion einer einzigen Schaffensperiode handelt, sondern um das Ergebnis eines Kontinuums von langer Dauer, während dessen die einzelnen Felsen immer wieder zur Anbringung von Zeichen und Zeichnungen aufgesucht wurden.

Für die Erstellung einer absoluten Chronologie fehlen, wie bei vielen anderen europäischen Fundstellen, zeitweisende Begleitfunde von archäologischem Material. Zwar konnte bereits 1920 der Wiener Prähistoriker Prof. Josef Bayer im Toten Gebirge aus einer in gleicher Höhe wie die Felsbilderstation gelegenen Höhle nicht nur zahlreiche Höhlenbärenknochen, sondern in deren Umkreis auch einige inzwischen verloren gegangene paläolithische Artefakte aufsammeln[2] und kamen in der von Professor Ehrenberg erforschten «Salzofenhöhle»[3] im gleichen Gebirgssystem ausser bearbeiteten Höhlenbärenschädeln auch mehrere altsteinzeitliche Geräte zutage, aber diese Fundstellen befinden sich doch nicht unmittelbar bei den Felsbilderstellen und bezeugen daher vorerst nicht mehr als die Tatsache, dass dieser gesamte Hochgebirgsbereich bereits sehr früh von Bärenjäger-Gruppen aufgesucht worden sein muss.

Viel deutlicher zeichnet sich aus den Inventaren der Felsbilderstellen die Schlussphase des vorgeschichtlichen Gravierungsbrauchtums in den österreichischen Alpen durch zwei Komplexe von Inschriften ab, die, ohne diese zu beschädigen, mitten unter die vielen abstrakten und figürlichen Motive hineingesetzt wurden, nämlich die senkrecht verlaufenden Schriftbänder von sieben rätischen Weiheinschriften an den Gott Castor bei einem Quellheiligtum im Gemeindegebiet von Steinberg in Tirol[4] und die dreizeilige gehülste waagrechte lateinische Inschrift einer Votivbekundung an den latinisierten keltischen Kriegs- und Heilsgott Mars Latobius, dessen Verehrung bisher nur aus dem südlichen Österreich bekannt war, in der düsteren Kienbachklamm bei Bad Ischl in Oberösterreich.[5] Denn die einen sind wegen der namentlichen Erwähnung eines Gefangenen aus dem Stamm der germanischen Usipeter, mit denen C. J. Cäsar im Krieg lag, nicht vor der zweiten Hälfte des letzten Jahrhunderts vor

Chr. möglich, und die anderen nicht vor der Besetzung des jetzigen Oberösterreich durch die Römer im Jahre 15. nach Chr., aber auch nicht nach Zusammenbruch der römischen Herrschaft in diesem Land im 4. nach-christlichen Jahrhundert. In diese Jahrhunderte um die Zeitenwende weist auch eine am Ofenauerberg in Salzburg entdeckte Zeichnung der Individualfigur eines Mannes in zeitgenössischer Tracht, die Zug um Zug mit der Bekleidung der germanischen und keltischen Kriegsgefangenen übereinstimmt, die auf den Reliefplatten des berühmten trajanischen Siegesmales von Adamklissi abgebildet sind.[6]

Für die Entstehungszeit der Gravierungen, die offensichtlich vor diesem Zeitraum liegen, ist man auch in Österreich ausschliesslich auf die Methode des Stil- und Motivvergleiches angewiesen, wobei sich unschwer ein deutliches Überwiegen jener figürlichen und abstrakten Motive erkennen lässt, die mit Bildern der nord- und südeuropäischen Verbreitungsgebiete, aber auch mit jenen der schweizerischen Fundstelle Carschenna korrespondieren. Dies trifft vor allem für die Pferde- und Hirschdarstellungen mit gerade und geschwungener Rückenlinie bzw. gefächertem Geweih zu. Bemerkenswerterweise kehren diese Figuren — worauf übrigens bereits Gallus[7] und Althin aufmerksam gemacht haben — vielfach auch im Ritzdekor von hallstattzeitlichen Urnen, wie jenen von Ödenburg, Warischberg, Lahse und einigen westpreussischen Gefässen, wieder, stimmen aber auch mit Einzelheiten der zeitgenössischen Figuralplastik überein, deren wichtigste gerade im österreichischen Alpenraum gefunden wurden, wie den Pferden an den Schmuckbeilen von Hallstatt,[8] den Reitern unter den Bleifiguren von Frög[9] oder den Hirschen und Reitern auf dem sogenannten Kultwagen von Strettweg,[10] die ihrerseits bekanntlich wieder mittelbare Zusammenhänge mit Stilelementen der oberitalienischen Kulturen von Este und Bologna-Villanova erkennen lassen.

In die gleiche Richtung weisen auch einige charakteristische Stilmittel, wie das der sogenannten «Draufsicht» auf einzelne Tiergruppen und die Darstellung der Pferdehufe als kreisrunde Dellen, wie sie am Hauptfelsen im Fundgebiet «Höll» (Abb. 1) ebenso beobachtet werden können wie an den genannten Urnen. Sehr bemerkenswert erscheint uns auch das Nebeneinandervorkommen von Schiffsdarstellungen mit doppelter Kiellinie und hochgezogenen Steven und die Wiedergabe von eigenartigen strahlenden Häusern, die jedes für sich charakteristisch sind für den skandinavischen, bzw. den oberitalienischen Motivschatz.

In dieselbe Entsehungszeit ab dem 2. Drittel des letzten Jahrtausends vor Christus sind offensichtlich auch eine Reihe von Baum-darstellungen zu setzen, die einerseits Pflanzen mit waagrechten Ästen zeigen, wie sie in gleicher Weise aus dem Norden, z.B. Kalleby, bekannt sind, andererseits aber auch fächerförmige Gebilde, die ihre Entsprechungen in den südeuropäischen Felsbilderbereichen haben. Hierher gehören wohl auch die zahlreichen Leitern[11] (Abb. 2), aber auch die konzentrischen Quadrate, die sogenannten «Mühlen»[12] (Abb. 4), sowie Kombinationsfiguren aus einem gefelderten Rechteck und einem seitlichen aufgesetzten Rad,[13] wie sie sowohl aus dem Valtellina als auch von einer Stele aus Bagnolo geläufig sind. Schliesslich sind in dieser Gruppe auch die eigenartigen Stilisierungen von anthropomorphen Figuren anzuführen, die aus einem Dreieck konstruiert sind, für die sich neben einzelnen Primitivformen unter den südeuropäischen Felsbildern insbesondere schöne Parallelen aus dem Dekor der Urnen von Ödenburg beibringen lassen.[14]

Wesentlich schwieriger einzuordnen scheint uns eine Reihe von Einzelfiguren, so eine grosse Idolfigur im Kegelschema an der Wand IV in der Kienbachklamm[15] mit Varianten in den Ybbstaler und Salzburger Fundstellen, die mit den bekannten südfranzösischen Menhirfiguren ebensolche Ähnlichkeiten aufweist wie mit der von einer Aureola umgebenen Gravierung von Pena Tu und den von Prof. E. Anati zusammengestellten Vergleichsobjekten, oder die Kombinationsfigur, bestehend aus einem neunspeichigen Rad mit darüber gesetzten M-Linien, die am Eingangsfelsen zur Notgasse angebracht ist (Abb. 3) und u.W. unter den bekannten prähistorischen Gravierungen nur Parallelen in den Felsen von Carnac[16] aufweist; oder die höchst merkwürdige, an der innersten Stelle der Kienbachklamm angebrachte Zeichnung eines menschlichen Paares (Abb. 4), das bei einfachster Umrissgestaltung dadurch ausgezeichnet ist, dass die gesamte Gesichtsbildung nur aus einem einzigen zyklopischen Auge besteht, wozu es eine Reihe von Vergleichsobjekten unter den paläolithischen Knochenplastiken aus dem Raume um Les Eyzies[17] gibt, ebenso aber auch in etwas abgewandelter Form unter den von Prof. Anati publizierten metallzeitlichen Gravierungen Spaniens.

Während die meisten der bisher genannten Motive den Betrachter vor allem auf die nord- und südeuropäischen Verbreitungsgebiete von Felsgravierungen blicken lassen, richtet sich unser Augenmerk für eine restliche Gruppe von Gravierungen nach Westeuropa. Dies trifft zu für eine große Abbildung eines liegenden weiblichen Torso mit stumpfen Beinen und nur undeutlich ausgeführter Gestaltung von Kopf und Oberkörper,[18] sodass sich sofort der Vergleich nicht nur mit den bekannten Venusstatuetten, sondern auch mit einem der Torsi von La Madeleine[19] aufdrängt, nur mit dem Unterschied, dass die

Abb. 2. Fundstelle Kienbachklamm bei Bad Ischl in Oberösterreich, Felsen IV. Gesamtansicht der Bildwand mit großer kegelförmiger Idolfigur (rechts unten), Rädern und Leitern. Phot. Ernst Burgstaller.

Ausführung des österreichischen Bildes erheblich plumper wirkt und damit deutlich einen epigonenhaften Eindruck erweckt. Eine gleiche Beobachtung wird man bei einigen anthropomorphen Figuren mit Vogelköpfen machen, die in der Kienbachklamm und in zwei Fundstellen in den Ennstaler Alpen angetroffen wurden,[20] nicht aber in der eleganten Wiedergabe der bereits mehrfach genannten — bisher neun Tierhäupter in grossflächiger naturalistischer Umrisszeichnung, von denen insbesondere die beiden einander folgenden Cerviden in den hochgelegenen Partien der Kienbachklamm und die Zeichnung eines Elches im Fundgebiet «Höll» unverkennbar spätpaläolitischen Charakter aufweisen, wenn auch selbstverständlich

Abb. 3. Fundstelle «Notgasse» in den Ennstaleralpen in Steiermark, Felsen I.
Kombinationsfigur aus Rad und M-Linien. Phot. Ludwig Lauth.

schon im Hinblick auf die lange Vergletscherung der Alpen an eine
unmittelbare Zeitgleichheit mit entsprechenden Vergleichsbildern in
Westeuropa nicht zu denken ist. Wohl aber muss in diesem Zusammenhang auf gleichartige Vorkommen unter den metallzeitlichen
Gravierungen in Skandinavien wie auch im sibirischen Raum hingewiesen werden, wie dies auch durch die jüngsten Veröffentlichungen
von Alexander Okladnikow nahegelegt wird.

Wird man in der endgültigen Zuweisung einzelner Bildgruppen
an bestimmte Zeiträume aber auch weiterhin noch sehr vorsichtig
sein müssen und stets auch die Möglichkeit von zeitlichen Phasen-
verschiebungen in der Verwendung bestimmter Stilformen in Be-
tracht zu ziehen haben, so dürfte aber doch auch bereits aus
diesen kurzen Ausführungen die grosse Spannweite der Stile und
Motive der österreichischen Felsbilder ersichtlich geworden sein, insbesondere aber auch deren Bedeutung in kulturgeographischer
Hinsicht, auf die auch Prof. Henri Breuil, dem wir noch erste Pro-

Abb. 4. Fundstelle Kienbachklamm, Felsen IX. Stilisierte Darstellung eines menschlichen Paares. Phot. Kurt Pietsch.

ben unserer Entdeckungen vorlegen konnten, und insbesondere Prof. Herbert Kühn nachdrücklich hingewiesen haben. Denn nun beginnt sich die so lange schmerzlich empfundene Fundlücke zwischen den nord-und südeuropäischen Felsbildergebieten im Raume von Mitteleuropa allmählich zu schliessen und durch das deutliche Zusammentreffen von spezifisch skandinavischen und spezifisch südeuropäischen Motiven auch die Kontaktzone abzuzeichnen, in der sich diese beiden grossen Überlieferungsbereiche begegnen und über die hinweg sich die Bevorzugung bestimmter Stilformen und Motivgruppen in ihrer charakteristischen Ausprägung aus dem oberitalienischen Raum nach den nördlich gelegenen Landschaften verbreitet haben könnte.

245

ANMERKUNGEN

1. *E. Burgstaller*, Felsbilder in Österreich. Linz a.d.D. 1972.
2. *J. Bayer*, Altpaläolithische Funde im Toten Gebirge in Oberösterreich. Die Eiszeit I (1925) 165.
3. *E. Ehrenberg*, Die palöolithische, prähistorische und paläoethnologische Bedeutung der Salzofenhöhle im Lichte der letzten Forschung. Quartär VI (1953) 19 ff.
4. *E. Vetter*, Die vorrömischen Felsinschriften in Steinberg in Nordtirol. Anzeiger d.phil.hist. Klasse d. Österr. Akademie d. Wissenschaften. Wien 1957, Nr. 24, 384 ff.; *K.M. Mayr*, Die rätischen Felsinschriften von Steinberg. Der Schlern 34 (1960) 309 ff.; ders.-, Eine neue Steinberg-Inschrift. Der Schlern 36(1962) 287 ff.
5. *K.M. Mayr*, Ein bedeutendes Ergebnis der Felsbilderforschung in Oberösterreich. Weiheinschrift an Mars Latobius. Oberösterreichische Heimatblätter XX (1966) 65 ff.
6. Eine Abbildung der Gravierung auf dem Ofenauerberg und die entsprechende Paralleldarstellung aus Adamklissi enthält *E. Burgstaller*, Felsbilder Tafel XXXI, Abb. 71, 72.
7. *S. Gallus*, Die figurenverzierten Urnen vom Soproner (= Ödenburger) Burgstall. Budapest 1934.
8. S. Katalog: Krieger und Salzherren. Hallstattkultur im Ostalpenraum. Mainz 1970, T. 68.
9. *W. Modrijan*, Die figurale Bleiplastik von Frög. Carinthia 1, 140 (1950) 91 ff.
10. *W. Schmid*, Der Kultwagen von Strettweg. Leipzig 1934, T. XVII ff.
11. Eine derartige Leitergravierung mit Markierungen zwischen den Sprossen zeigt auch Abb. 76 in *E. Burgstaller*, Felsbilder Tafel XXII.
12. s. die entsprechenden Abbildungen bei *E. Burgstaller*, Felsbilder Tafel XLII, Abb. 102—105, XLIII, Abb. 106.
13. s. Abb. 135 und 136 in *E. Burgstaller*, Felsbilder Tafel LI.
14. s. *S. Gallus*, Die figuralverzierten Urnen, Tafel XVII f.
15. s. auch die grosse Abbildung dieser Figur in *E. Burgstaller*, Felsbilder Tafel XXII und die Zusammenstellung des Vergleichsmaterials S. 56.
16. *M. et St. J. Péquart et Z. Le Rouzic*, Corpus des Signes Gravés des Monuments Mégalithiques du Morbihan. Paris 1927. Tafel 78 (Dolmen di Petit Mont).
17. *E.F. Greenman*, The Upper Palaeolithic and the New World. Current Anthropology 1963, 41 ff. Tafel 6.
18. Wiedergaben dieser Gravierung enthält *E. Burgstaller*, Felsbilder Tafel XIX, Abb. 42; Tafel XX, Abb. 43.
19. s. entsprechende Wiedergabe des Bildes von La Madeleine bei *S. Giedion*, Ewige Gegenwart. Köln 1962, 363; *M. König*, Das Weltbild des eixzaitlichen Menschen. Marburg 1954, Abb. 75.
20. Abbildungen der Gravierungen von Vogelkopffiguren bei *E. Burgstaller*, Tafel XXII, Abb. 48, 49.

Rock paintings in northwest and north Australia

BY AGNES SUSANNE SCHULZ[1]

My last experiences in studies of rock-paintings were in Australia, in the northwest Kimberley-District and in the continent's most nor-thern part, Arnhem-Land.

Of special interest were the people still living there, who are not too far from the state of mind from which the art of rock-painting arose. Another interesting feature are two special picture themes: in the Kimberleys the «wondjina», in Arnheim-Land, the so-called X ray animals (Fig.) I also found it important to be able to distinguish some style-differences in the way of representing animal and humanlike fi-gures as they appear in the older and the more recent layers of the rockpaintings in question.

[1] Agnes Susanne Schulz starb unterwartet in der Weihnachtsnacht 1973 in ihrem Heim in Elba. Wir werden stets unsere hochgeschätzte Kollege in dank-barer Erinerung bewahren.

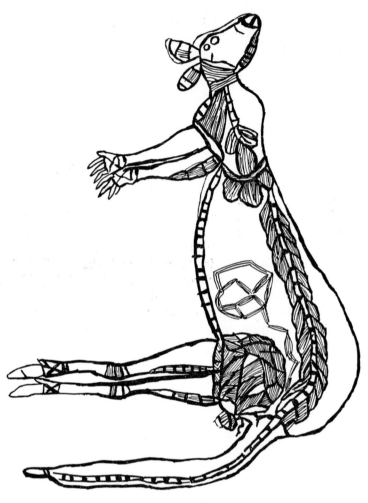

Inyaluk (Südöstliche Gruppe), Arnhem-Land, Nord-Australien. «X-ray» —
Känguruh; weisse und violett-rote Malerei.
Kopie: Agnes Susanne Schulz, 1954/55.